I0901059

IMAGES
of America

BIG SKY

ON THE COVER: EMMETT CRAIL, EARLY 1940S. Emmett Crail and horses are on his ranch in the meadows of the West Fork of the Gallatin River. He is standing in the area that now contains the homes of the Big Sky Meadow Village and the Arnold Palmer–designed Big Sky Golf Course. Lone Mountain, the iconic figure of Big Sky and home to the ski resorts, rises 5,000 feet above the meadow. At 11,166 feet, it dominates the landscape. (Historic Crail Ranch Conservators.)

IMAGES
of America

BIG SKY

Jeff Strickler and Anne Marie Mistretta in
cooperation with the Historic Crail Ranch Conservators

ARCADIA
PUBLISHING

ISBN 978-0-7385-9514-6

Published by Arcadia Publishing
Charleston, South Carolina

Printed in the United States of America

Library of Congress Control Number: 2012932886

For all general information, please contact Arcadia Publishing:
Telephone 843-853-2070
Fax 843-853-0044
E-mail sales@arcadiapublishing.com
For customer service and orders:
Toll-Free 1-888-313-2665

Visit us on the Internet at www.arcadiapublishing.com

This book is dedicated both to the members of the Historic Crail Ranch Conservators and to the Gallatin Canyon Women's Club for their preservation efforts.

CONTENTS

Acknowledgments

We must first acknowledge the Historic Crail Ranch Conservators of the Big Sky Community Corporation, whose archival collection of photographs from the Crail family provided the basis of this book. We would particularly like to thank its chairman, Al Lockwood, whose encouragement and enthusiasm greatly influenced the creation of the book. To the many volunteers of the Historic Crail Ranch Conservators, and the Gallatin Canyon Women's Club before them, who have worked so long and hard at the preservation of the history of the Big Sky area, we express our appreciation.

Many people, friends, and descendants of the original pioneers graciously gave their photographs and memories to help with this book. We value our long-term relationship with A.F. Crail's grandson Frank, who donated hundreds of photographs and numerous artifacts to the Crail Ranch Museum. Sara Anderson, granddaughter of Pete Karst, was a treasure trove of information, as was Cindy Larsen, Pete's granddaughter from his second wife. Ken McBride's son Don also opened his family albums for our use. John Richardson of the 320 Ranch, PJ Wirchansky from the Lone Mountain Ranch, and Mike Scholtz of Buck's T-4 gave the historic files of their organizations and added much to the telling of the tale. Fred "Skip" Pessl and his daughter Liesl provided the background, pictures, and diaries of Freddy Sr., whose purchase of retirement property up Beaver Creek bridged the space between the homesteaders and Chet Huntley's formation of the resort. Their hospitality was greatly appreciated. Beth Naert, Bill Erwin, and Kevin Kelleher provided photographs and stories, and Scott Carpenter, historian and archeologist, supplied important leads and assistance. In addition to the above, interviews were conducted with longtime canyon residents Donna Klindt and Shirley Luhrsen as well as Elaine Hume, Adrian Inabnit, and Marcia Pablo from the Gallatin National Forest Heritage Program; Larry Lahren of Anthro Research; and Bob and Vivian Schaap, who created the Lone Mountain Ranch. Also, the oral history tapes and interviews and the scrapbook belonging to Dorothy Vick, as well as the land, census, and voting records held at the Gallatin County Courthouse, were essential.

We also would like to thank John Russell and the staff at the Pioneer Museum in Bozeman, Montana; Steven Jackson of the Museum of the Rockies; and Kim Scott at the Renne Library for all their help. Their extensive collections of photographs and memorabilia were essential in filling the gaps and completing the story of Big Sky.

We owe thanks to Arcadia Publishing for the concept and production of its Images of America series. It will add not only to the historical preservation of Big Sky, but also to all of America's history of the past 150 years.

Except as indicated, the images in this volume appear courtesy of the Historic Crail Ranch Conservators (HCRC), the Pioneer Museum in Bozeman, Montana (PM), and Sara Anderson's Karst collection and Isabelle Durnam album (S. Anderson).

INTRODUCTION

Big Sky conjures up images of skiing, golf courses, high-end homes, and private resorts. As the home of "The Biggest Skiing in America," its powder snow, 5,500 acres, and 4,350 vertical drop have put Big Sky on the map as a destination resort. However, prior to 1970, when famed newsman Chet Huntley and his business consortium started the ski area, there was no Big Sky here. The name actually came from Pulitzer Prize–winning and native Montana author A.B. "Bud" Guthrie's popular 1947 novel *The Big Sky*. He gave the rights to the name to the State of Montana, which now calls itself The Big Sky Country. Gov. Forrest Anderson authorized the use of the name to Chet Huntley, and the resort community was born.

Now home to 2,400 people, this unincorporated area of both Gallatin and Madison Counties is generally recognized to stretch along the Gallatin River Canyon and its tributaries some 19 miles from Karst to the 320 Ranch and up the valley of the West Fork from the Gallatin River to the ski resorts on Lone and Pioneer Mountains. With Big Sky, Moonlight Basin, and Lone Mountain Ranch, as well as the exclusive and private Yellowstone Club, driving the economy, a small community has expanded to accommodate this tourist business. Fishing guides and dude ranches, banks and boutiques, fire departments and doctors, realtors and restaurants, gas stations and golf courses—all have sprung up in the past 42 years to augment the motels, hotels, and condominiums of the resort. The modern history of the resort and Big Sky is well told elsewhere. The purpose of this book is to describe the area before there was a Big Sky, where the reader will find a history in microcosm of the settling and development of the American West.

Prior to 1970, the middle section of the Gallatin Canyon and the tributaries that lie halfway between Bozeman and West Yellowstone were just locations named by the rivers and mountains. People lived on the West Fork, in the Gallatin Canyon, by Moose Creek, Cinnamon, or up Beaver Creek. It was a land hemmed in by the high peaks of what is now the Lee Metcalf Wilderness and the coniferous country of the Gallatin National Forest. Life was settled on the creek and river bottoms.

But it was not all wilderness. The Gallatin Canyon and the West Fork were home to the wide variety of people and pursuits that characterized the pioneer American West. There is evidence of an Indian presence that goes back thousands of years. Mountain men trapped beaver in its streams, mining and timbering brought many men to the area, and dude ranching was very successful. Some of these original businesses are still in operation, and new ones have developed that have led to and supported the skiing industry that now dominates Big Sky. There were also several hardy families that homesteaded this country, bringing dry-land farming and ranching to the difficult climate between 6,000 and 7,000 feet in the northern Rockies.

The Crail family established itself in the West Fork basin in 1902, where the Big Sky Meadow Village and the Arnold Palmer–designed golf course now stand. Through the Crails' eyes, the reader witnesses frontier life and the daily operation of a pioneer homestead. Although the life was hard, even by contemporary standards, the photographs show a joy in this life and a true love of the land on which these people chose to live. There were a few other families that homesteaded in the flat alluvial creek and river bottoms. Together they helped form a small, tight-knit community with schools, a social fabric, and a common lifestyle. Some of these homesteaders are chronicled here, but evidence of them has faded with time. The Crail Ranch persisted as an active operation until the resort opened, and since the Crail archives have provided us with the most comprehensive documentation, they form the basis of frontier life description.

Other industries were at work in this canyon as well. Dude ranches were quite successful and continue to this day. Karst Kamp burned and is no more, but the name can be seen daily on the big busses and airport shuttles that ply Highway 191. The B-K became the Lone Mountain Ranch—still dude ranching in the summer but now a world-class Nordic ski resort in winter. The 320 Ranch continues dude ranching in the summer and, along with the Rainbow Ranch and Buck's T-4, provides accommodations and restaurants to serve skiers and summer tourists.

Lumbering was one of the early industries that led to the opening of the canyon. Most of these operations failed, but small-scale timber operations still continue, and the "diapers" of snow-covered clear cuts on the mountains can be seen from the ski slopes. Mining, especially for gold, was on most of the pioneers' minds. Despite the prospectors' efforts, no substantial lode was ever found, and, except for the asbestos mine, no real profit ever came from these ventures. The lack of mining, along with the narrow, rugged, remote Gallatin Canyon, made large-scale timber extraction unprofitable and travel prohibitive. This helped to preserve the pristine beauty that is seen here today.

Recreation is a natural human behavior, even with the rough life of the homesteaders and ranchers. Most of these pursuits continue to this day. Trapping and hunting were prominent activities in the late 1800s, and big game season still brings flocks of hunters to the local outfitters to hunt for elk, deer, and moose. Rocky Mountain bighorn sheep, mountain goats, and grizzly and black bears can occasionally be hunted with special permits, and one can even still shoot a bison for a fee on the Flying D Ranch. Fishing has always been popular in the Gallatin River and its tributaries. Home to the native Westslope cutthroat trout as well as rainbow trout and whitefish, this river was made famous by the movie *A River Runs Through It.* Trail rides, picnics, dances, and tours of nearby Yellowstone Park all enriched the lives of the pioneer families, just as they do our own today.

Hopefully, through these photographs, we will paint a picture of life in this area from 1890 to 1970, up to the beginning of the resort and the community known as Big Sky today. With examples of mining, logging, dude ranching, farming occupations, and the recreation and the home life on the frontier, we hope to create an image of pioneer life that was fairly typical of the northern Rocky Mountains and Montana. It is a history that we have come to love, enjoy, and value and one that we hope the reader will come to appreciate as well.

Enjoy!

One

"Before Barbed Wire"

Early Contact

The first part-timers in Big Sky were various bands of Indians at the hunter-gatherer level who used the area for at least 9,000 years, during their seasonal search for resources. Shoshone, Bannock, Nez Perce, Crow, and many other Indian bands trekked along a north-south axis on the Gallatin Crest, an important use and travel zone extending from Yellowstone National Park to the Gallatin and Paradise Valleys. Indian campsites have been located on the Gallatin at confluences with many creeks. Indian bands used the Gallatin Basin as a shorter travel route between other occupation areas in the Paradise and Madison Valleys to the east and the west of Big Sky. Unfortunately for history, critical archaeological evidence was destroyed by gold prospectors and highway improvements.

When the Corps of Discovery passed through the Gallatin Valley, north of here, in the early 1800s, guiding them was the Shoshone Sacajewea. Her knowledge of the area was critical to the team charged with initial exploration for westward expansion. The Cut-tuh-o'gwa (Shoshone for "swift water") became the Gallatin River, named after the secretary of the treasury during Lewis and Clark's exploration. The name of the river is not the only thing that would change as a result of the arrival of the Europeans and Eastern Americans. The Indians' way of life, and oftentimes their utter existence, would be seriously altered.

After the US Geological Survey of 1871, Ferdinand V. Hayden chronicled his analysis of the Northern Territories, documenting the geology, geography, flora, and fauna. The expedition mapped the Gallatin Canyon and other drainages.

Legends abound of the mountain men who passed through the territories, scouting, guiding, hunting, and trapping—men like John Colter, Jim Bridger, and Jedediah Smith. A few resourceful men settled in the Gallatin Canyon, at least for a time, leaving behind their colorful stories.

After the 1872 establishment of Yellowstone National Park, the trail paralleling the Gallatin River was widened and lengthened every few decades. Ultimately, the road not only gave visitors access to the park, but by the early 1900s, it also opened the Gallatin Canyon and Basin for development.

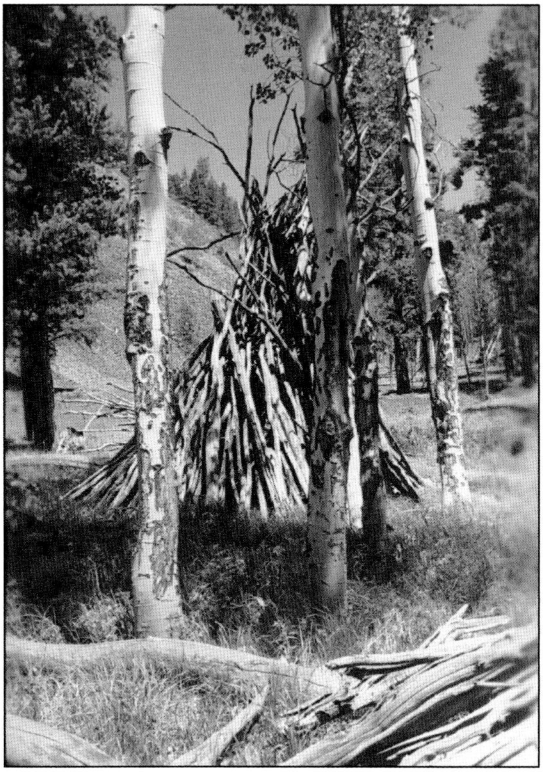

Wickiup. Indian bands built these conical structures assembled from poles and threaded with pine boughs and used them for storage and sleeping. Although most wickiups have been destroyed by fire and the elements, several remain in southwest Montana. This one was photographed in Gallatin Canyon. (PM.)

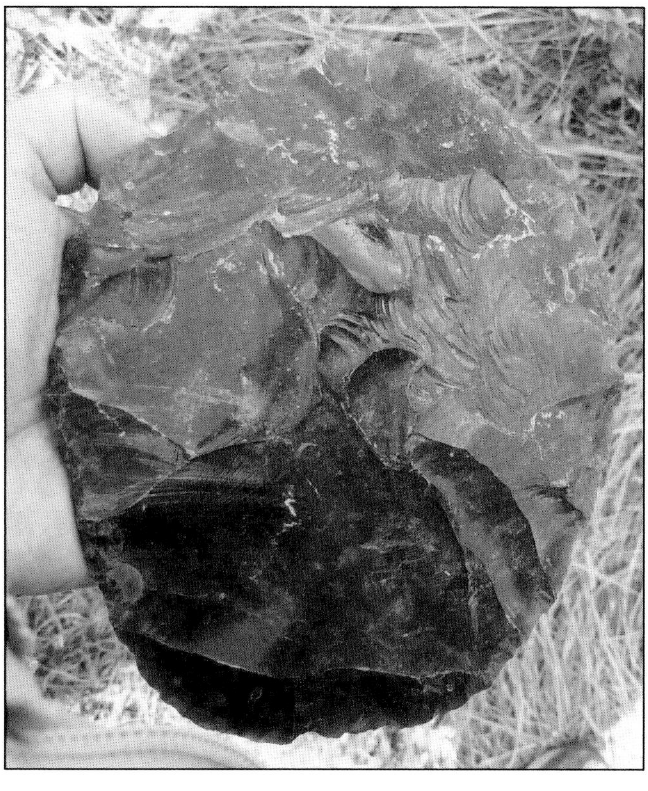

Obsidian Biface Tool Blank. This biface, approximately 3,800 years old, was used as a tool or as material for making finished implements such as blades, scrapers, and projectile points. Lithic scatter, stone tools and chips scattered on a site surface, constitutes the most frequently found evidence of Indian presence in the area. Unfortunately, much archaeological evidence within the Gallatin Canyon area is permanently lost. (Scott Carpenter, InteResources, Bozeman.)

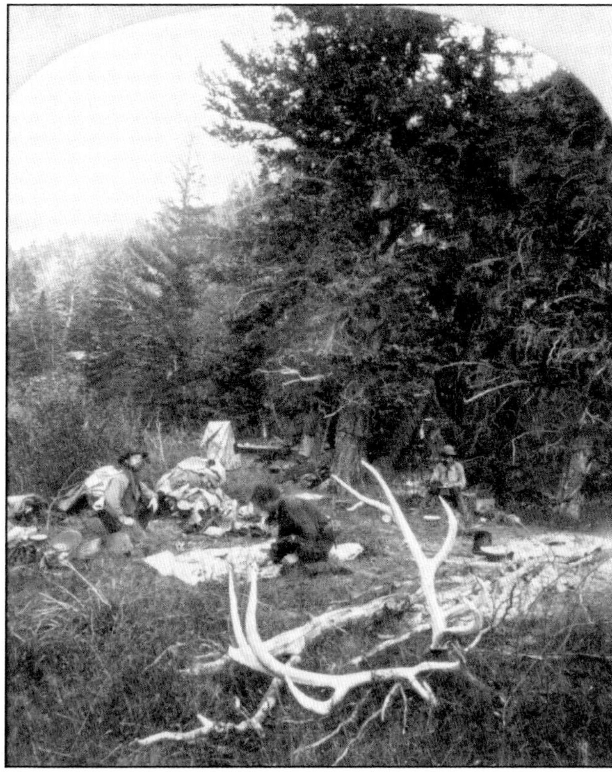

Camping on the Gallatin (Right); 19th-Century Survey Crew (Below). Pioneer photographer William Jackson captures members of the Hayden Survey Expedition of 1872 in this stereopticon scene. Conceived by the 1853 Pacific Railroad Bill, the US Geological Survey of the Territories led to the creation of Yellowstone National Park. The proposed railroad required another survey in 1881. (Right, US Geological Service and Museum of the Rockies; below, PM.)

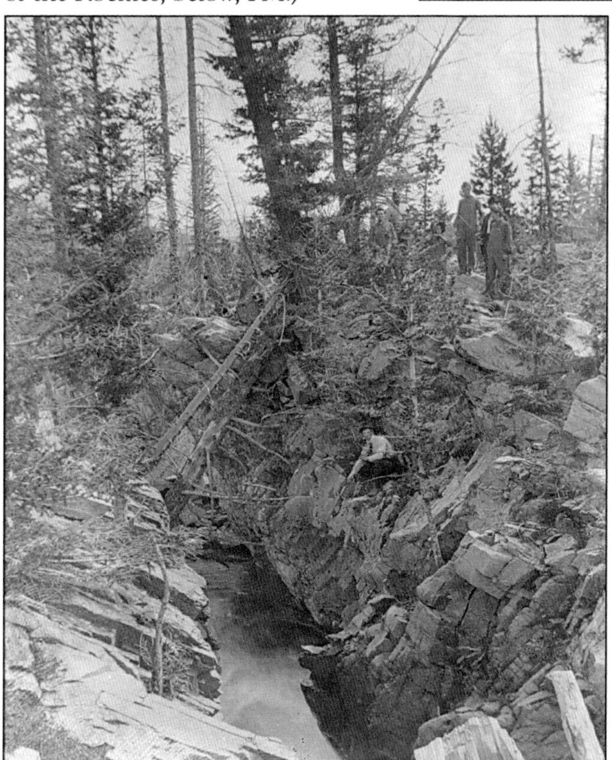

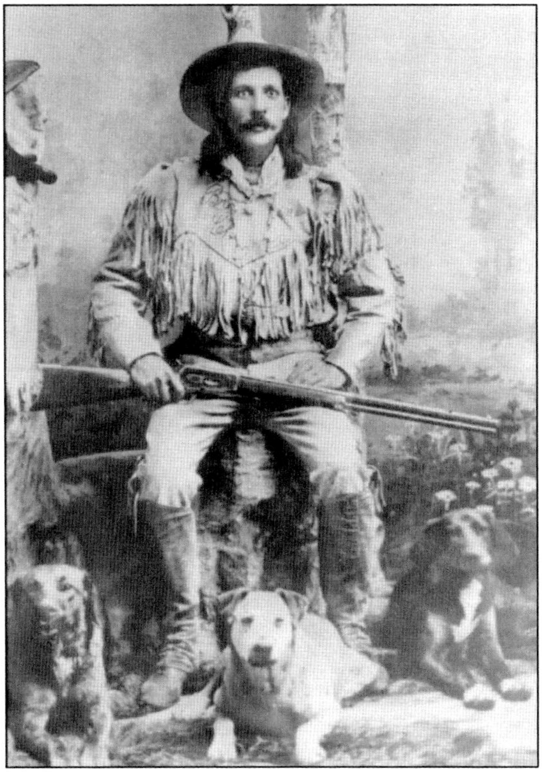

Charles "Buckskin Charley" Marble. In the early 1880s, Charles Marble escorted game hunters through the canyon. In 1886, he guided Teddy Roosevelt along the Gallatin, camping near Sage Creek before heading into the Madison Range. He and his wife, Lizzie, lived at Taylor's Fork and later owned a taxidermy and novelty shop in Livingston. Marble's memoirs are held at the Theodore Roosevelt Center. (Museum of the Rockies, x84.4.635.)

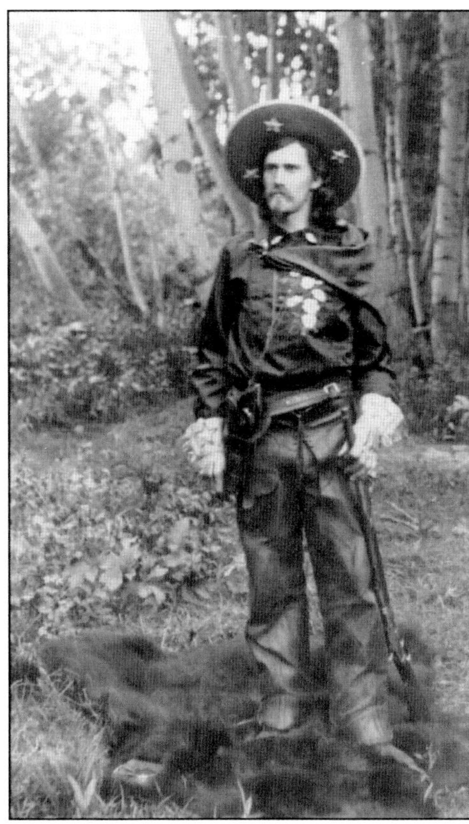

"Rocky Mountain" Dick Rock. Richard "Dick" Rock ran a dude ranch near Black Butte with Vic Smith. Rock trained elk to harness and sleigh. A buffalo hunter and hunting guide, he ranched with both Smith and Buckskin Charley. He relocated and finally settled in the Island Park–Henry's Fork area of Idaho but died after being gored by his own trained buffalo. (Museum of the Rockies, x84.4.632.)

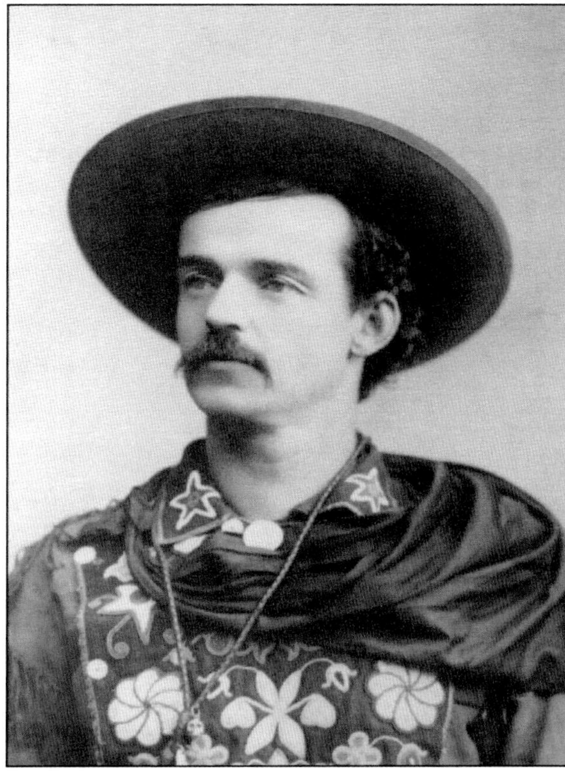

"Yellowstone Vic." Victor Grant Smith is possibly the best-known local mountain man. He was an Army frontier scout, dispatch rider, buffalo hunter, guide, and "trick shot" with Cole's traveling circus. Smith's memoir as a frontiersman, *The Champion Buffalo Hunter,* was recently rediscovered. His stories of adventures with Theodore Roosevelt are authenticated in Teddy's 1904 letter, archived at the Theodore Roosevelt Center. (Museum of the Rockies, x84.4.633.)

Jack Smith. Smith arrived in 1872 to hunt. He built on the west side of the Jack Smith Bridge, just north of the Highway 191 and Lone Mountain Trail junction, and ran the first canyon cattle in 1893. Nels Murray boasted that he killed Indians on Smith's ranch. Smith's son Charlie homesteaded a stock ranch near present-day Buck's T-4. Here, Jack Smith poses along with Helen and Grace Trent. (PM.)

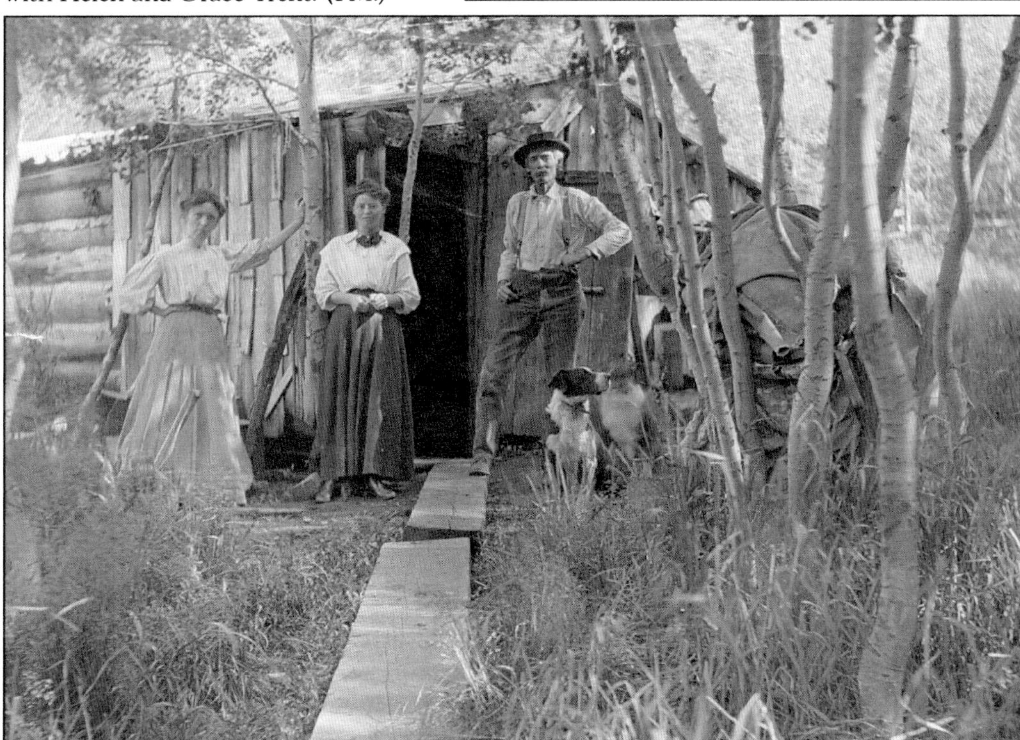

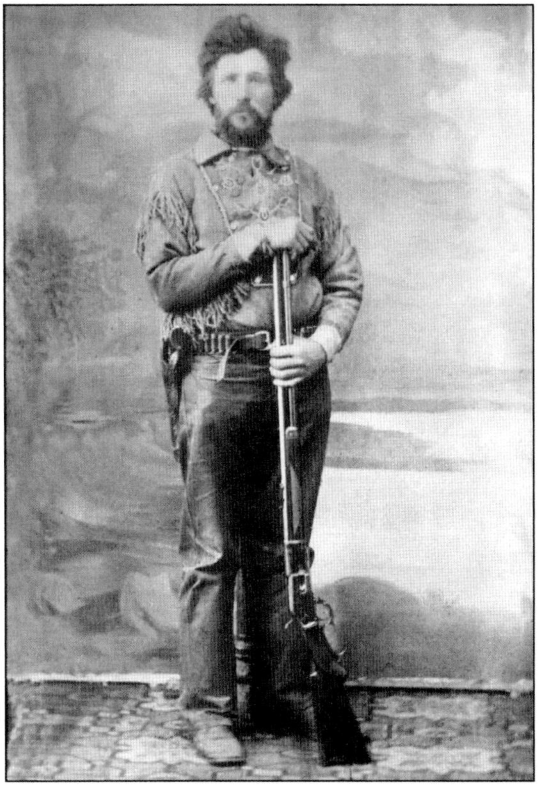

Nels Murray (Left) ; Building the Gallatin Road (Below). Trapper Nels Murray built the first pack trails up the Gallatin Canyon in the mid-1800s. In the photograph below, unidentified road construction crewmen work with a horse-drawn horizontal blade to scrape a level road in the Gallatin Canyon. Following the trails of the Indians, hunters, and prospectors, the first primitive road was excavated for the passage of wagons carrying goods and people. (Left, Museum of the Rockies X85.22.18; below, S. Anderson.)

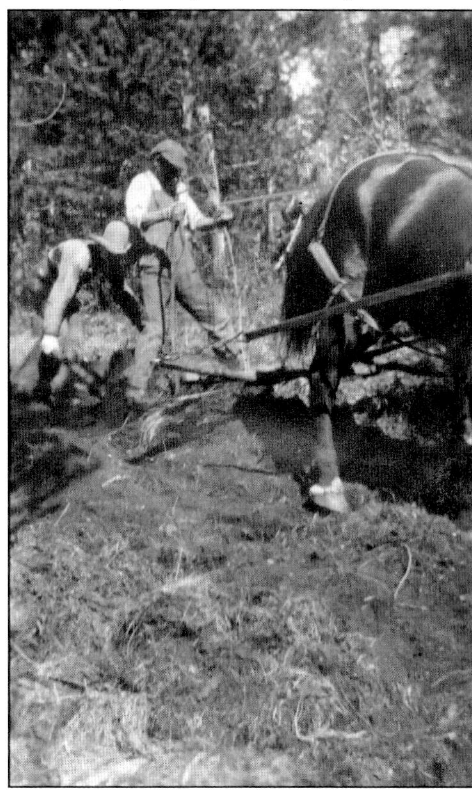

Two

"Ridin' Down the Canyon"

Travel

The high, rocky cliffs and narrow river canyon along the Gallatin provide modern-day tourists with a beautiful and scenic drive. However, these same features greatly inhibited development of the area.

The first people, Indian and white, came through the canyon on foot or horseback along a narrow, difficult trail that has been described as a "dizzy bridle path." Trappers, prospectors, and hunters established temporary camps or small shacks that were used on a seasonal basis, and the trail was slowly widened during the 1890s.

The first road was cut in 1901 to supply the Cooper Tie Camp in the Taylor Fork south of Big Sky. Pete Karst got his start driving mail, people, and freight to the logging camp, and the road allowed settlers to gain access to homestead sites in the fertile basins. Travel was still difficult, and the road did not follow the river as it does today. Rather it diverted away from the stream to avoid the cliffs, sometimes rising 150 feet above the river. At Sagebrush Flats, one particularly bad hill, the old cars with gravity-fed fuel lines had to back up the hill and carry extra water for the radiator boil-overs.

Although Bozeman entrepreneurs surveyed and pushed for a railroad through the Gallatin in 1881, the difficulty of the terrain and the completion of the Union Pacific from Idaho Falls to West Yellowstone discouraged the investment. The Milwaukee Railroad branch to Gallatin Gateway encouraged Gallatin County officials to authorize finishing the road from Taylor Fork to West Yellowstone to take advantage of tourism to Yellowstone Park. This section was completed in 1911.

Major road improvements continued from 1919 to 1930, and asphalt was laid in 1953, driven by the needs of tourism and the Corcoran lumber operation. Today as US 191, the canyon is filled with the traffic of tourists and the huge long-haul trucks headed north to I-90. As a sad and ironic end of the homestead era, in 1970 Ed Durnam was killed by a semi as he drove his tractor across the road.

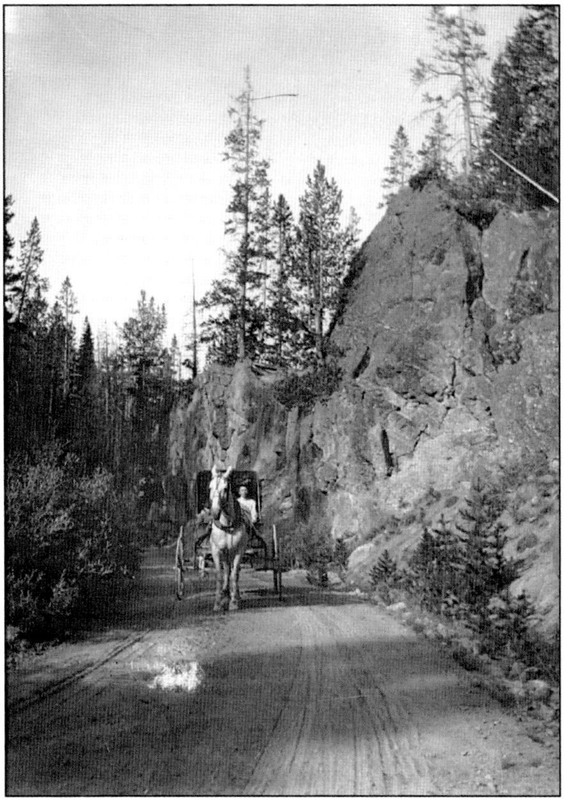

Horse and Surrey on Road (Left; Horse and Buggy on Road (Below). Horse-drawn vehicles provided the primary transportation in the early decades of the 20th century. Even with the advent of the automobile, horses were more reliable and used in snow and difficult situations well into mid-century. (Both, PM.)

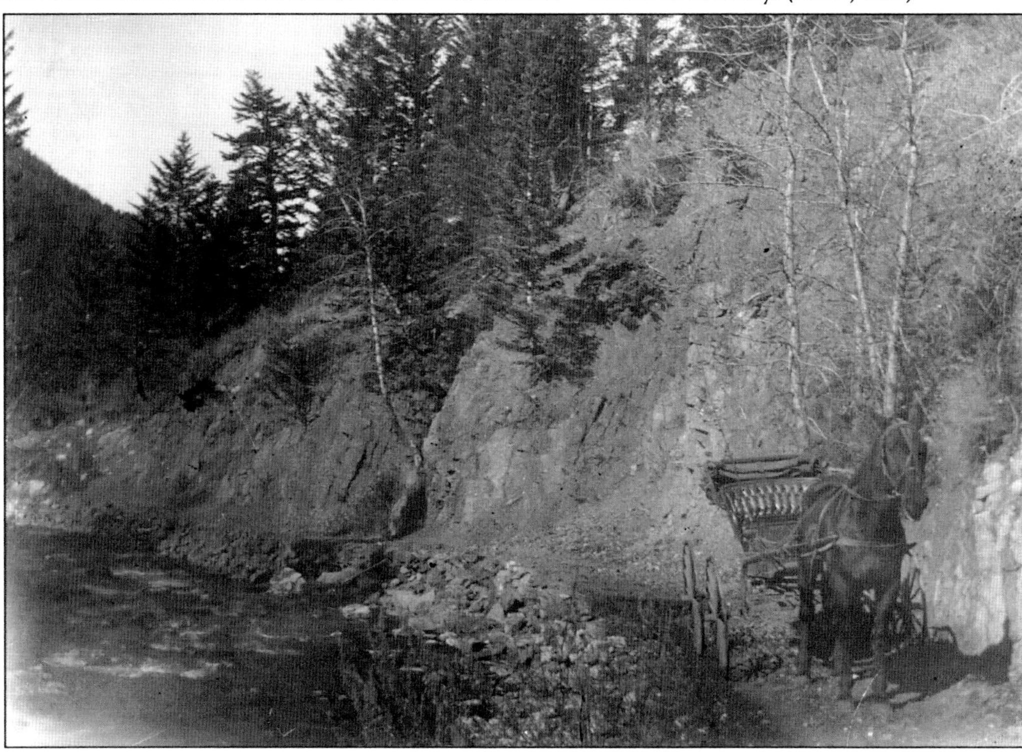

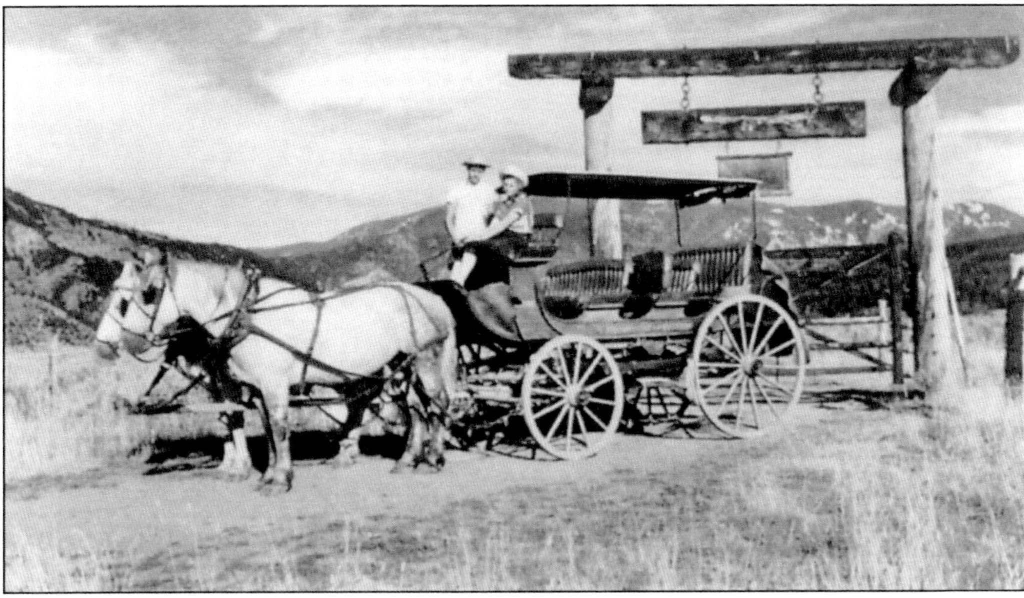

STAGECOACH AT THE B-K (ABOVE); STAGECOACH AT KARST (BELOW). Although stagecoaches were used for tourist rides at the various dude ranches, they were not regularly used in the canyon. In the 1947 photograph above, Dr. David Sacks of Pennsylvania drives the stage for fun at the B-K Dude Ranch. In the photograph below, Pete Karst takes visitors for a ride at the Karst Kamp. Actually, before automobile use, Pete hauled mail, people, and supplies to the Cooper Tie Camp in a canvas-covered freight wagon. (Above, Lone Mountain Ranch; below, PM.)

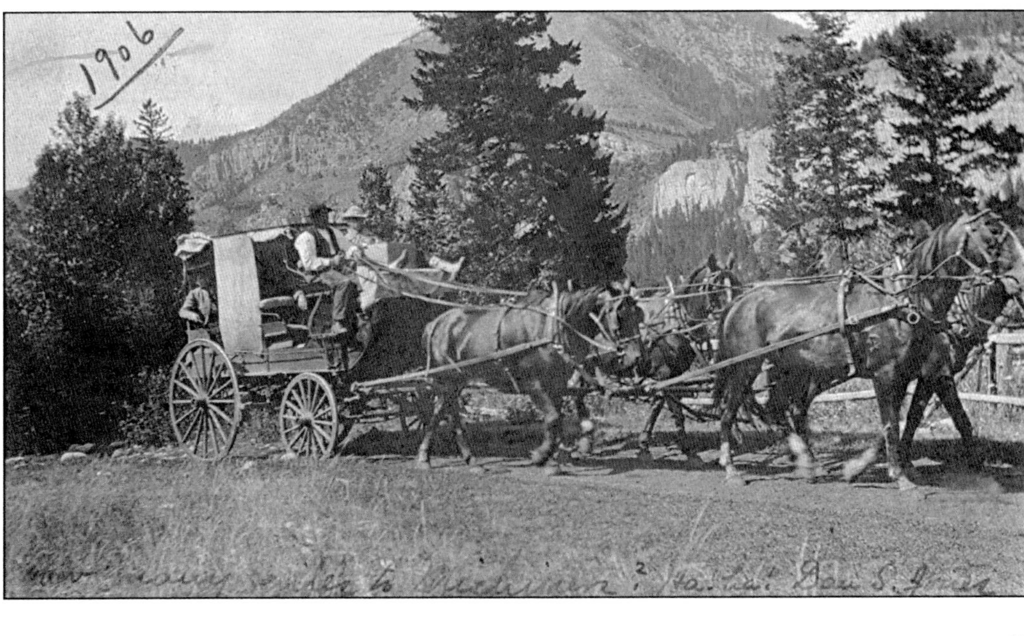

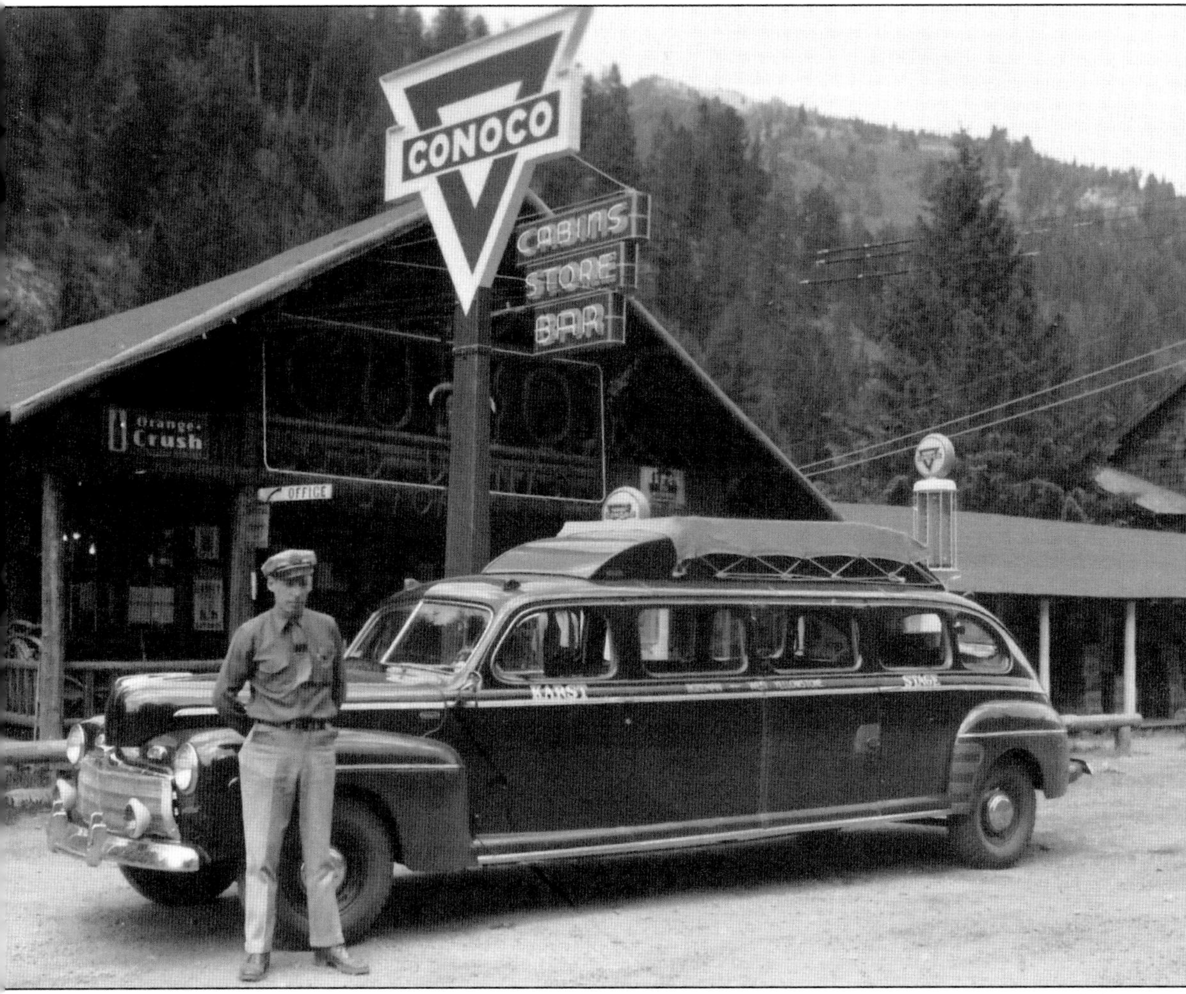

A Karst Bus in 1946. Pete Karst started regular passenger service with two pioneer Cadillacs from Salesville (now Gallatin Gateway) to West Yellowstone in 1913. A trip that now takes under two hours was a two-day adventure each way, with an overnight at Karst's Cold Spring Camp. This later expanded to three times a week. Driver Horatio Hencke is pictured in this 1946 photograph. Karst Stage busses still deliver tourists from Bozeman and the airport to the resorts. (S. Anderson.)

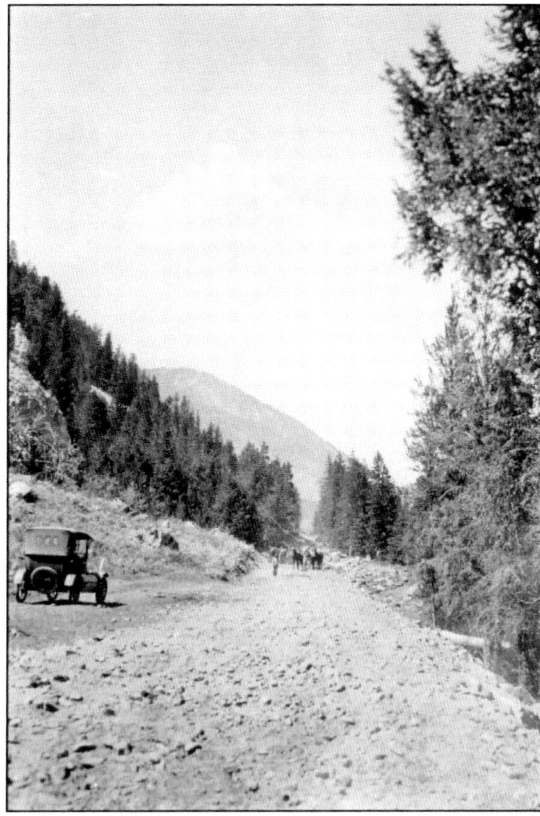

Car and Horses on the Road (Right); Primitive Roads (Below). The automobile caught America by storm. Although on the primitive canyon roads where repairing three flats per trip was the norm, automobiles were still very popular. Billy Lytle was the first to bring a personal car into the Gallatin Canyon in 1915, but by the 1920s, most of the Gallatin ranchers and homesteaders had cars. (Both, S. Anderson.)

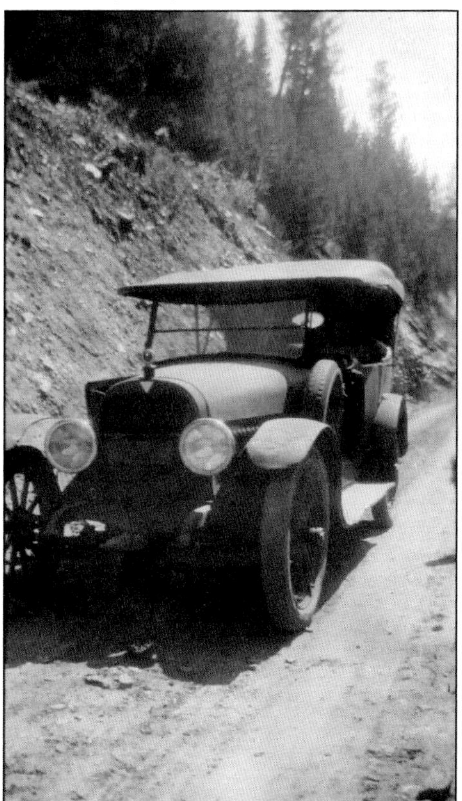

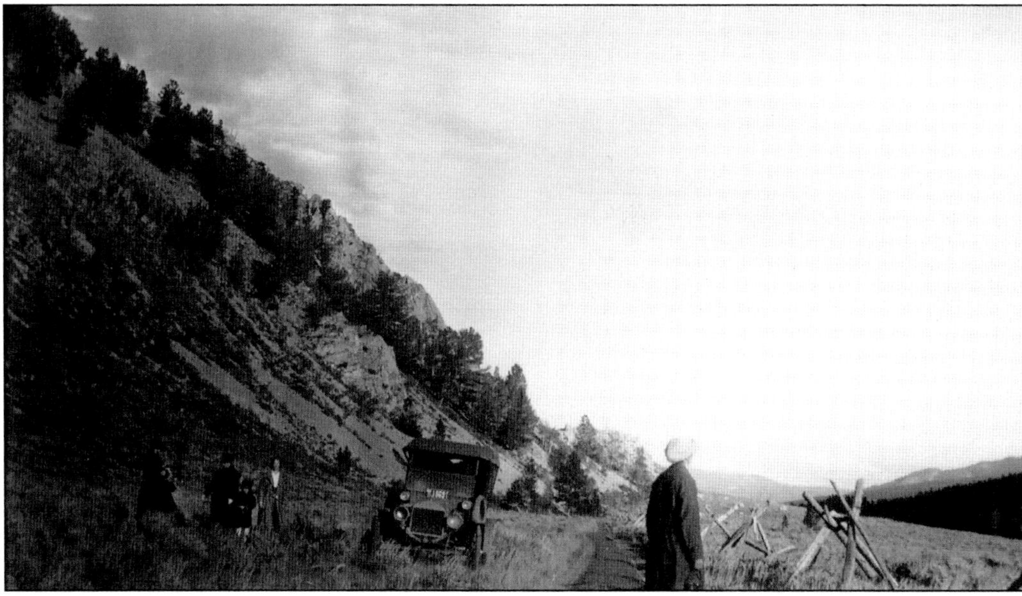

UNIDENTIFIED CRAIL RANCH VISITORS (ABOVE); WEST FORK ROAD (BELOW). Some roads were no more than two tracks through the sagebrush. Although graded relatively level, they turned to gumbo mud after a rain and were nearly impassable with snow. The unidentified visitors to the Crail Ranch are taking a break to enjoy the view and get some relief from the jolting ride, while the two-track West Fork Road heads up the basin toward Lone Mountain. (Both, HCRC.)

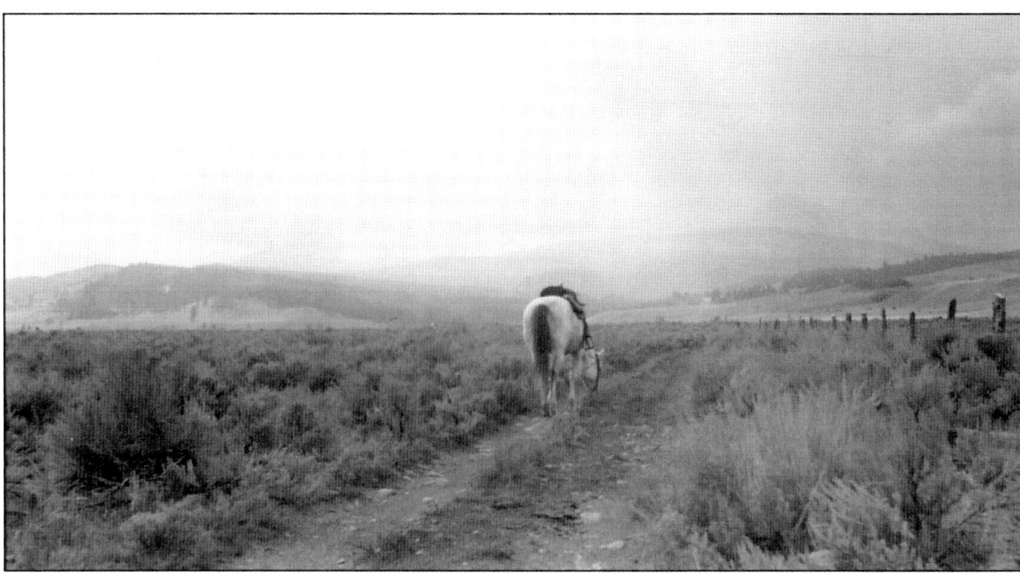

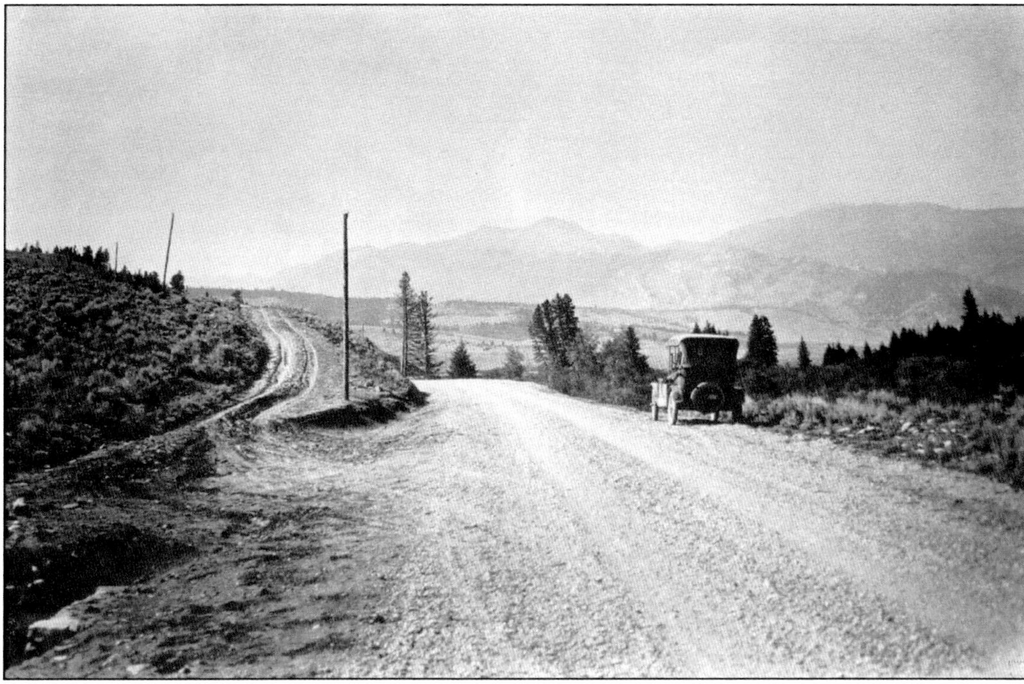

OLD AND NEW ROAD (ABOVE); HIGHWAY ALONG THE GALLATIN (BELOW). Even the main road was nearly impassable in its "improved" condition. Continuous work went on from 1919 through 1930. A major upgrade was launched in 1939 bringing the roadbed down to the river and eliminating the big hills such as Sagebrush Point. Another was begun in 1952 with the laying of an asphalt surface. (Above, PM and the US Forest Service; below, S. Anderson.)

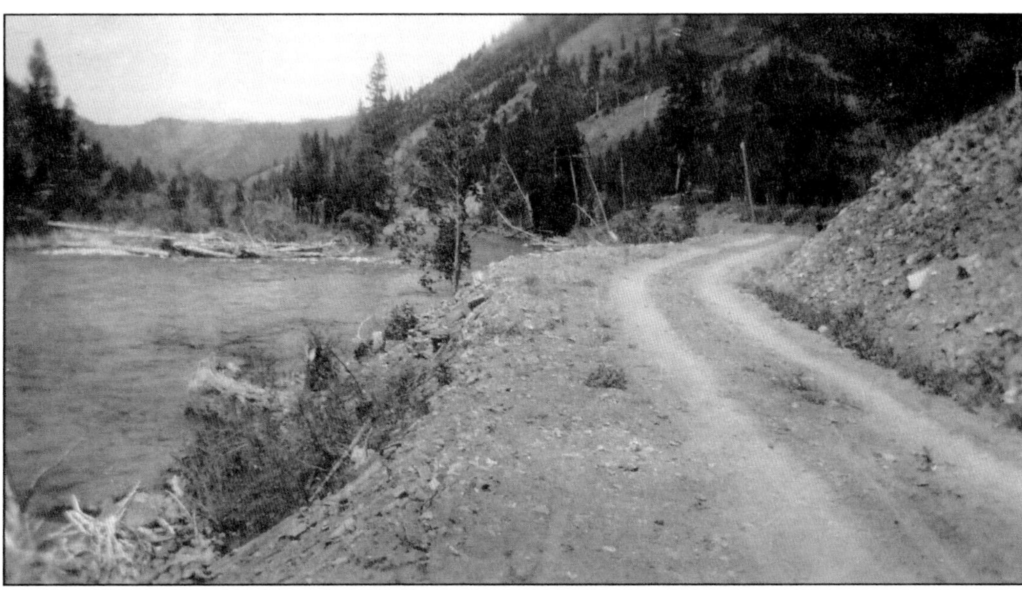

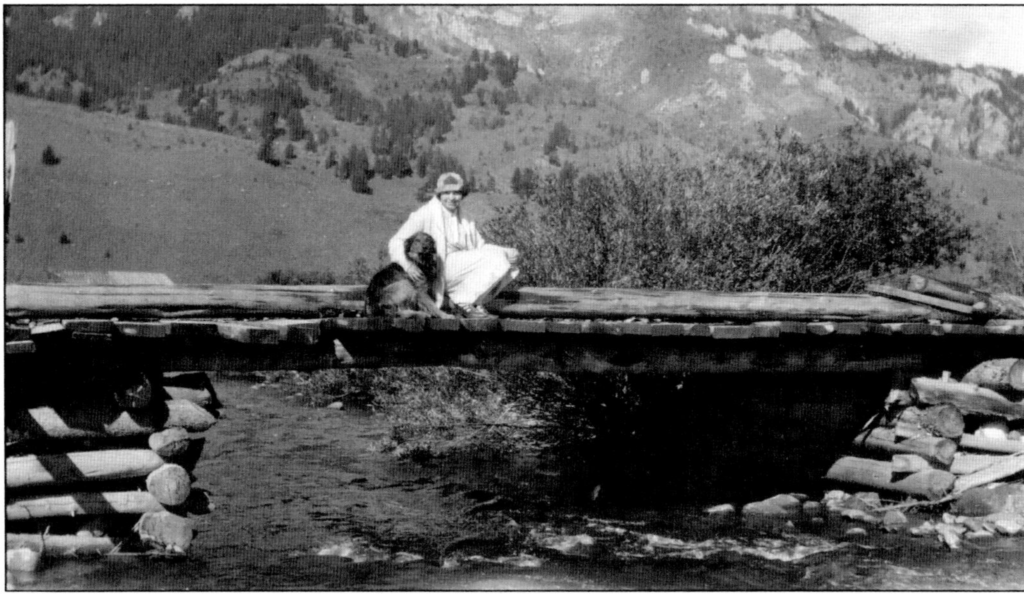

Lilian Crail on Bridge (Above); Pole Bridge with Buggies (Below). Bridges were essential to cross the river and side streams. Pole bridges, as shown here, were typical and carried people, horses, carriages, and cars in relative safety. If swept away in high spring runoff, they were easily rebuilt. The first permanent concrete bridge on the Gallatin was constructed over Squaw Creek (now Storm Castle Creek) by the New Deal's Civilian Conservation Corps in 1936. (Above, HCRC; below, PM.)

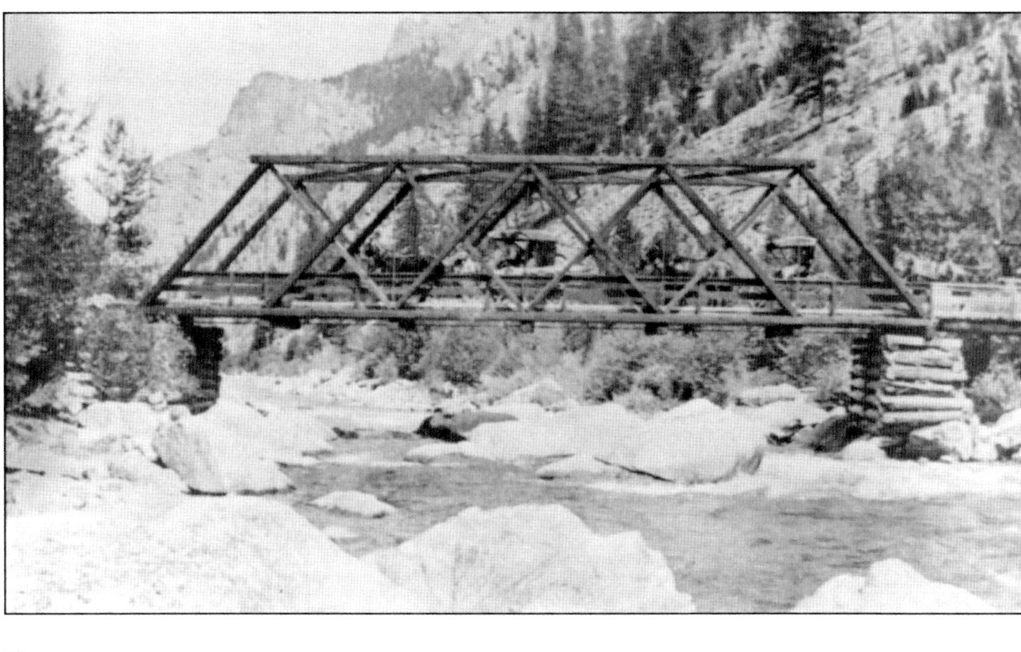

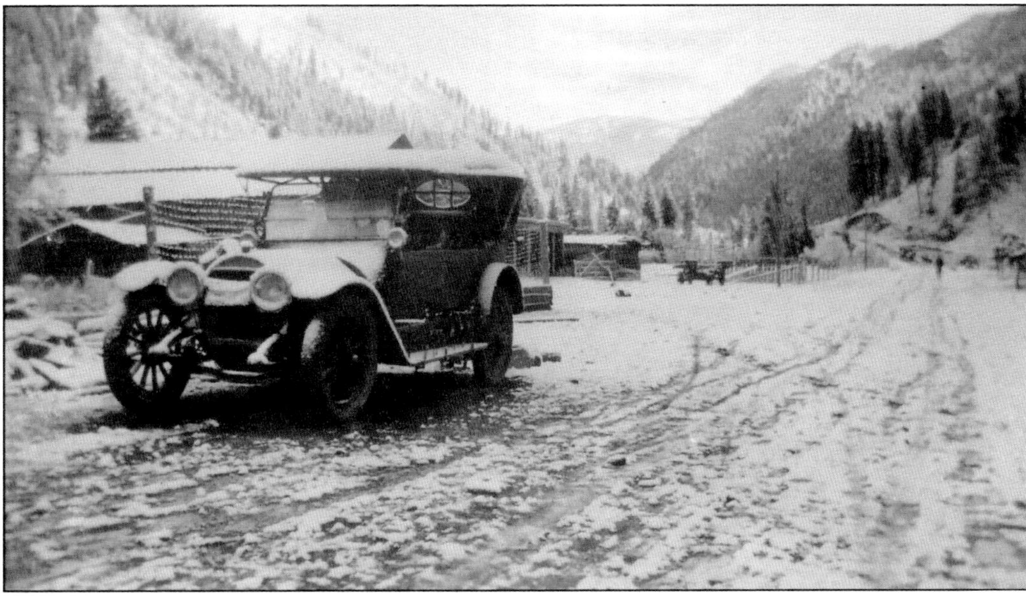

First Snow at Karst Ranch (Above); "No Snow Removal Beyond Here." (Below) Before the modern highway, snow made automobile travel impossible. Ranchers with sheep or cattle to feed holed up at home until the thaw. Dude ranches, summer cabins, and hunting camps closed for the season, and after winterizing the buildings, the families retreated to Bozeman. The road was plowed as far as Karst Kamp by the mid-1930s, but winter travel was not assured until after World War II when, for 22 years, George Lemon, working for the Montana State Highway Department, plowed the road. (Above, S. Anderson; below, PM.)

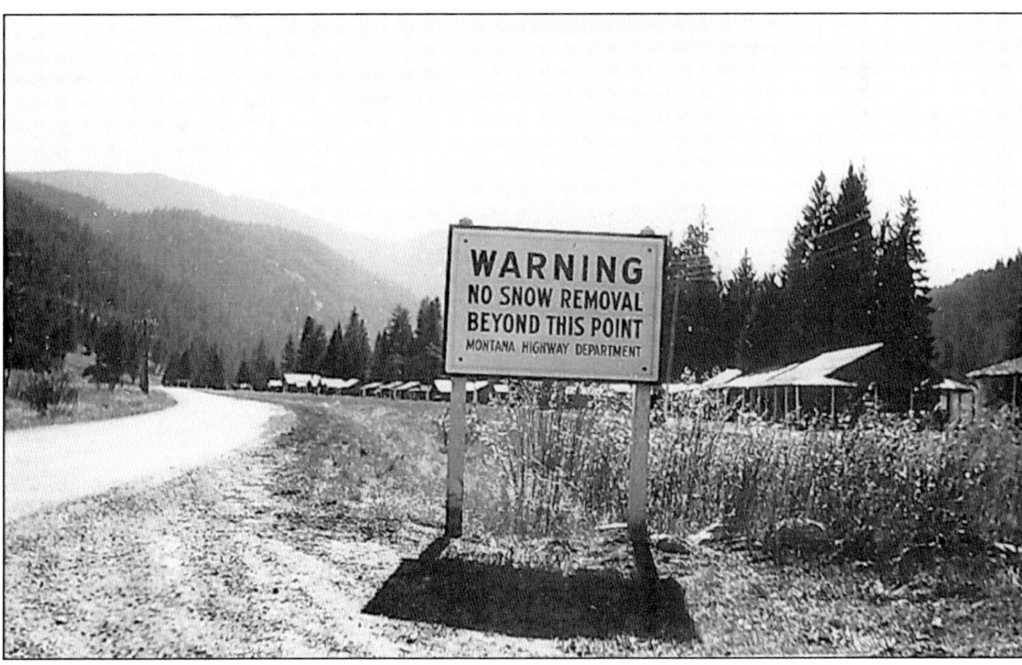

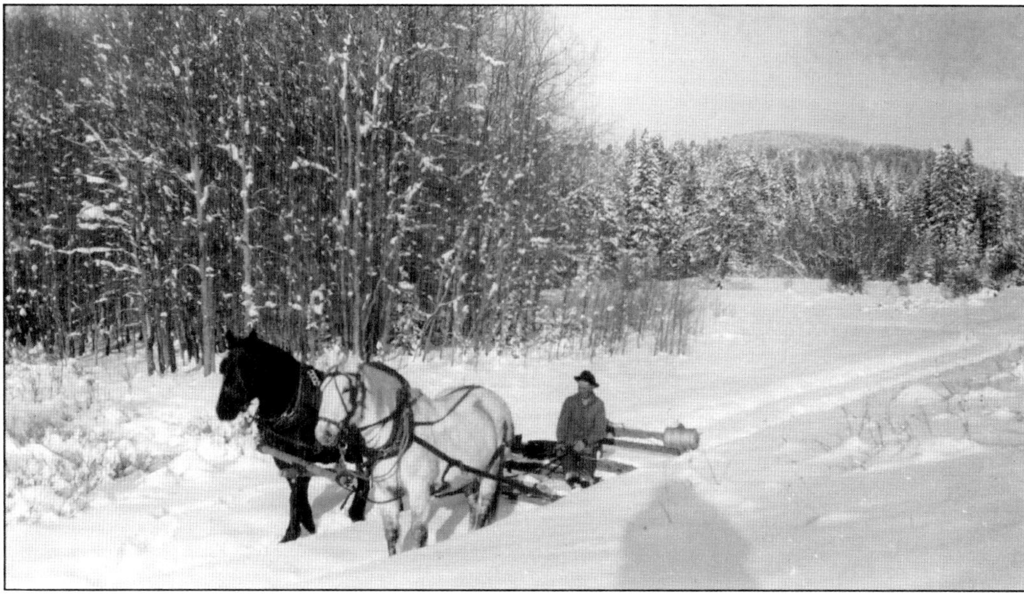

Winter Travel on the Crail Ranch (Above); Sledge and Horses, 1928 (Below). Those who stayed in the Gallatin Canyon and Basin found ways to deal with the isolation. Horse-drawn sleighs and sledges provided a means of travel. Above, Emmett Crail is on a sledge near the current 18th hole of the Big Sky Golf Course. Below, Arthur Foster regularly delivered mail to the Eldredge Post Office. Originally located at the Cooper Tie Camp on the Taylor Fork, the post office moved when the tie camp folded in 1907 to the 320 Ranch, where it remained serving the canyon until 1936. It was then absorbed by Gallatin Gateway where the postal service is today. The Big Sky community currently has its own contracted post office but no home delivery. (Above, HCRC; below, PM.)

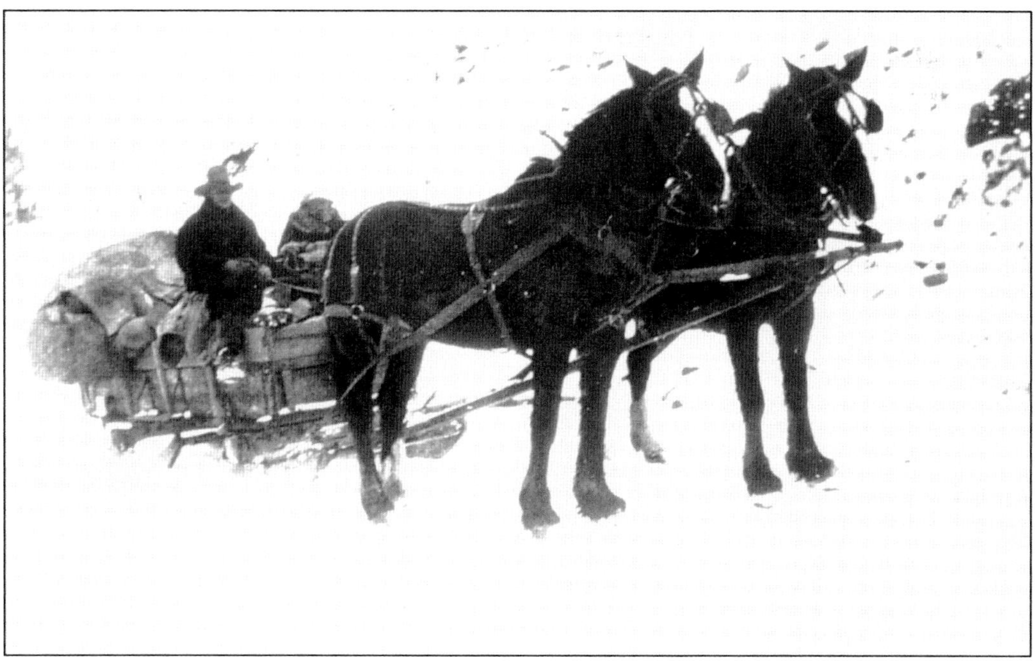

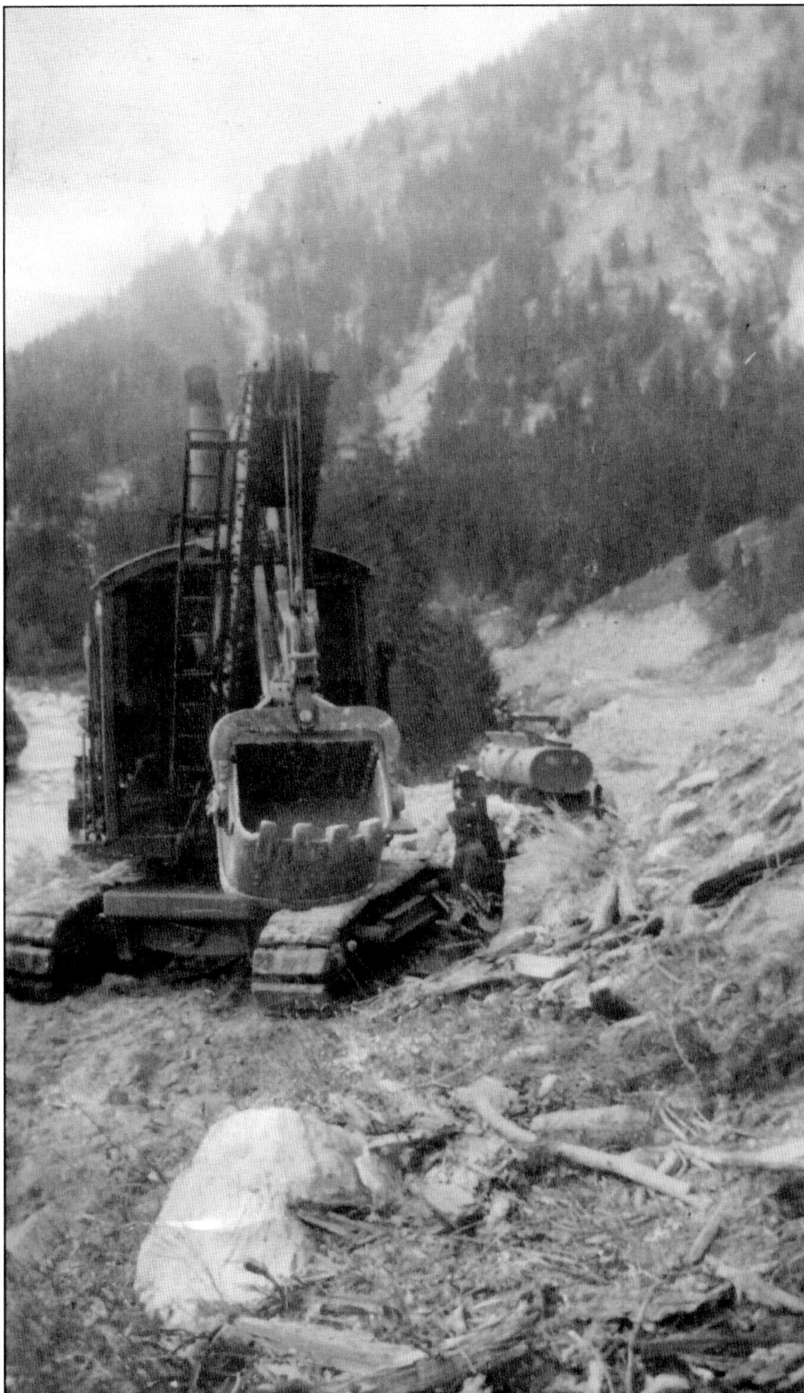

Steam Shovel. Serious improvements in the road were almost a constant job. Here, a steam shovel can be seen working the hillside. The new road cuts are visible in the background. The addition of gravel in 1939 and later asphalt, along with improved maintenance and automobiles, made transportation more modern and accessible. (S. Anderson.)

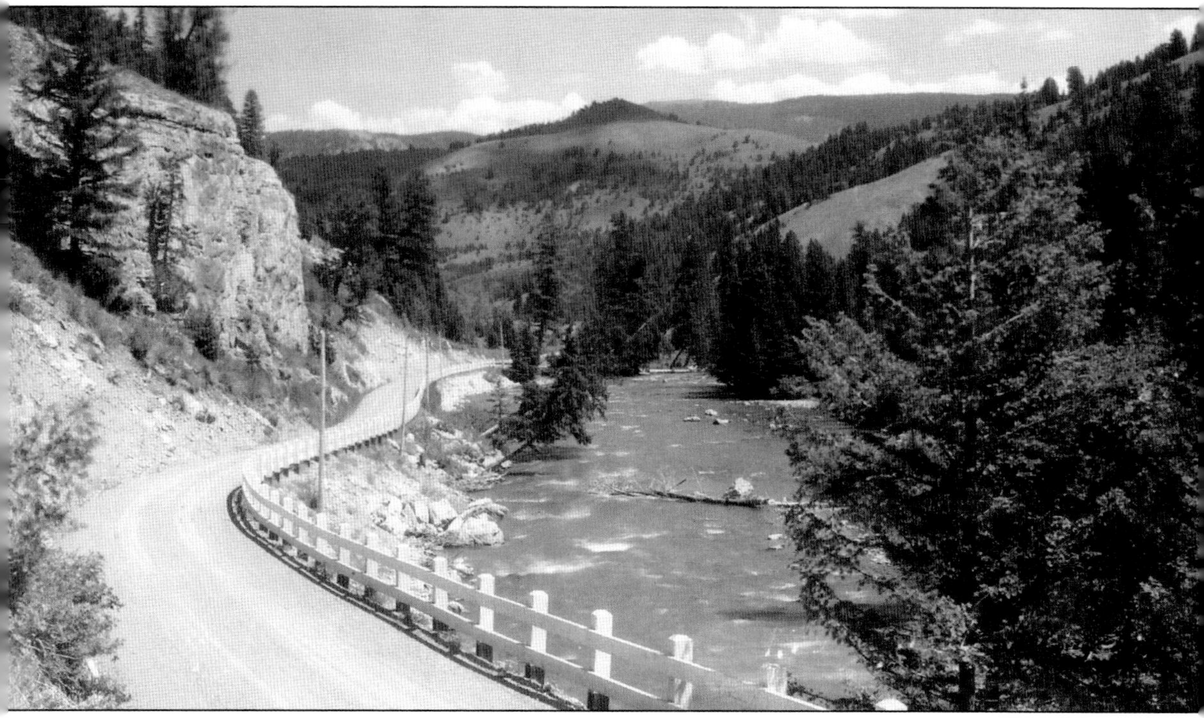

GRAVEL ROADBED WITH GUARDRAILS. Gravel was added with the improvements in 1939. Blacktop was not laid until the improvements of 1952–1953. To this day, it remains one of the most dangerous highways in Montana. (HCRC.)

Three

"Chasing Rainbows" Mining and Logging

Gold fever affected this area as it did much of Montana. There were even a couple of "gold rushes" that lured men from Bozeman to reported strikes. None lasted more than a few days as none struck pay dirt. Most of the pioneer homesteaders report looking for gold in the streams. Tom Michener found some and even went so far as to start a company, the Hercules Dredging Company, in 1914 to mine the West Fork basin and the upper Gallatin River. However, his partners were shot and killed by Andrew Levinski in January 1917. Levinski's acquittal on the basis of self-defense and claim jumping, along with the lack of profitable quantities of gold, put an end to the venture. Silver and copper were found in small amounts, and useable coal up the Taylor Fork was also mined. None proved worthwhile, and all the mines were abandoned. The one profitable mineral mined was asbestos. Pete Karst discovered a seam on the hill west of his ranch in 1908, which he began mining in 1924 and continued until 1947.

Logging was intermittently successful, and roads to the logging camps opened up the area for ranches and homesteads. The first operations were the Cooper Tie Camps of 1904–1907. Lumbermen spent the winter cutting logs that were dragged to the creek bottoms. The creeks had been dammed, and with the spring runoff, the dam was blown and the logs floated down the Gallatin to the sawmill in Central City, near present-day Gallatin Gateway. Transportation and labor problems forced Cooper to close, but the roads remained. A later operation took place at the B-K from 1950 to 1955. Don Corcoran from Minnesota bought the ranch and started a large pulp mill. The needs of this timber industry was said to be one of the primary reasons that the road was improved and asphalt laid. However, the Corcoran mill was also not commercially viable and closed in 1955. Logging trucks are still occasionally encountered on US 191 as small-scale timber cutting and forest thinning continue to this day.

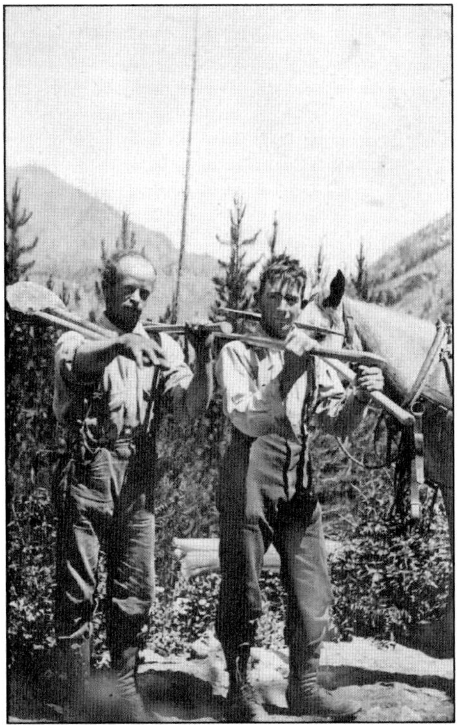

Postcard of Unidentified Miners (Left); a Placer Mine (Below). There were placer claims throughout the West Fork basin from 1880 through 1945, but the reported annual output seldom exceeded a few ounces. With the lack of good "color," serious miners headed off to richer strikes. It was the possibility of gold that brought Tom Michener to the Gallatin. A miner died in Bozeman around 1889, and his son told of a lost sluice box at a rich placer strike. Although the sluice box and the strike were never found, the tale brought Tom and others to the area and started a legend that fueled speculation for nearly two decades. It was this tale and the search for the gold that led Strauss Miller and Gladstone Stevens to their deaths at the Andrew Levinski claim near the present-day ski resort. (Left, HCRC; below, PM.)

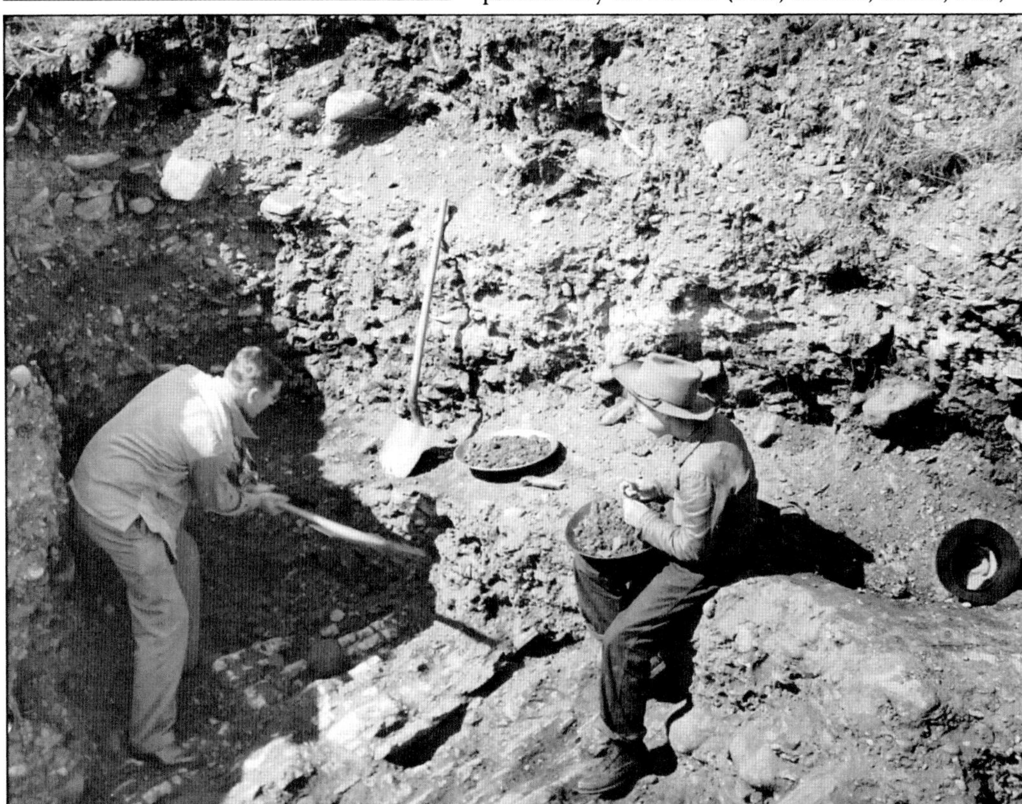

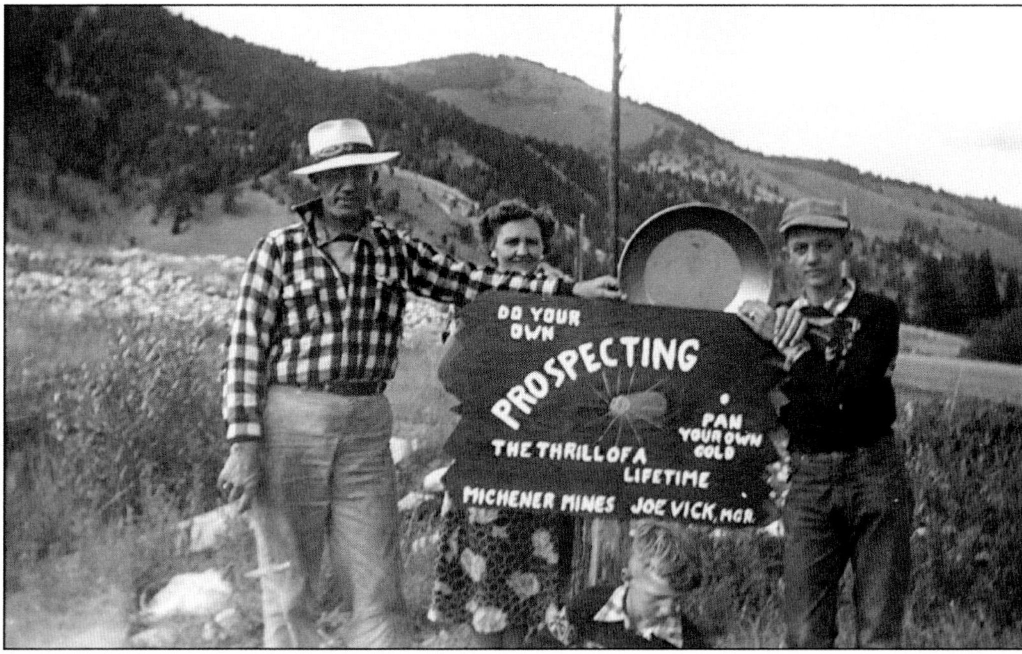

Prospectors at the Michener Camp (Above); Panning for Gold (Below). There were many small placer claims in the early decades of the 20th century. Three residents claimed to be miners in the 1910 census, none in 1920, and only two in 1930. Tom Michener filed 45 claims and Pete Karst 39, but only one in the whole basin was ever patented. Tom left in 1919 for brighter dreams in New Mexico, but Dorothy Vick, his daughter, and her husband, Joe, returned to the Gallatin in the late 1930s and reopened the homestead and mining claim. It did not produce much gold, but it brought in profits from the visitors who paid to pan for it. In the above photograph, the Wilding family poses, and below, dudes work the site as artist John Stewart Curry watches. (Both, PM.)

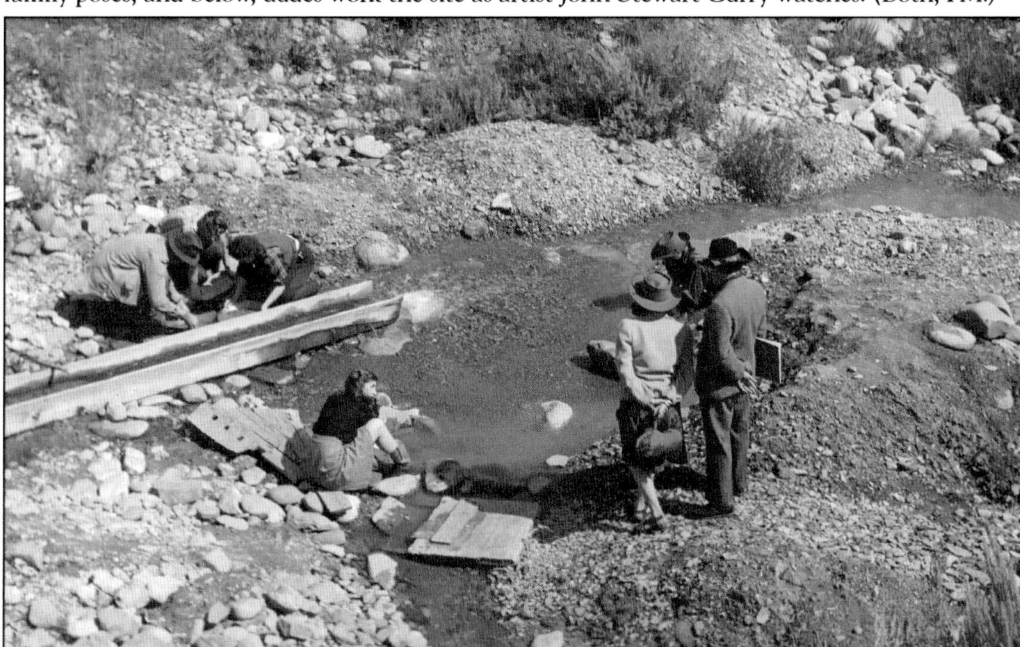

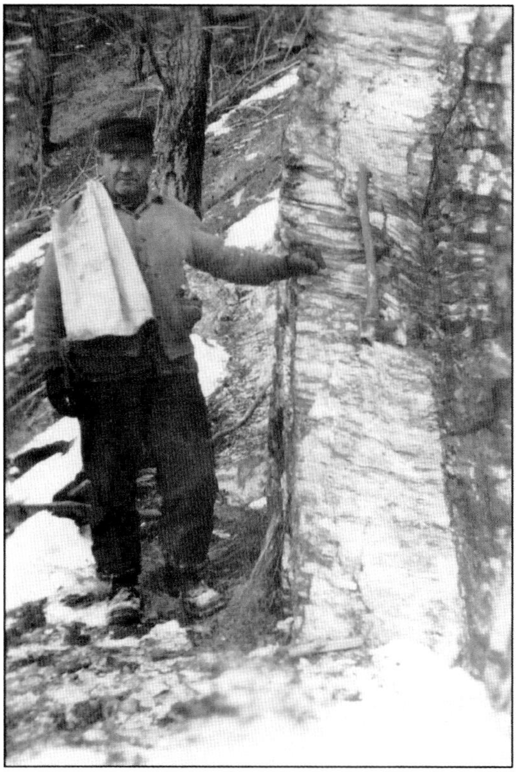

Pete Karst at His Mine (Left); Asbestos Flume (Below). The seam of asbestos that Pete Karst discovered in 1908 on the hill to the west of his camp provided a small-scale but profitable extraction for over 20 years. Mining started in 1924 and continued until 1947. The flume and the mill at the river are gone, but the closed mine adit, or entrance, can be reached by a US Forest Service trail to this day. (Left, S. Anderson; below, Museum of the Rockies, X85.2.190.)

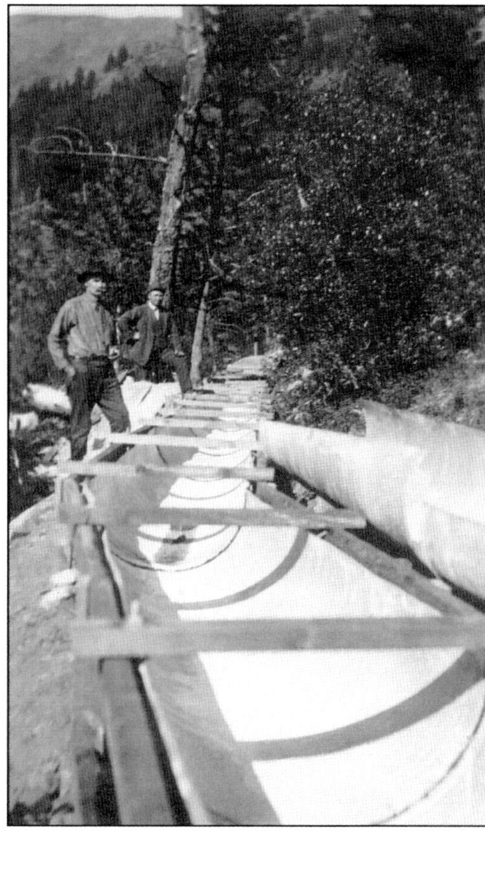

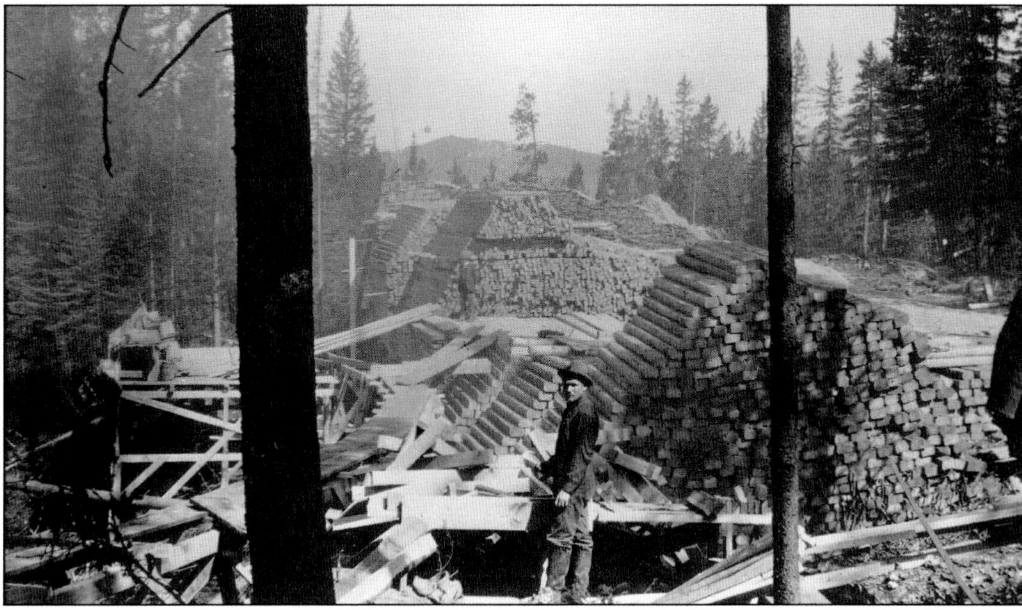

Piles of Ties (Above); Unidentified Loggers (Below). The Cooper Tie Camps operated from 1904 to 1907. Three were located in the Taylor Fork drainage south of Big Sky, and others were on Buck Creek and the West Fork. Each camp had 50 men with subcontractors hiring 30 to 40 people each. Cooper provided railroad ties for construction of the Northern Pacific Railroad that was being built through Montana at that time. Labor disputes, the panic of 1907, and the completion of the rail line ended profitability. It was before the time of adequate motorized travel, so all work was done by horse and hand as seen here. (Above, Museum of the Rockies x83.13.549; below, Ophir School archives and PM.)

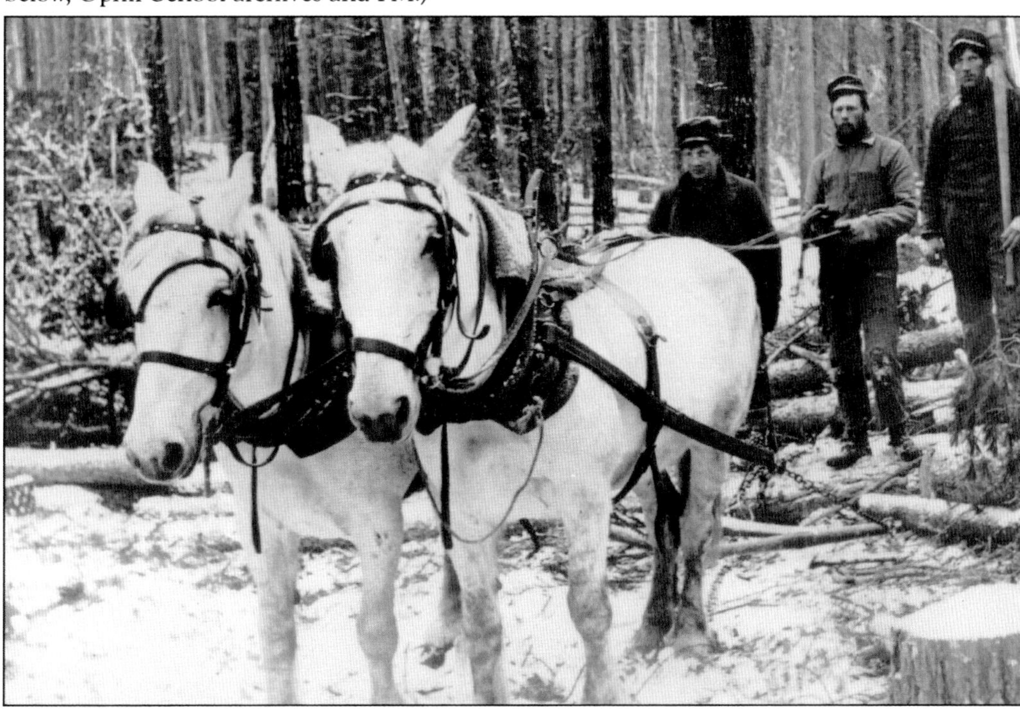

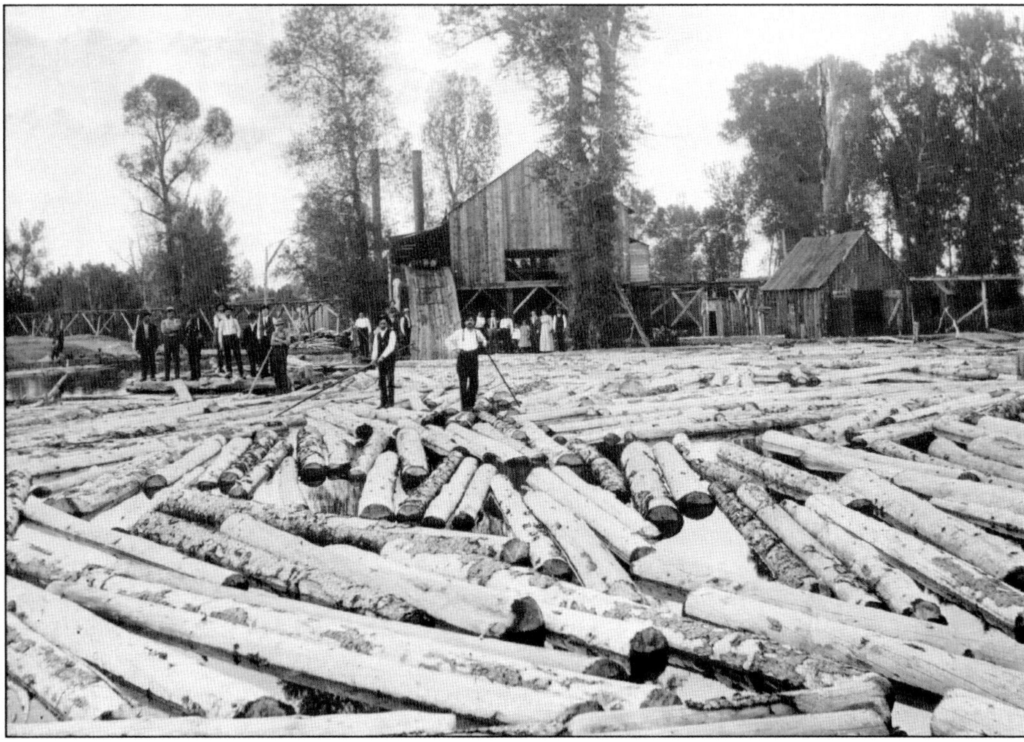

End of the Float (Above); Logs at Moose Creek (Below). Logs were cut all winter and dragged to the dammed creek bottoms. In the spring, the dams were breached, and men rode the logs or followed in boats all the way through the Gallatin River rapids. Long steel hooks were used to loosen the log jams that formed, and the flotilla continued on to the sawmill at the end of the rail spur at Central City, south of Bozeman, pictured above. Cooper closed his camps in 1907, but the photograph below from the 1930s shows that logging continued through the Depression. (Above, Museum of the Rockies x83.13.835; below, S. Anderson.)

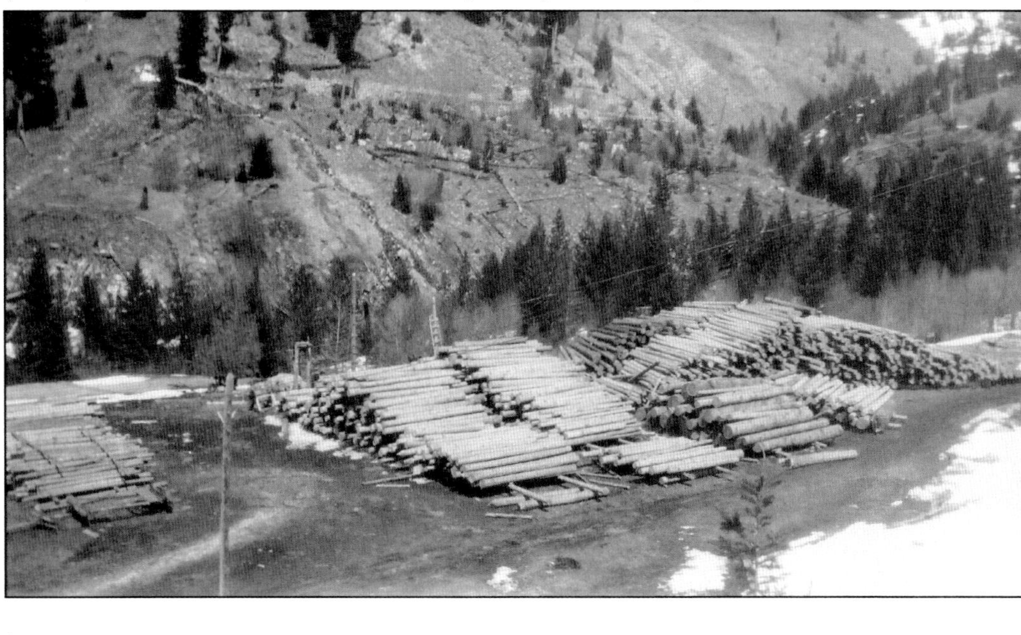

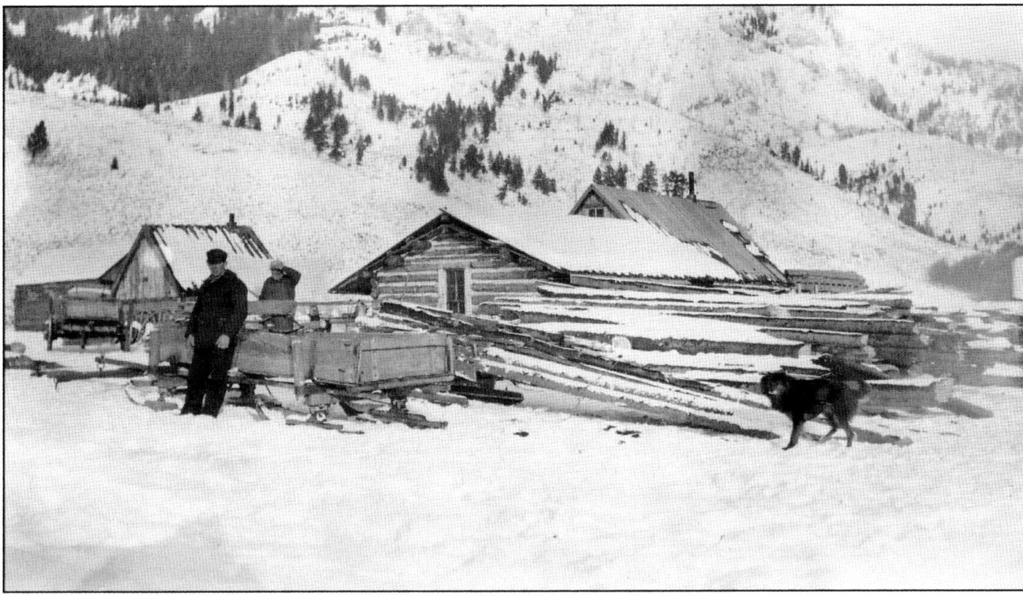

Lumberyard at Crail Ranch (Above); Emmett Crail at His Sawmill (Below). Because of the remote nature of the homesteads, many had their own small sawmills. Here, Emmett Crail and unidentified hands are cutting beams. The beams and planks were used for shingles and siding for the houses and for barn construction. Eugene Crail was a trained carpenter who built the schoolhouse and several cabins for his neighbors. (Both, HCRC.)

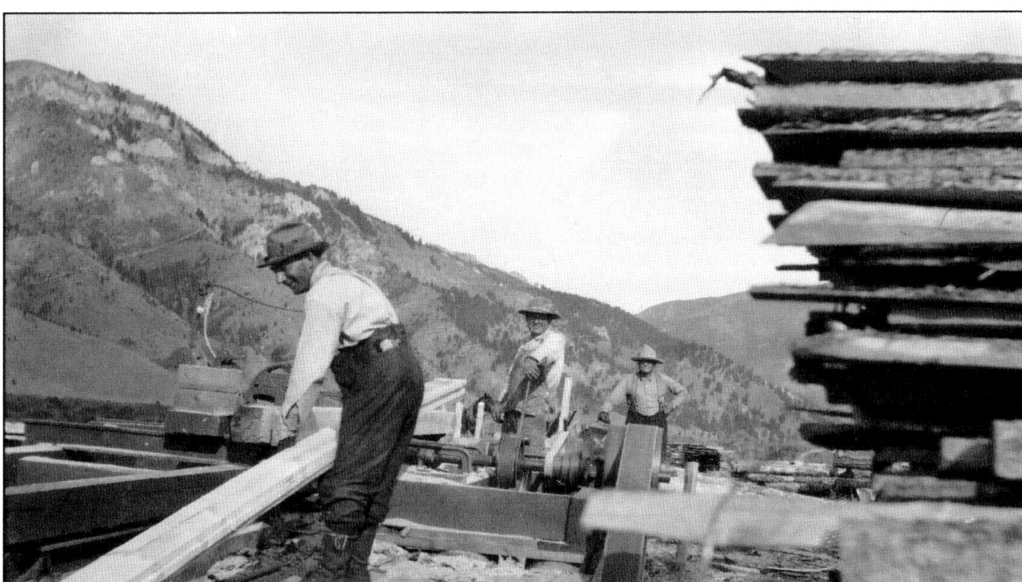

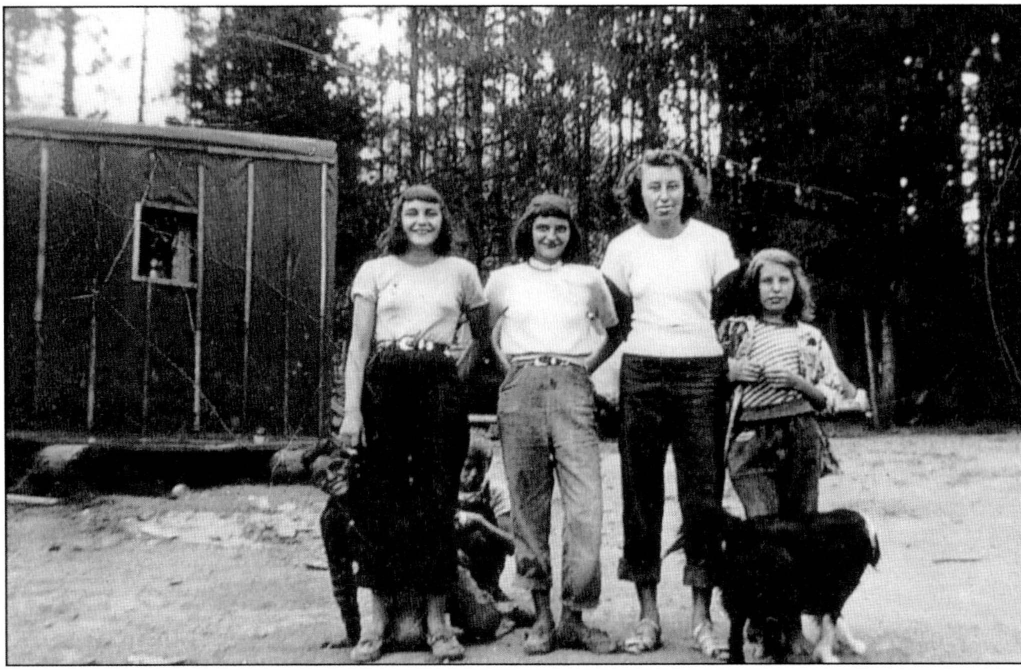

Tar Paper Shacks (Above); Dragging the Shack on Skids (Below). The area's last serious timber operation was the Corcoran Lumber Camp at the B-K. The employees were "housed" in these 9-by-12-foot tar paper shacks. During the most active year, there were over 80 camp children in Ophir School, so school that year was held at the B-K. One, who returned as an adult guest at the ranch, reminisced about the cold and drafty shacks. Another told of returning to get her homework and finding the shack gone. She had to follow the skid trail in the snow to locate her home. Below, Ken McBride, with Jean and Don riding, drags a shack to a new location in 1953. (Above, Lone Mountain Ranch; below, the McBride family collection.)

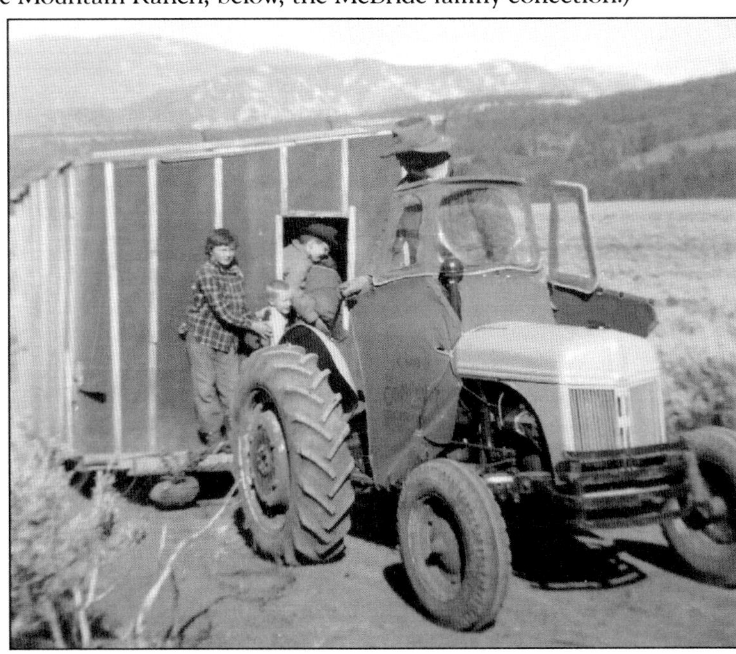

Four

"Come a Ti-Yi-Yippie Yippie Yea"

Ranching

The people who came looking for a place to live and to settle the land were typical of the homesteaders throughout Montana. They may have had a minor interest in logging or mining, but they primarily pursued agriculture.

The high altitude of the upper Gallatin and West Fork had long winters and deep snow that, with the exception of the Durnam lettuce field, was not conducive to growing crops. As a result, farmers raised hay, sheep, and cattle. Hardy breeds were necessary, and a large haying operation was needed to overwinter the animals, which could require up to two tons of hay per cow.

Although many of the people in the area raised animals, the Crail and 320 Ranches continued to the present era and were well documented photographically. As a result, there is an authentic documentation of haying before machines and an accurate record of the cattle operation from branding in the spring, to the summer range, to the winter corrals.

The geography of the area limited where ranching could be pursued, as only the wide open creek basins and river bottoms were suitable for hay. The first major cattle operation was in 1898 in the Taylor Fork south of Big Sky where Marshall Cunningham and Hans Behring ran several thousand head. The 320 later used this area as a summer range. The Crails and their successors used the West Fork basin, and Ken McBride ran sheep there until the Meadow Village appeared with the creation of the ski resort. Several of the original ranches, such as the Stillman, Lytle, and Waters places, disappeared from history. Most of the others became dude ranches. The 320 and the Lone Mountain Ranch (formerly the B-K) continued with the guests helping to run a working cattle ranch, while others such as the Half Way Inn/Rainbow Ranch and the current Buck's T-4 turned to short-term stays featuring trail rides, fishing, and hunting.

Big Sky's ranching roots have been captured in these timeless photographs from the archival collections of the early 20th century.

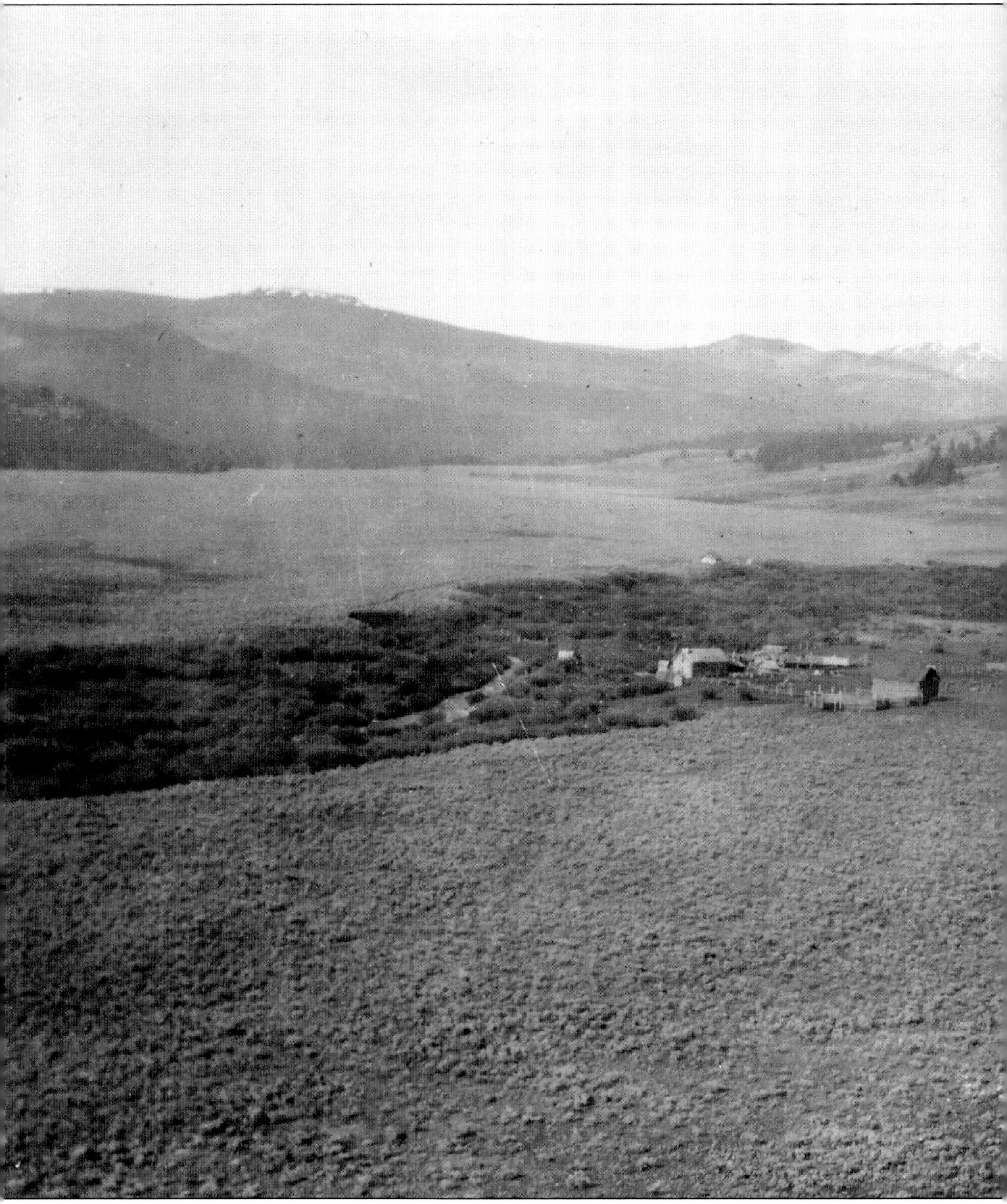

Crail Ranch, c. 1920. Beautiful and remote, the Crail Ranch spreads across the Basin of the West Fork. Then over two miles from the nearest neighbor, today this scene is filled with the links of the Arnold Palmer–designed golf course and the homes, condos, and businesses of Big Sky's Meadow Village. When Frank Crail bought the homestead from Daniel Inabnit in 1901, it

was a one-room cabin and 160 acres. Over the next 49 years, the ranch expanded to 960 deeded acres and 10 structures, including a two-story house, a forge, sawmill, piggery, chicken coops, springhouse, and barns. Even so, electricity did not come until 1948, and indoor plumbing was added by the Humes after they purchased the ranch in 1950. (HCRC.)

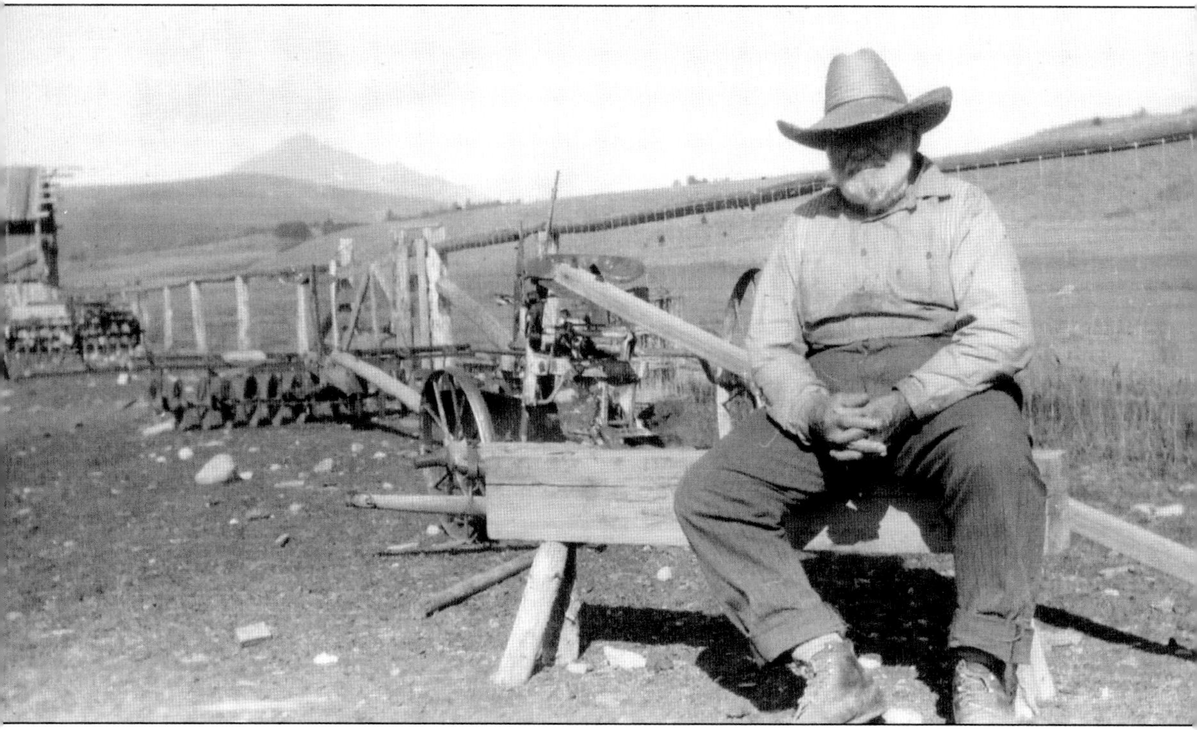

A.F. Crail and Equipment. Augustus Franklin "Frank" Crail, in the early 1920s, sits on a sawhorse in front of a disc harrow and dump rake. Lone Mountain rises in the distance. (HCRC.)

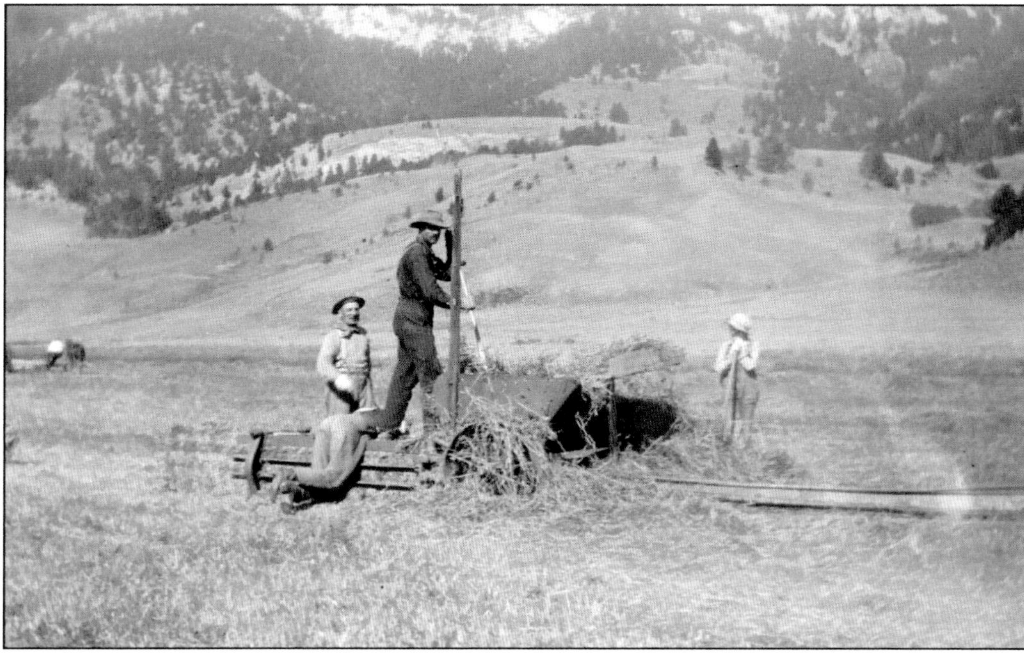

Baling Hay, 1915. Bert Stillman, standing between two unidentified hands, demonstrates that much of the work was done by hand. The Waters Ranch, shown here, was east of the river and Ophir School and is now owned by the State of Montana for the Gallatin elk herd's winter range. (Ophir School archives.)

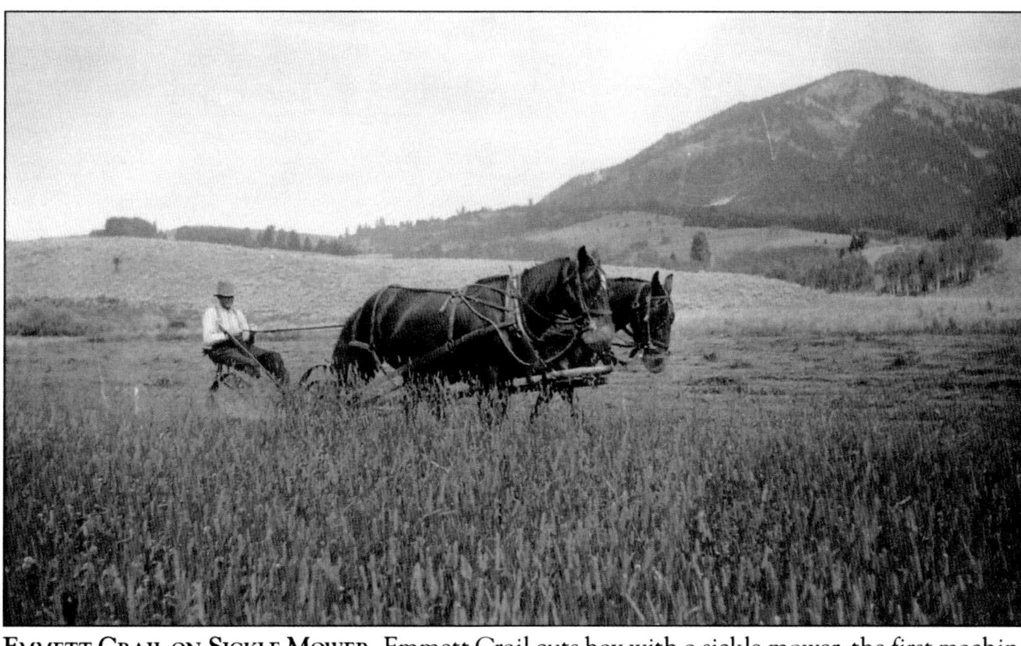

Emmett Crail on Sickle Mower. Emmett Crail cuts hay with a sickle mower, the first machine in the multistep haying process. The toothed sickle bar extends to the right side with the back-and-forth blade action operated by the wheels' motion. The horses are able to walk on the mowed strip. (HCRC.)

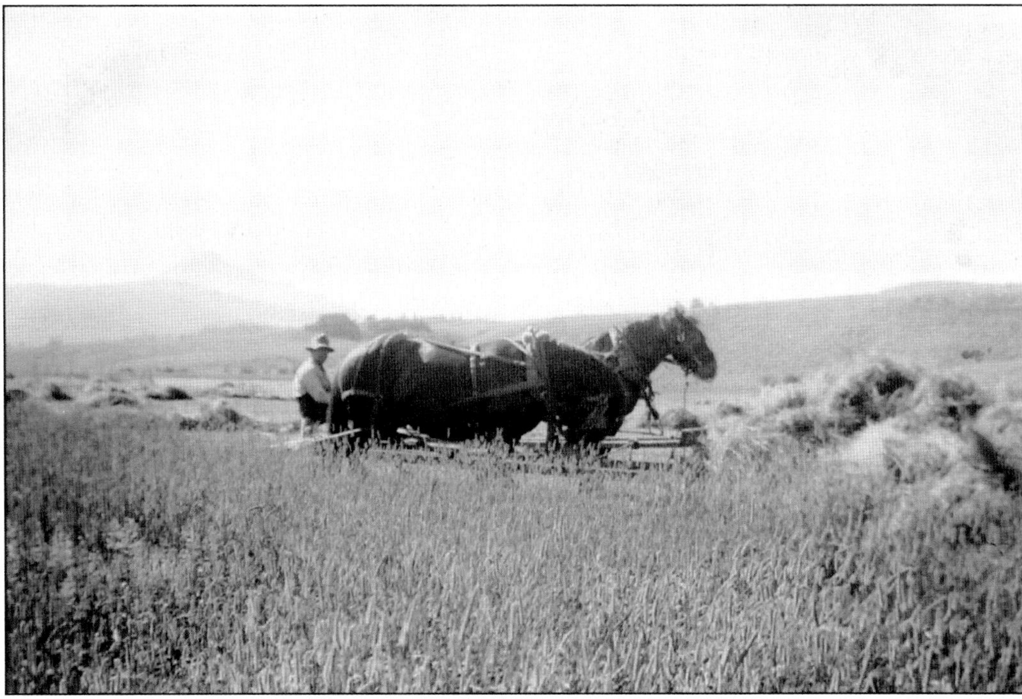

EMMETT CRAIL ON A BUCK RAKE (ABOVE); BUILDING THE HAYSTACK (BELOW). The long, curved teeth of the horse-drawn dump rake, also called a sulkey rake, seen in the background on page 38, turned the cut hay over and moved it into windrow piles where it would dry. When the hay was dry, the team of horses pushed it ahead into piles for the hay stacker using the comb-toothed buck rake. In the photograph below, the boom derrick, a crane adapted for haying and also known as a Mormon derrick, lifts the hay onto a stack. Ranch hands, called stackers, stood on the stack to level the hay. (Both, HCRC.)

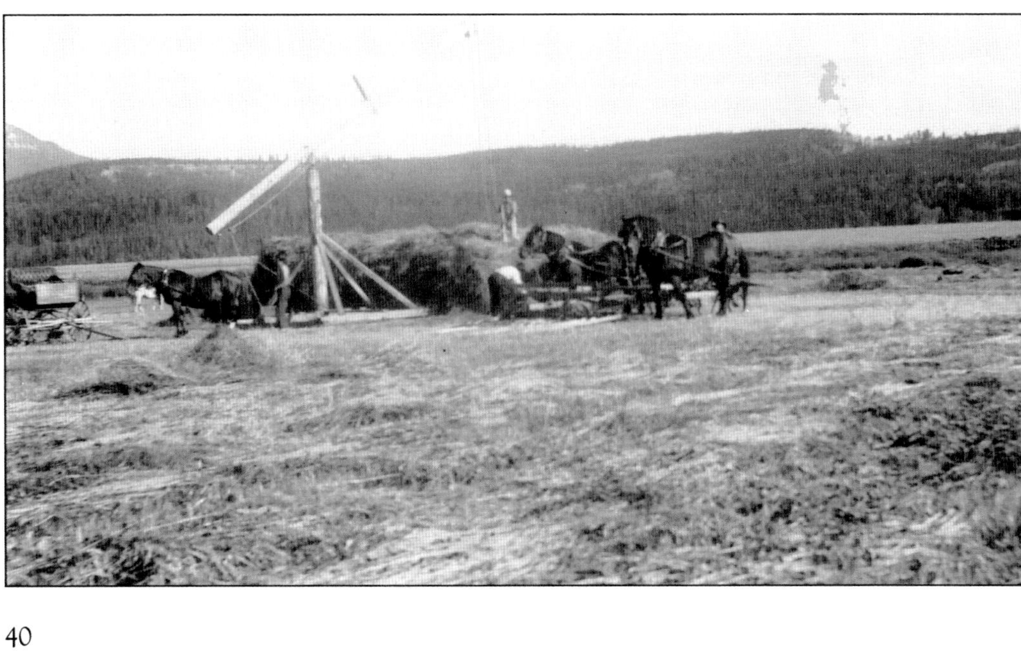

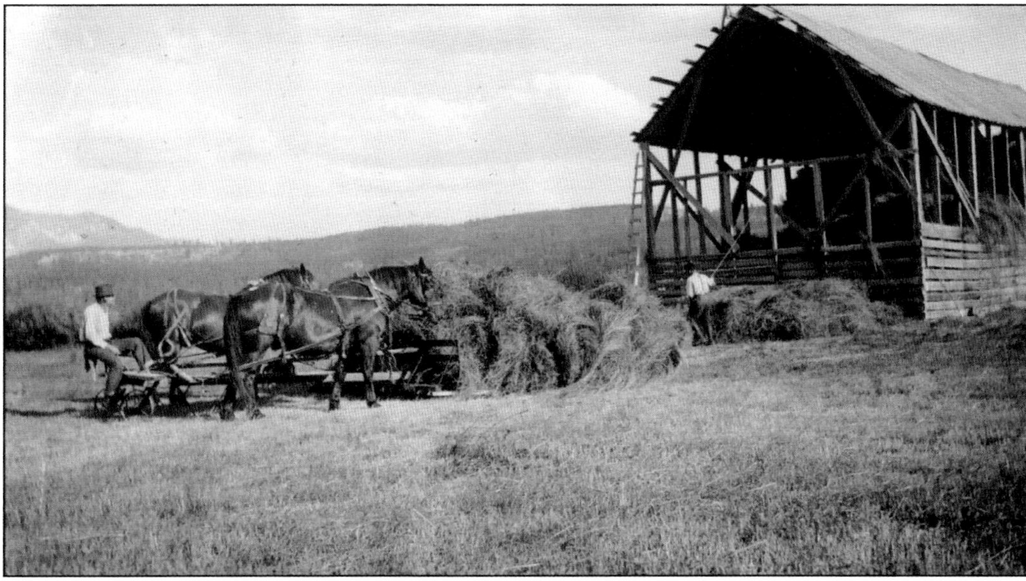

Buck Rake and Drying Shed. In this photograph, a buck rake pushes hay to the drying shed. This type of pole barn was particularly useful because of the heavy snowfall in the basin. (HCRC.)

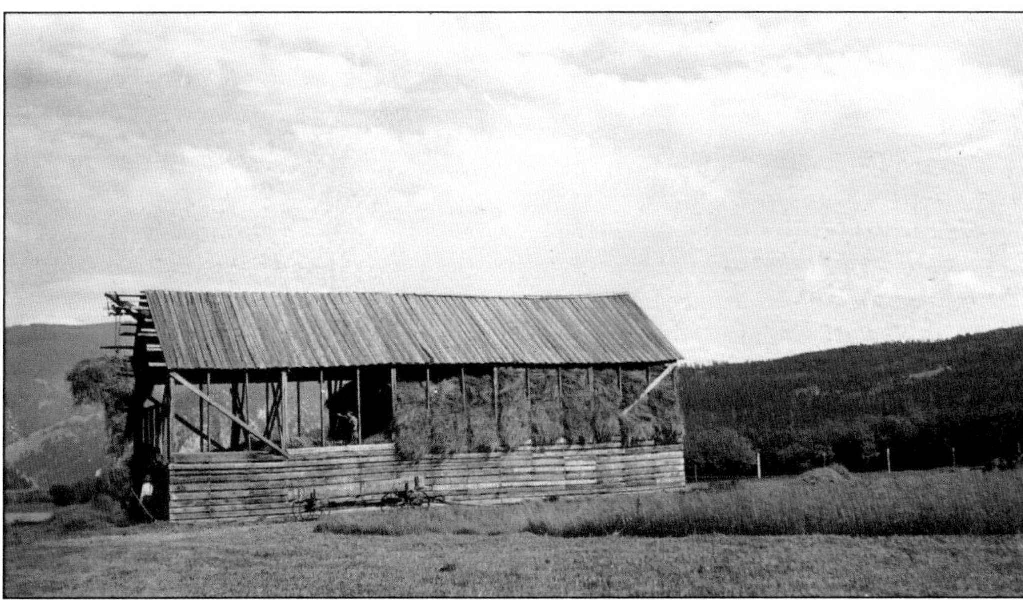

Drying Shed or Hay Barn. Note the pulley and grappling hook, adapted from the boom derrick, that allowed for efficient filling of the open-sided drying shed. (HCRC.)

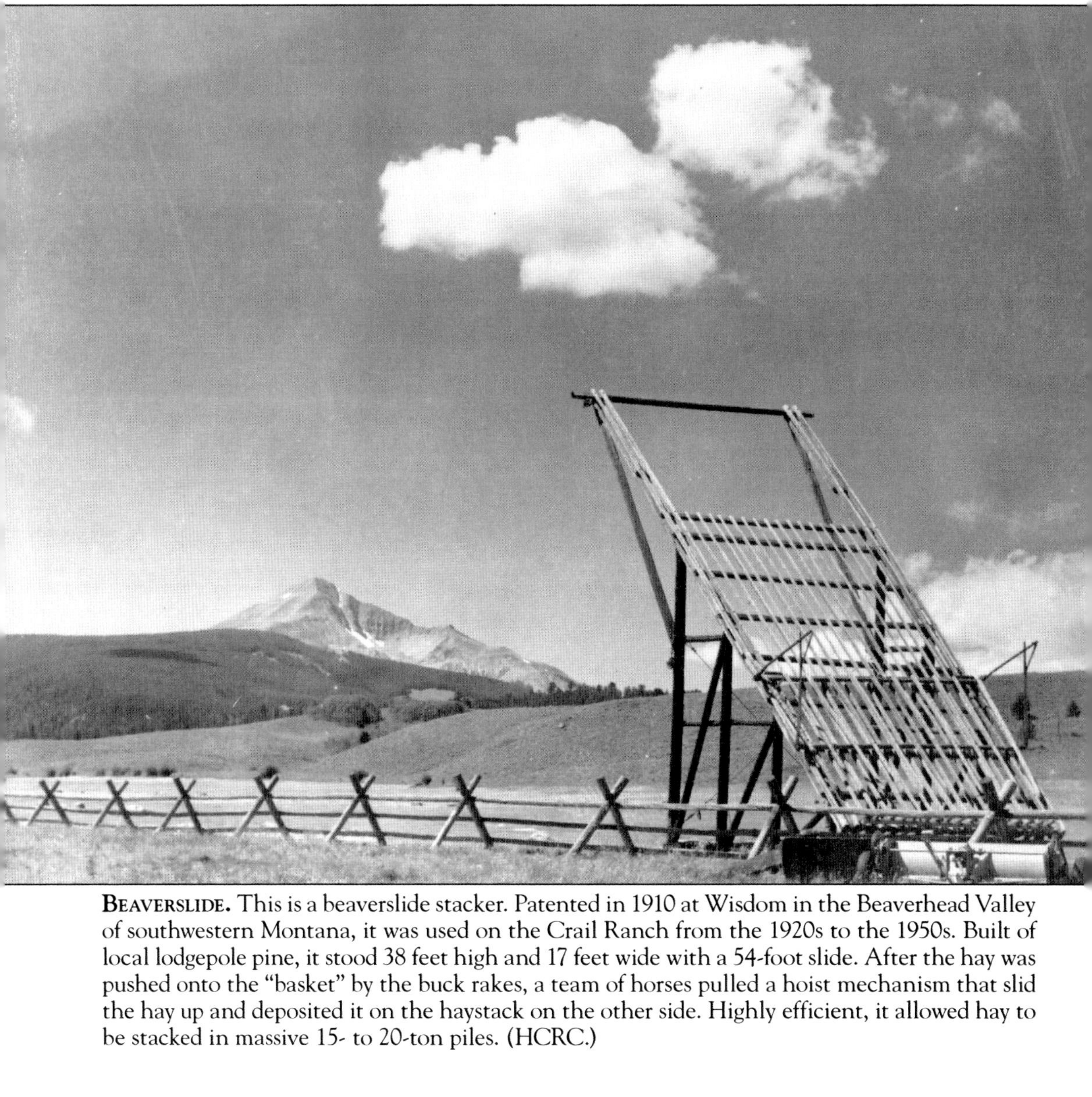

BEAVERSLIDE. This is a beaverslide stacker. Patented in 1910 at Wisdom in the Beaverhead Valley of southwestern Montana, it was used on the Crail Ranch from the 1920s to the 1950s. Built of local lodgepole pine, it stood 38 feet high and 17 feet wide with a 54-foot slide. After the hay was pushed onto the "basket" by the buck rakes, a team of horses pulled a hoist mechanism that slid the hay up and deposited it on the haystack on the other side. Highly efficient, it allowed hay to be stacked in massive 15- to 20-ton piles. (HCRC.)

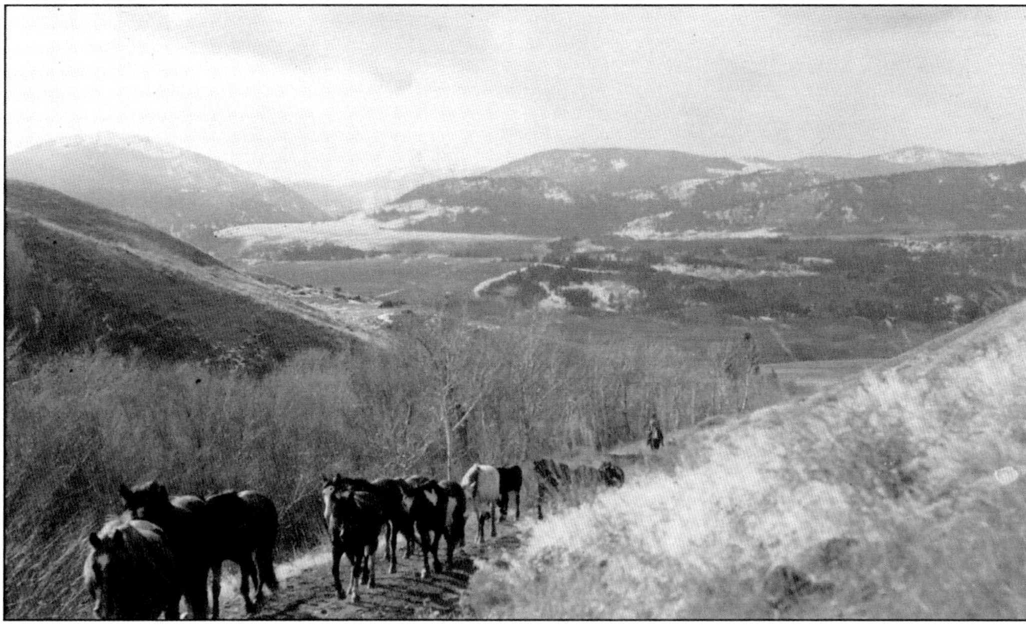

Moving Horses (Above); Horse Herd in Pasture (Below). Horses were essential to running a ranch. They dragged plows, mowers, and rakes, pulled wagons for transportation, and were saddled to carry folks for hunting, livestock management, and pleasure. Pictured are the Crail horses in the early 20th century. (Both, HCRC.)

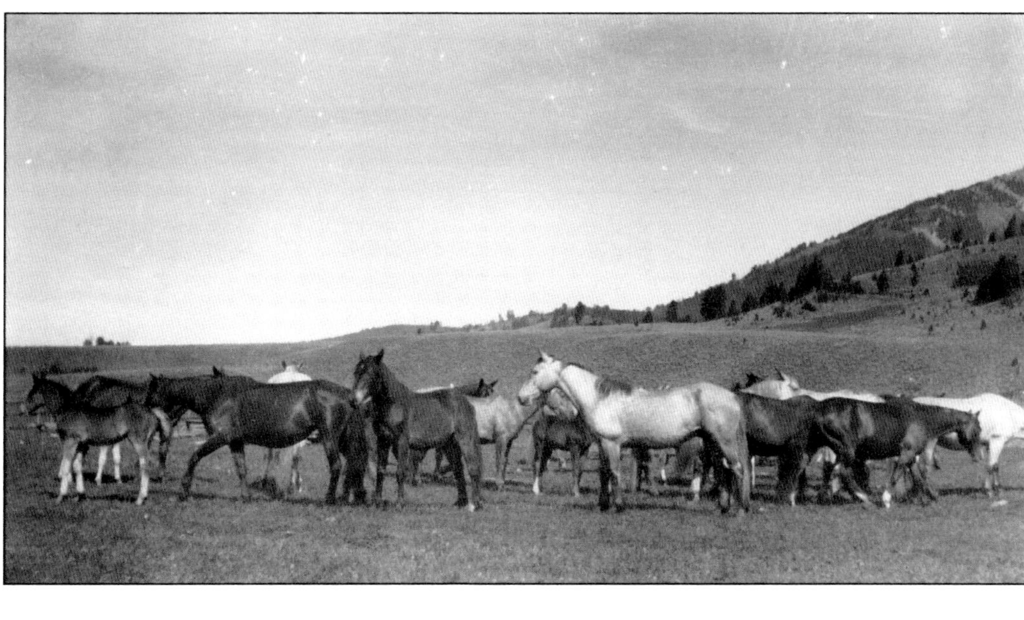

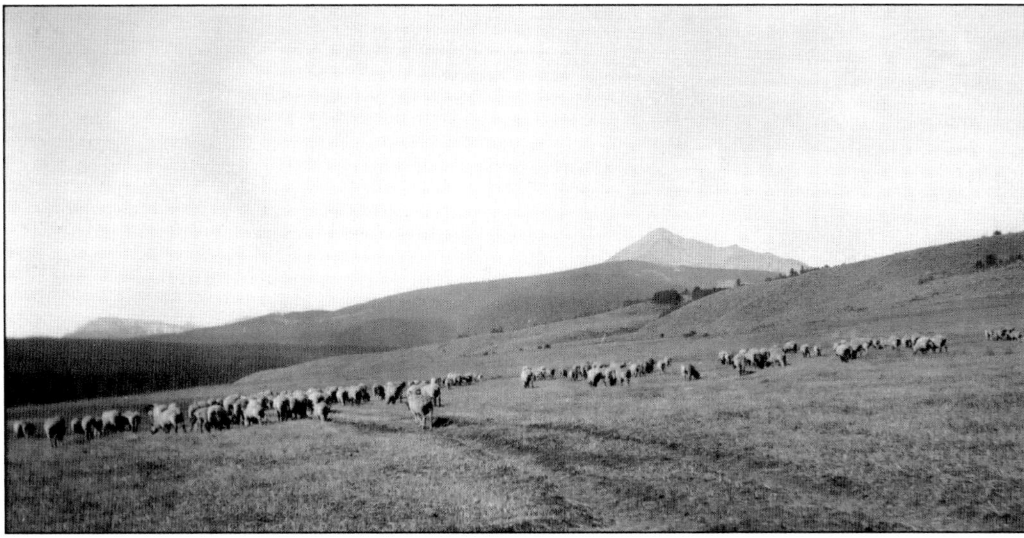

Crail Sheep Herd (Above); Ken McBride with Sheep (Below). A.F. Crail homesteaded the West Fork in 1902 and ran primarily sheep until his death in 1924. His son Emmett continued with sheep until 1934 when he switched to cattle. Sheep remained prominent in the West Fork until modern times. Ken McBride, until he developed the Westfork project in the 1970s, kept a flock at his place, the 5-K, where the fire and ambulance stations are now located. (Above, HCRC; below, McBride family collection.)

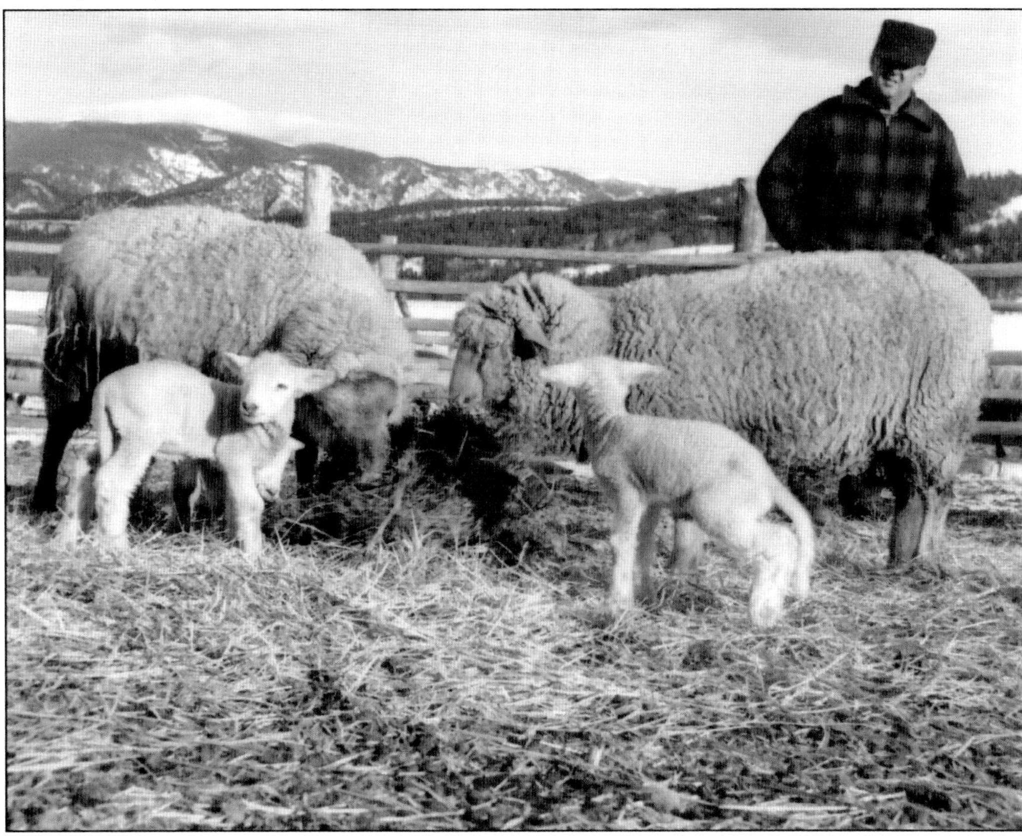

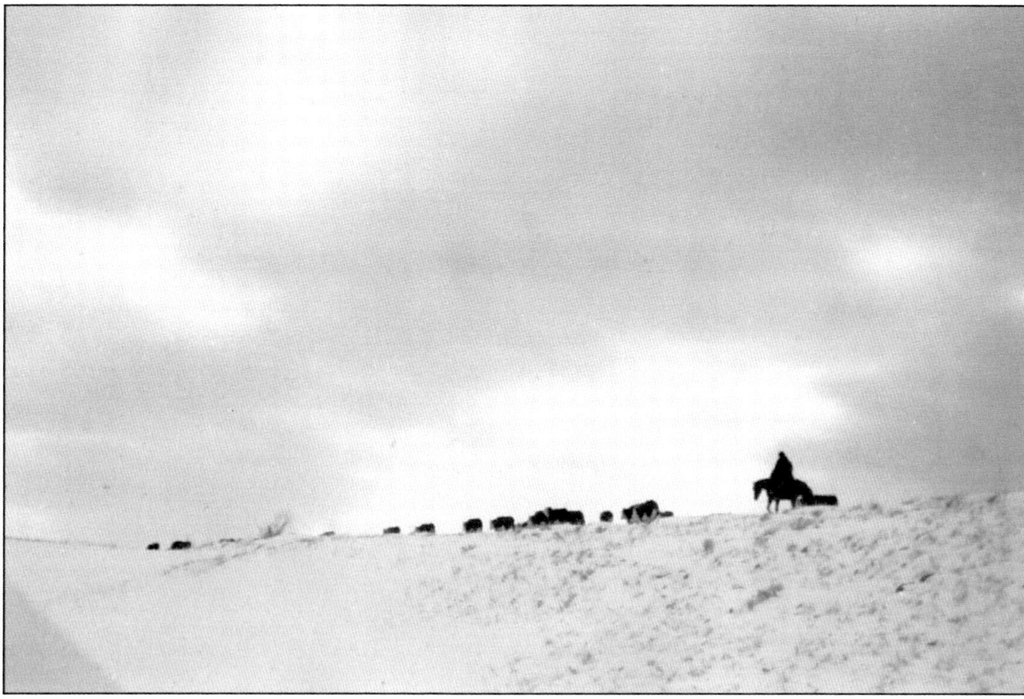

Moving the Herd in Winter (Above); Spring Calves (Below). Emmett Crail inherited the ranch in 1924 and shifted the focus to cattle. (Both, HCRC.)

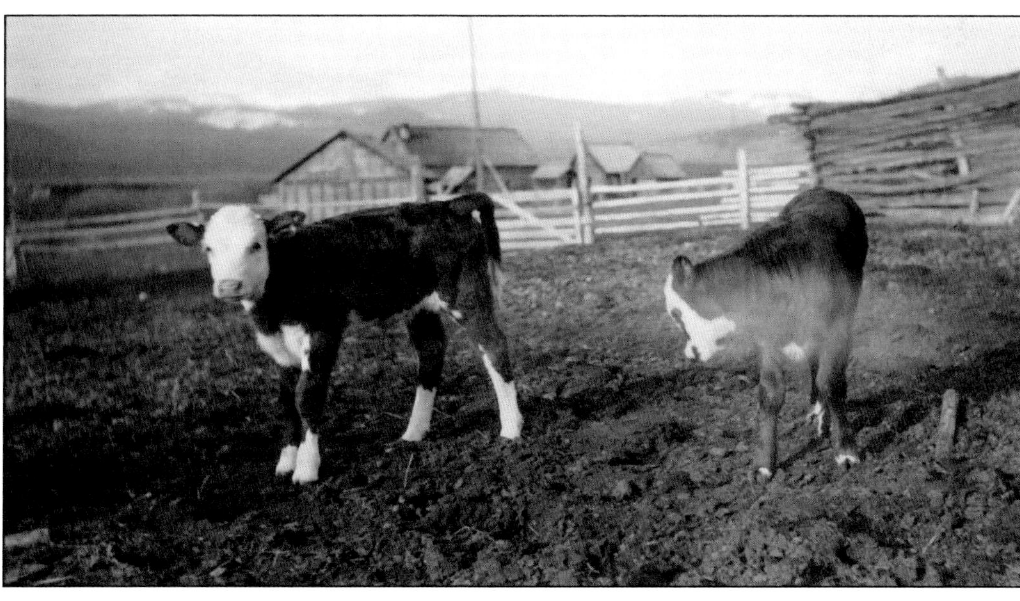

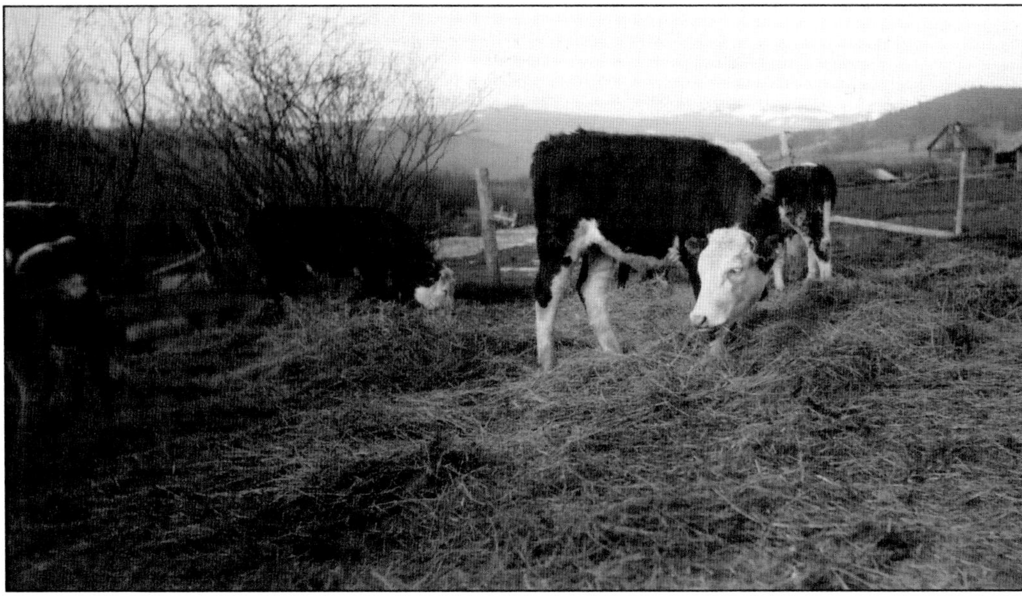

Cattle on Hay in Spring (Above); Ready for Summer Pasture (Below). Cattle would be fed hay until the grass had grown enough to support them. After the calves were born, the herd would be moved to summer pasture on leases on Northern Pacific Railroad or U.S. Forest Service land. The private land could then be used for growing hay for the following winter. (Both, HCRC.)

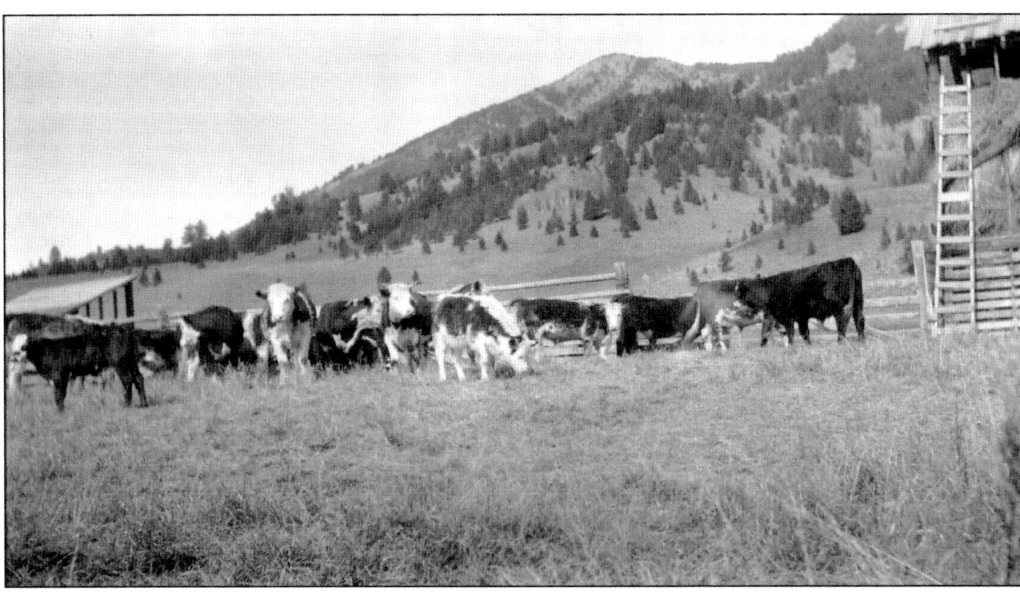

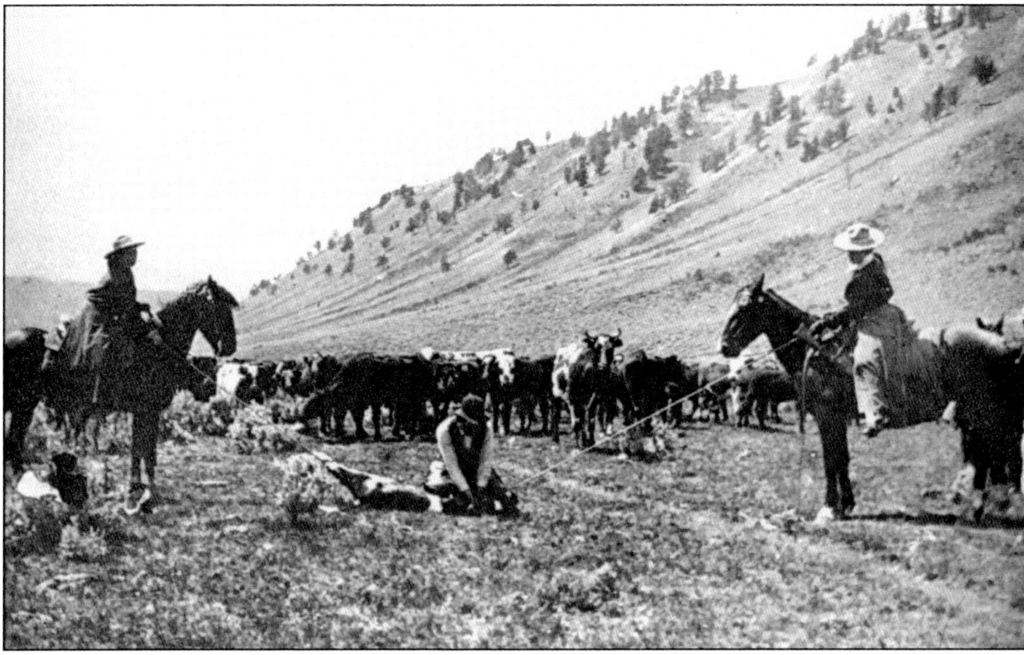

SEYMOUR CUNNINGHAM TYING A CALF (ABOVE); CUTTING PRIOR TO BRANDING (BELOW). The springtime cattle roundup brought the animals to the home corral for branding, castration, and treating. The above photograph shows the traditional calf-roping technique that has been replaced by herding into chutes. (Above, the Museum of the Rockies X84.4.623; below, 320 Ranch.)

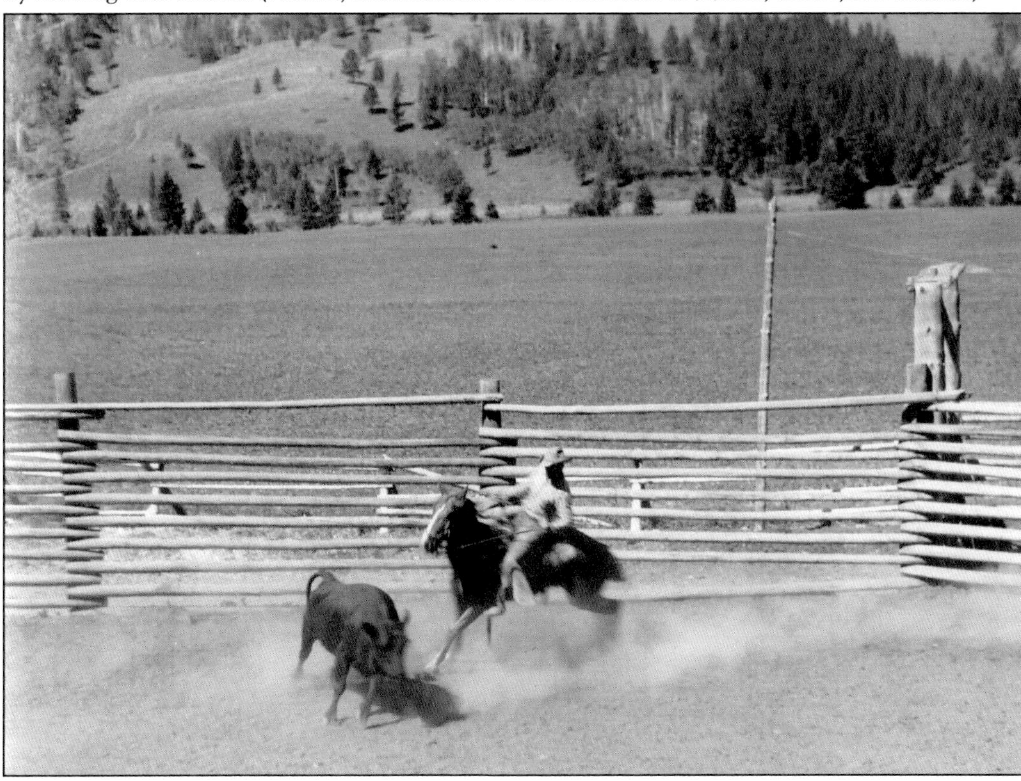

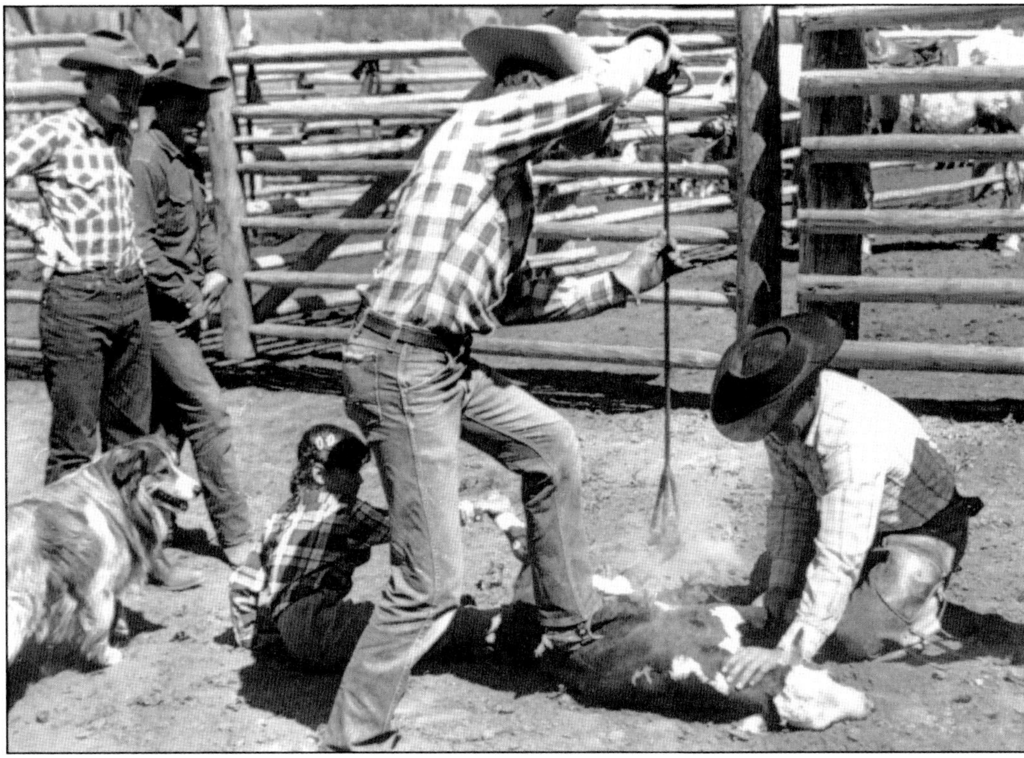

Jim Goodrich Branding (Above); Using a Kerosene Burner (Below). In the 1950s photograph below, a kerosene furnace has replaced the coals of a bonfire for heating the branding iron. The coffee can holds disinfectant to paint on the brand. (Above, PM; below, 320 Ranch.)

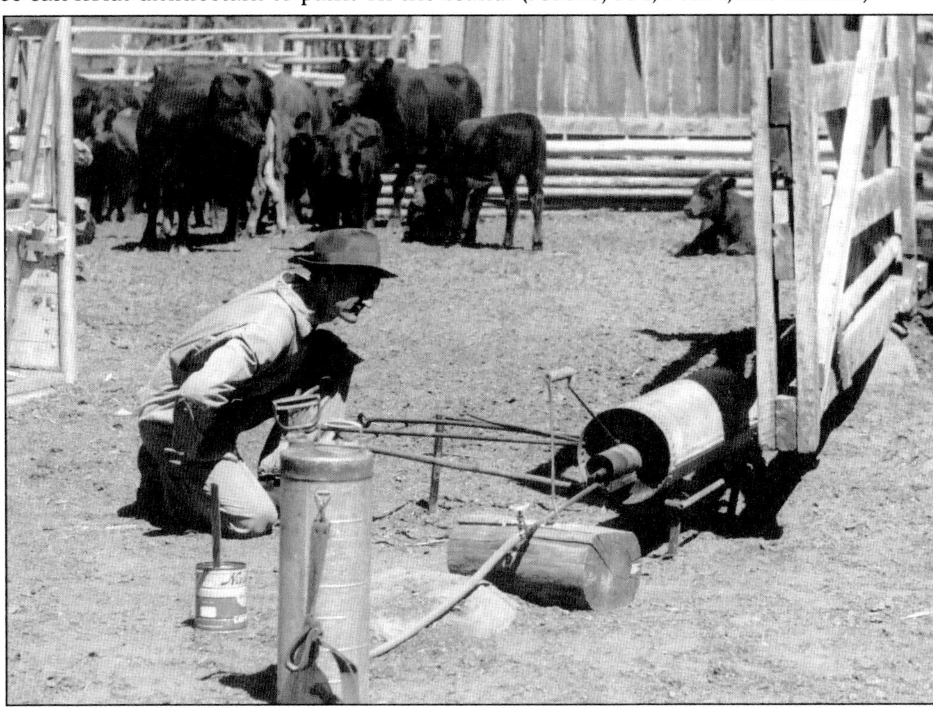

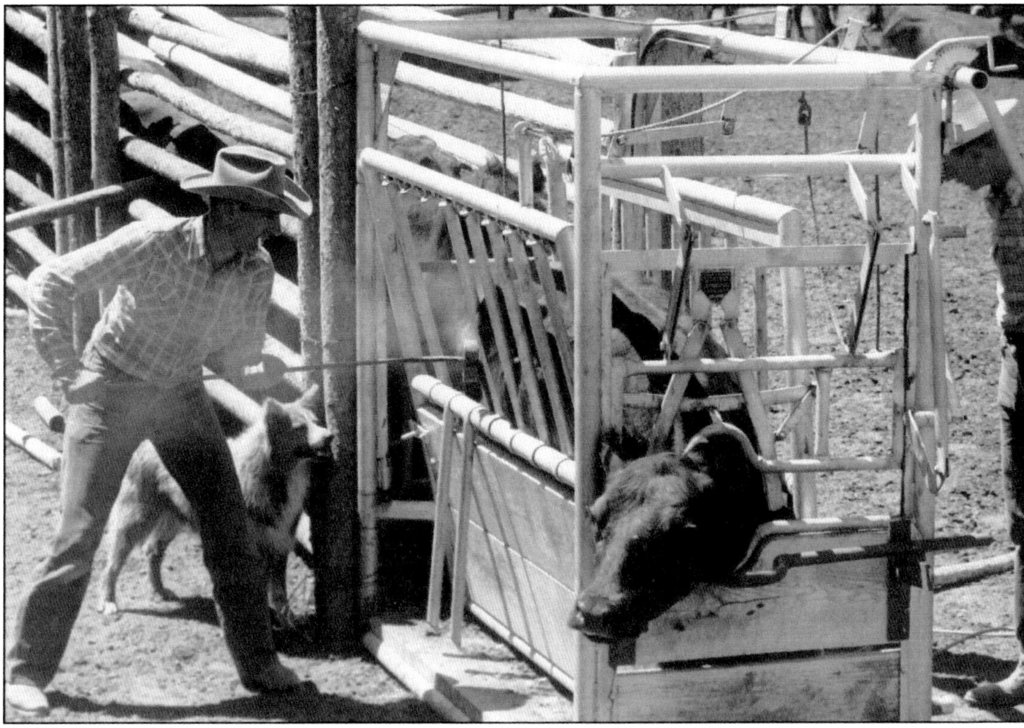

Branding in a 1950s Chute (Above); Cattle Drive down US 191 (Below). The branding chute in the above photograph was a much safer way of handling the cow than bulldogging. Chuck, the shepherd dog, seems to have some suggestions. In the photograph below, the branded cattle are driven down US Highway 191 to the summer range. Currently, RVs and semis in summer have a similar effect on traffic. (Both, 320 Ranch.)

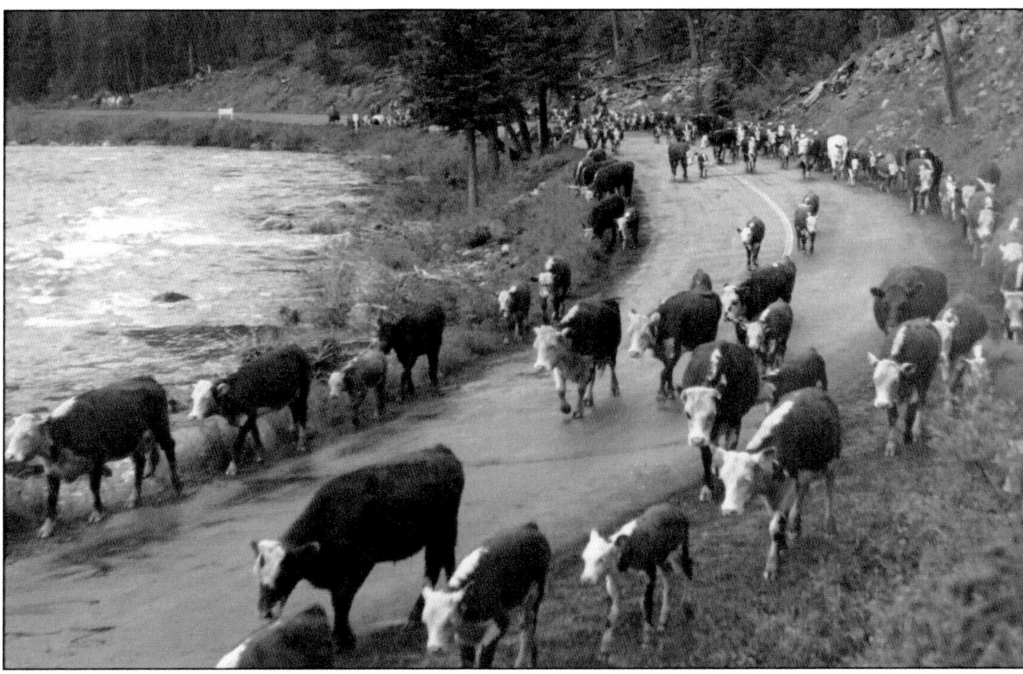

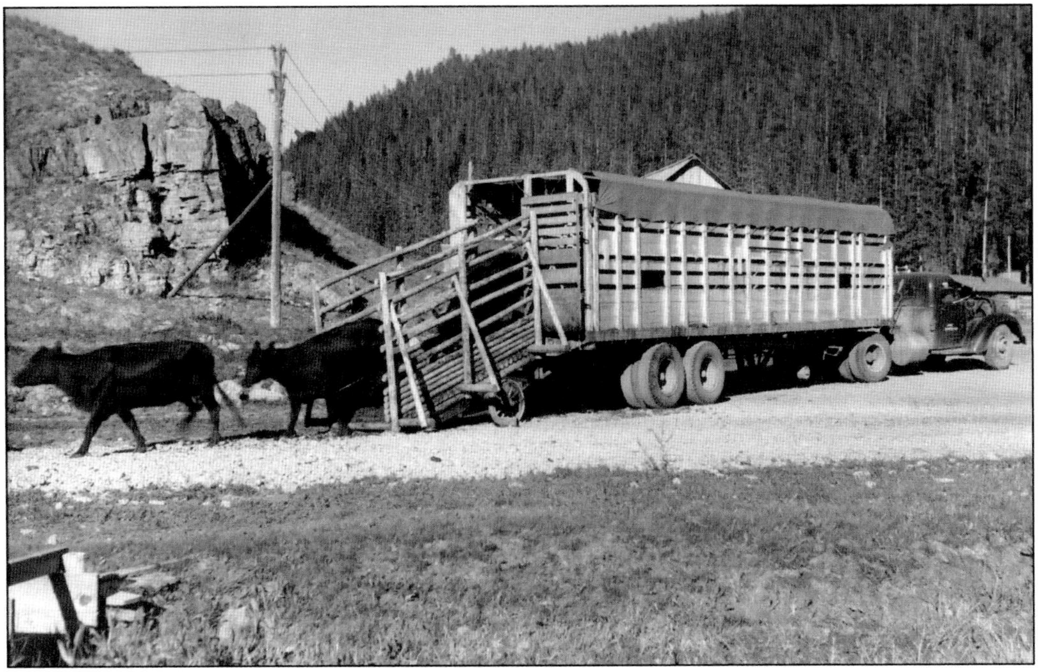

TRUCKS REPLACE THE CATTLE DRIVE (ABOVE); SUMMER RANGE (BELOW). In the photograph below, the 320 cattle are on summer range in the Taylor Fork where Cunningham and Behring started cattle operations in the 1890s. This is now home to the 9 Quarter Circle Ranch. As more private land limited grazing and traffic increased, truck transport supplanted the cattle drive. (Both, 320 Ranch.)

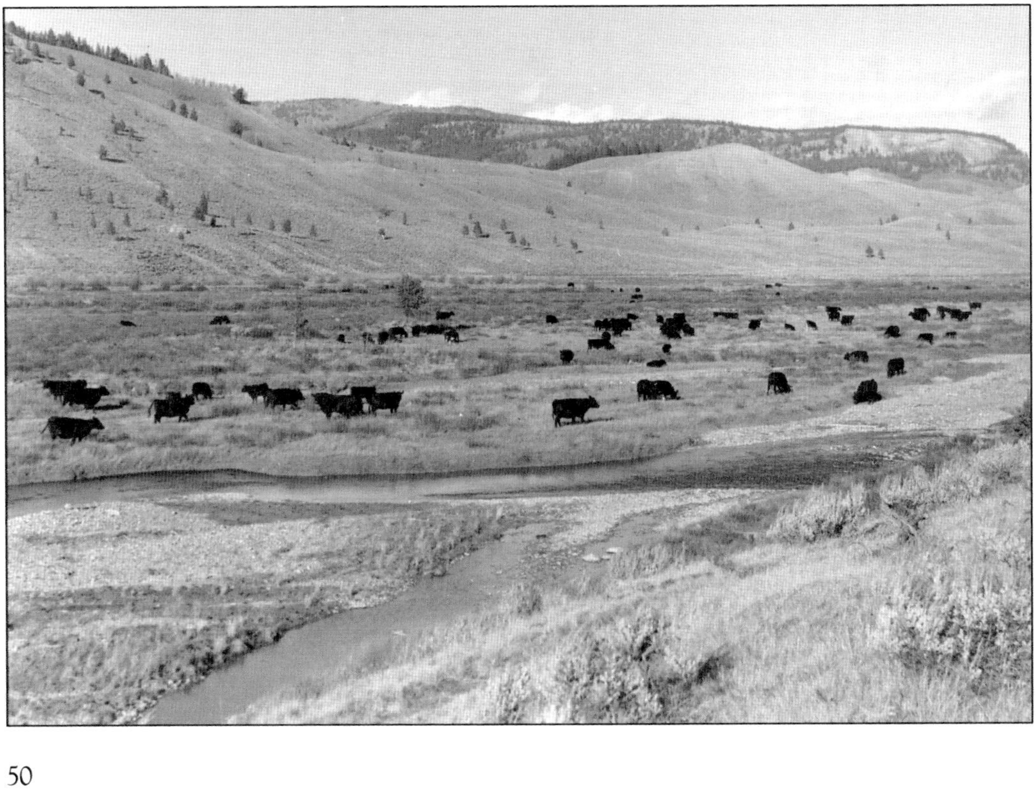

Five

"Sweet Montana Home"
Homesteading

A series of federal acts opened undeveloped areas to ranching. The 1862 Homestead Act granted a quarter section (160 acres) to ranchers who lived on the land for five years. The 1877 Desert Land Act followed, giving 640 acres to ranchers who irrigated. The Land Revision Act (1891) designated the canyon as Gallatin National Forest, leaving meadows for homesteading.

By the 1880s, ranchers and herds struggled up the crude canyon logging road during the summer, seeking grazing in drainages like the West Fork, Buffalo Horn, and Taylor Fork. By the late 1890s, a few ranchers, such as the Augustus Franklin Crail family, had begun building cabins and establishing 160-acre homesteads.

The 1909 Enlarged Homestead Act increased land that could be deeded to a homesteader. Few who acquired land through homesteading understood the challenges they would face: arid climate, ravaging grasshoppers, the impacts of a distant war, and the Depression.

Homesteading life was difficult for ranchers. Lacking infrastructure, they built their homes and ranch buildings from local lumber, after erecting their own sawmills. They often crammed large families into exceedingly small structures that were poorly insulated against Montana's extreme cold and excessive heat. Ranching in the Gallatin Basin, which was 50 miles through an unforgiving canyon to the closest town, required hardiness, self-sufficiency, and spirit. In 1900, US census workers did not venture through the canyon. By 1910, the census precinct for this area was named "Gallatin National Forest" and listed 40 residents. The Ophir School, established before the 1920 census, lent its name to the precinct that boasted 42 residents. A name emerged finally by 1930—Basin—after the basin-like drainage from the mountains that created the West Fork of the West Gallatin. The community might have had a name, but the census reported only 35 residents, a 20-percent drop in population.

The population had tripled by 1940, but just eight of those "families" had been in the area since the early 1900s. Only the hardiest met the homesteading challenges, survived, and in many ways thrived, etching an existence and a community into the forest.

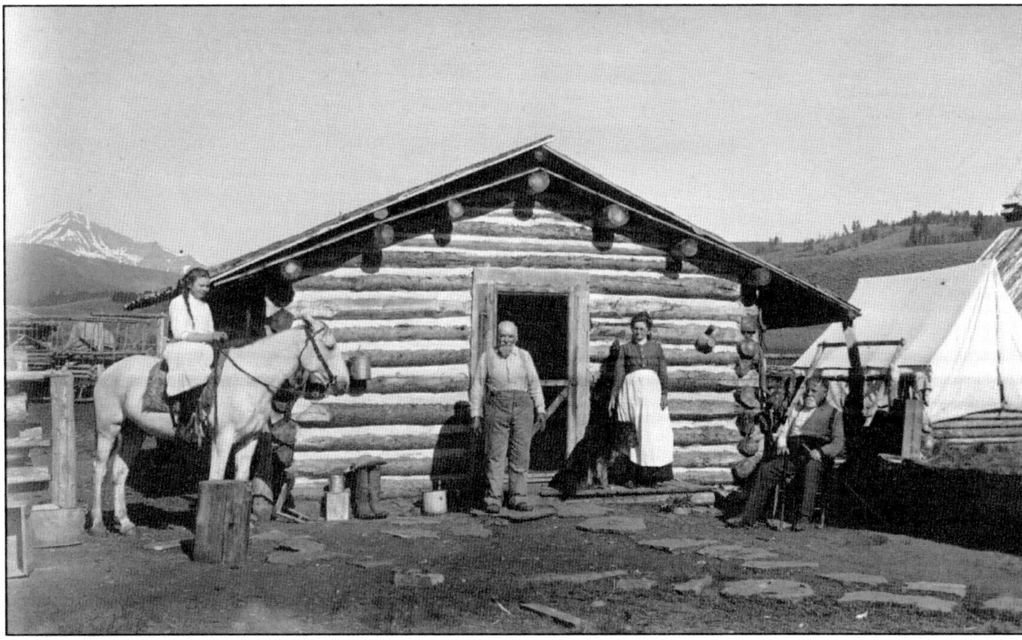

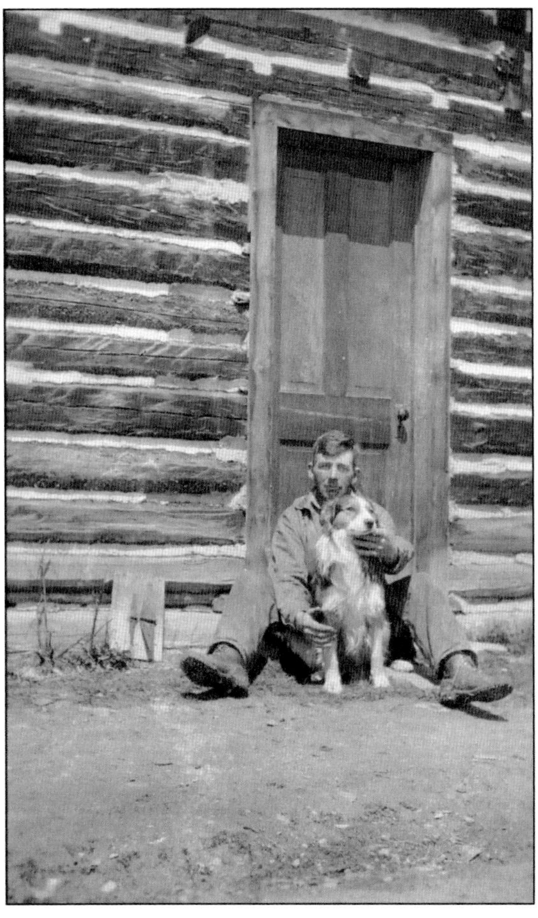

AUGUSTUS CRAIL FAMILY AND CABIN. In 1901, A.F. Crail purchased a homestead and cabin from Daniel Inabnit for $1 an acre. He and Sallie then moved their three children from Bozeman. The family lived in this 255-square-foot cabin for years before building a larger home. Abraham Creek, Sallie's father, outside the cabin to the right of Frank and Sallie, enjoys watching Lilian ahorse. (HCRC.)

EMMETT OUTSIDE THE RANCH HOUSE. After 20 years as sheepherders, the Crails started raising cattle. They grew their hay to the north of the meadow in what is now called the Hay Meadows subdivision. Self-sufficient ranchers, they also ran a lumber mill. Emmett worked the ranch until 1950, when at 61, he sold the 960 acres to Jack and Elaine Hume. (HCRC.)

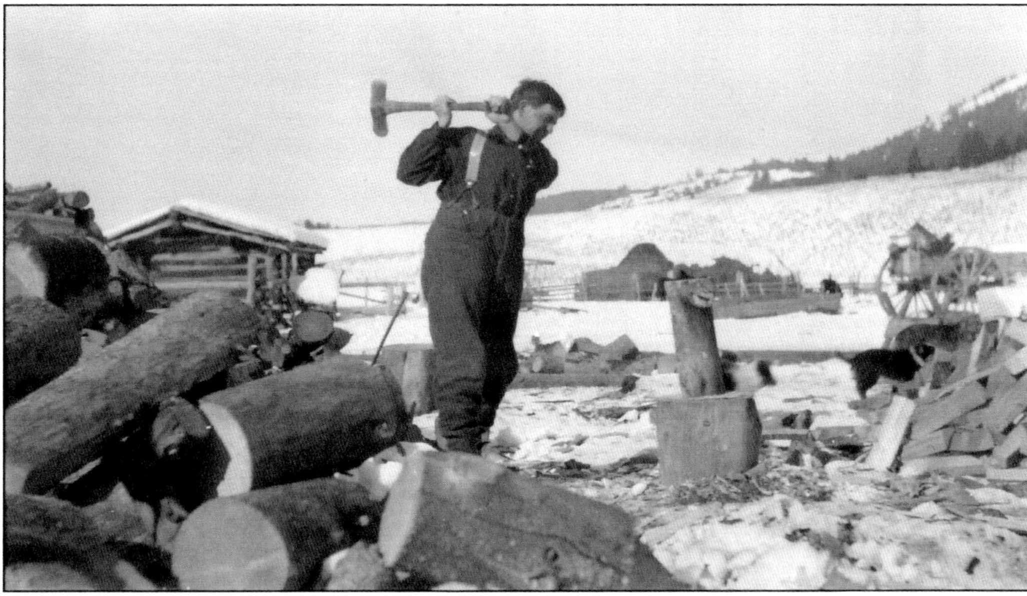

Eugene Crail Splits Cord Wood. Oldest child Eugene was 14 when the family moved to the Gallatin Basin where he ranched alongside his father and brother Emmett. A Montana Agricultural College (later Montana State University) graduate in steam engineering, Eugene returned to the family homestead after service in World War I. He was a skilled carpenter and constructed the first community school, the first B-K buildings, and the Rockhaven Church. (HCRC.)

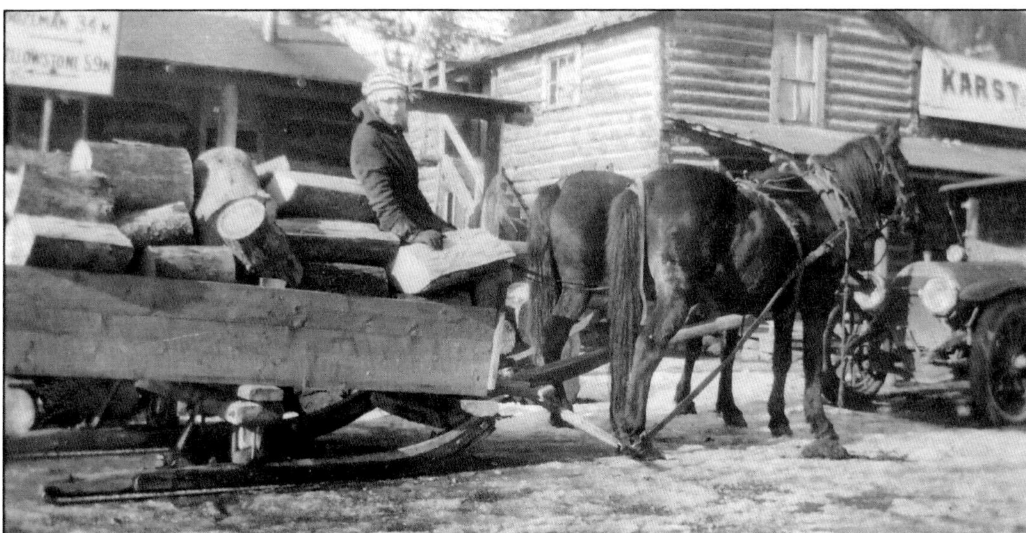

Isabelle Karst Hauling Wood. Wood was necessary for heating homes and cabins, fencing, and building materials. It was plentiful in the surrounding forests, but great amounts of time and effort were needed for cutting, hauling, and stacking. (S. Anderson.)

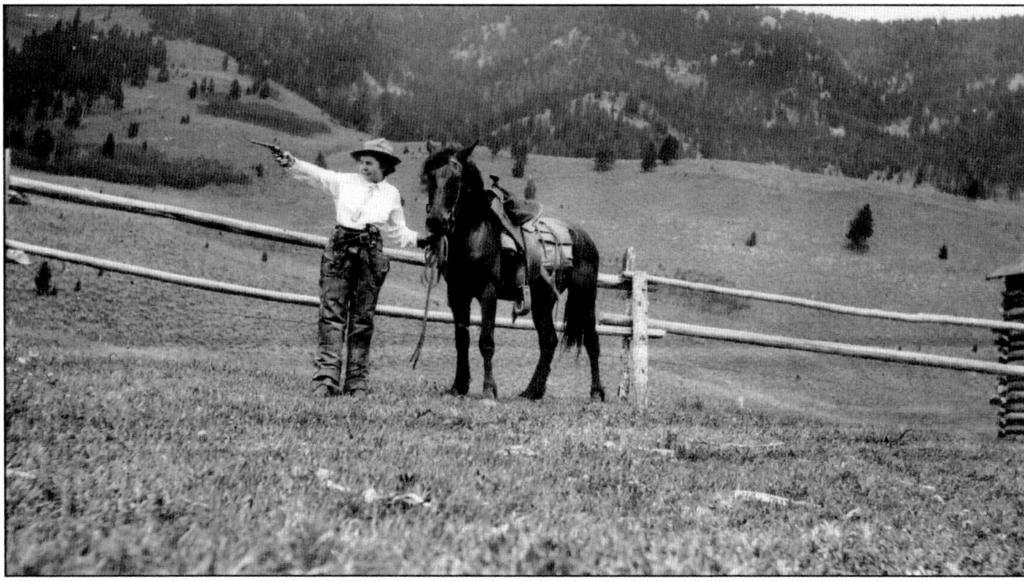

LILIAN CRAIL, A WESTERN WOMAN (ABOVE); ISABELLE KARST ON TRAPPER (BELOW). Lilian grew up on the ranch. Like most ranch women of her day, Lilian was as comfortable riding a horse and handling a gun as she was with needlework and cooking. Like her mother, Lilian loved animals. Ultimately, she moved to Chicago to attend nursing school. Isabelle was Pete Karst's step-daughter and grew up in the canyon. She married Ed Durnam and lived, worked, and raised her own children there. (Above, HCRC; below, S. Anderson.)

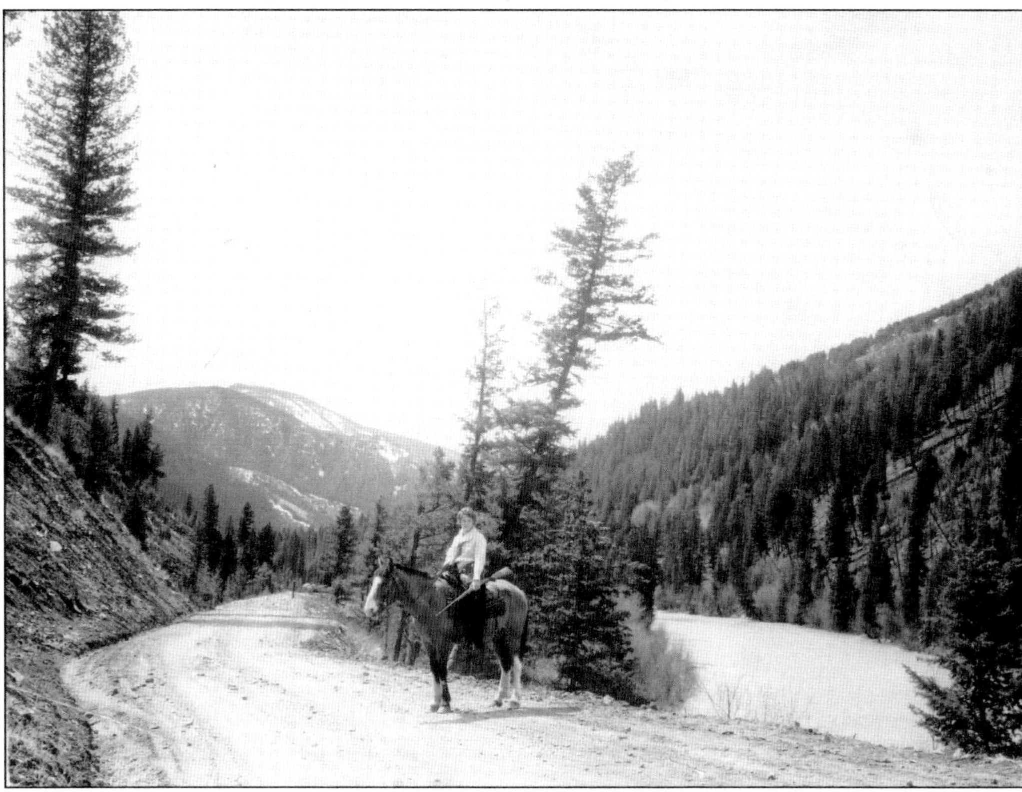

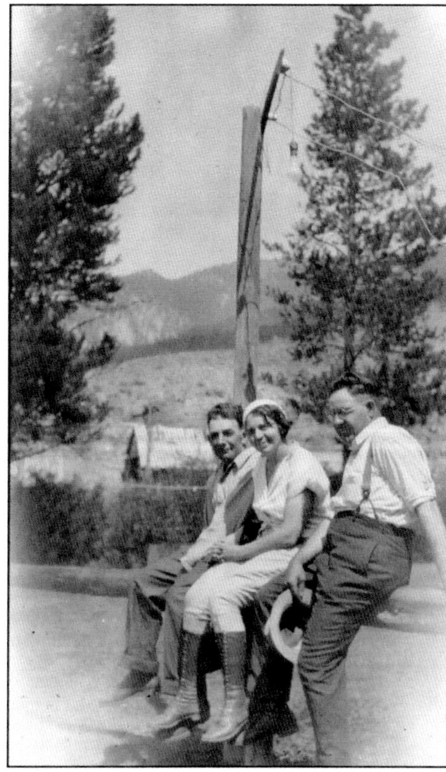

Self-Sufficiency and Limited Amenities. Emmett, Lilian, and Eugene Crail (pictured from left to right) relax under an electrified lamp. Until 1948, when Montana Power ran electricity through the canyon, many ranches produced their own with generators. Some were gas powered, like the 320 Ranch's old Cadillac engine. Others, such as Karst Kamp, had small hydropower turbines. Even in the 1950s, homes in the meadow depended on canyon neighbors for telephone service. (HCRC.)

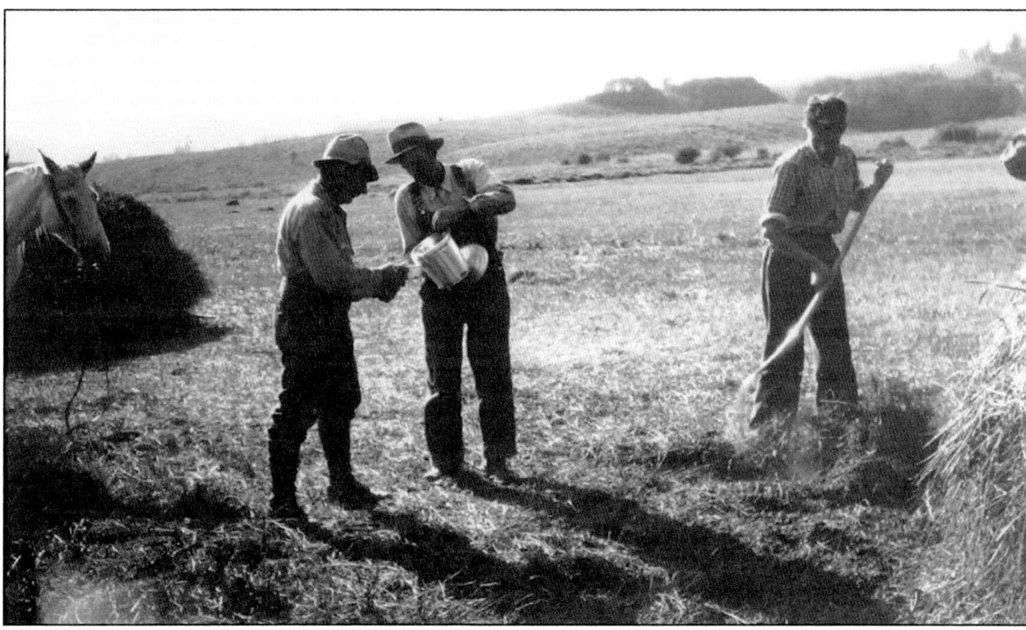

A Haying Milk Break. The haying operation was labor intensive, especially prior to the introduction of the beaverslide. A ranch needed to put up more than one ton of hay per head of cattle. Here, Emmett and ranch hands take a milk break. Most homesteads had their own milk cow, but Donna Klindt remembers buying her family's milk by the pailful from the Half Way Inn store. (HCRC.)

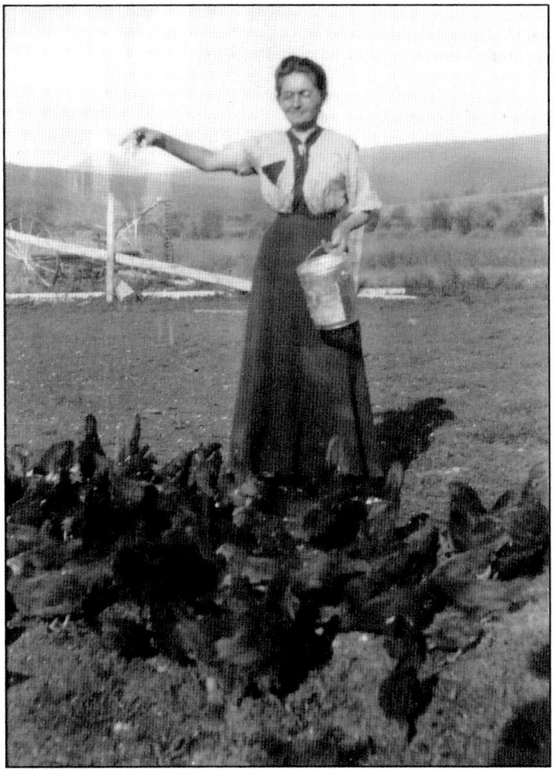

Sallie Creek Crail Feeds Chickens (Left); Sallie's Quilt (Below). One of the most valuable homestead animals, chickens provided eggs, meat, and down feathers. Sallie, despite her prior city life, embraced life in the remote Gallatin Basin. She was an accomplished quilter. This 1901 quilt took first prize in a Chicago competition. Sallie also taught guitar at Daughters' College in Fulton, Missouri, prior to her marriage and move to Montana. (Both, HCRC.)

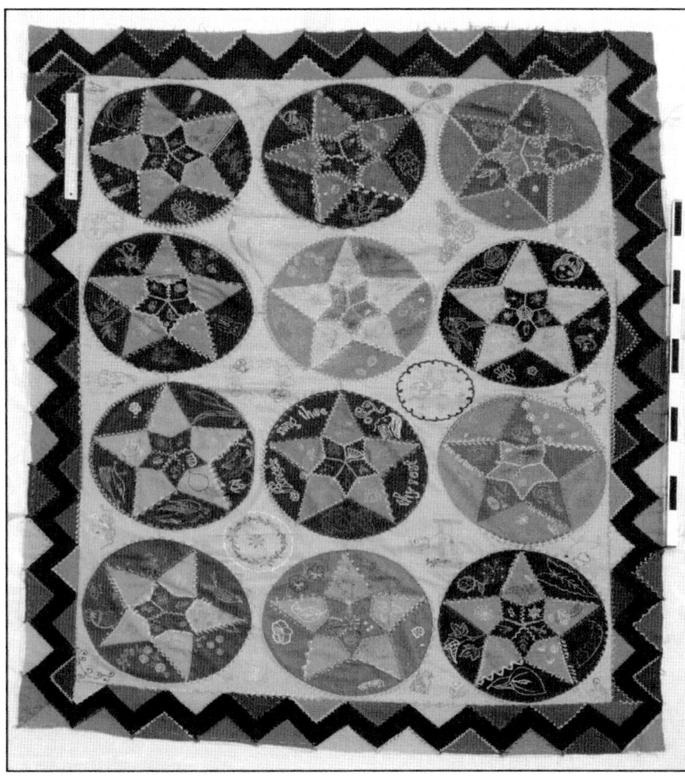

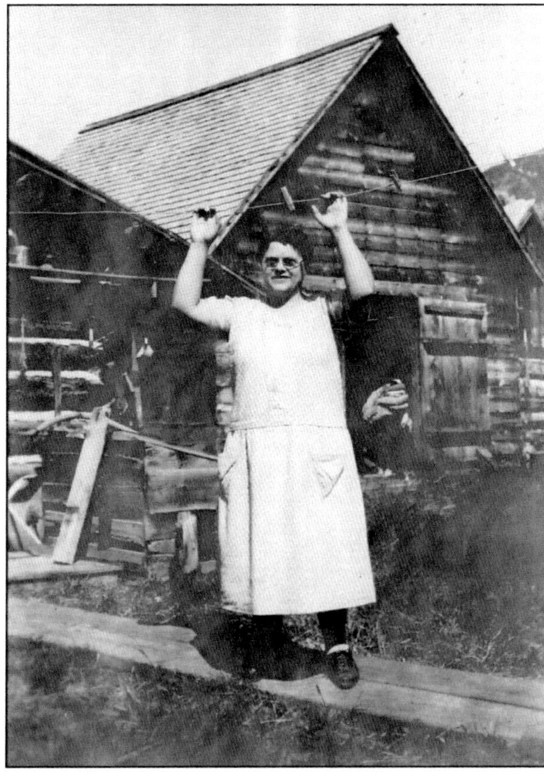

ANNIE BRENEMAN HANGS CLOTHES. Butte schoolteacher Annie Breneman married Emmett after a courtship of several decades. After hang-drying clothes that were washed and wrung by hand, Annie would iron them with a heavy, stove-heated or gas-fueled iron. Although a handwritten caption on the photograph reads "No dinner to-day," the reality is that the homesteading woman would then prepare dinner on a gas or wood-fired cook stove. (HCRC.)

WASH DAY AT 320 RANCH. The 320 Ranch staff always found time to have meaningful conversation. By the 1930s, thirty percent of the area's residents claimed dude ranching or summer resort as their work, displacing mining and trapping as the major employment areas. (PM.)

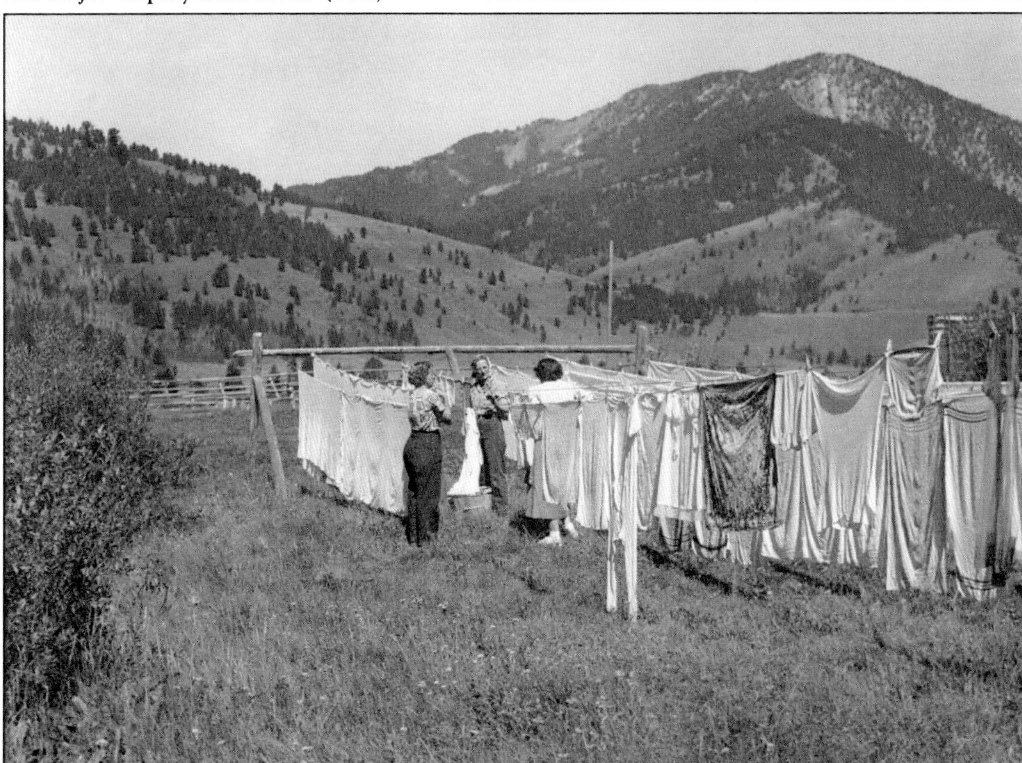

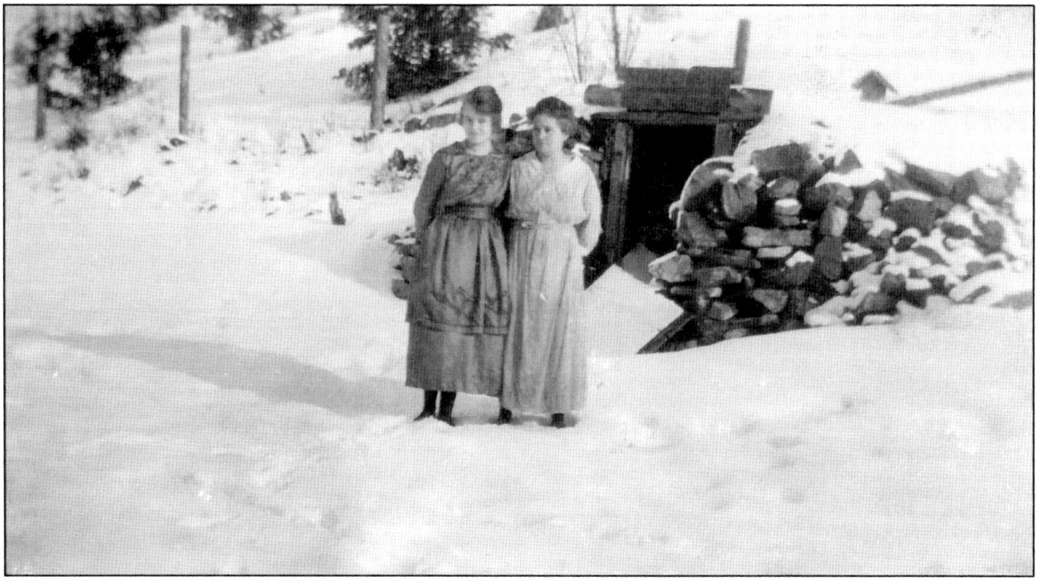

At the Root Cellar. Proper storage was essential to keep foods throughout the year. Root cellars dug into hillsides insulated from heat and cold. Springhouses were built over the flowing cold mountain streams to provide another method of refrigeration. (S. Anderson.)

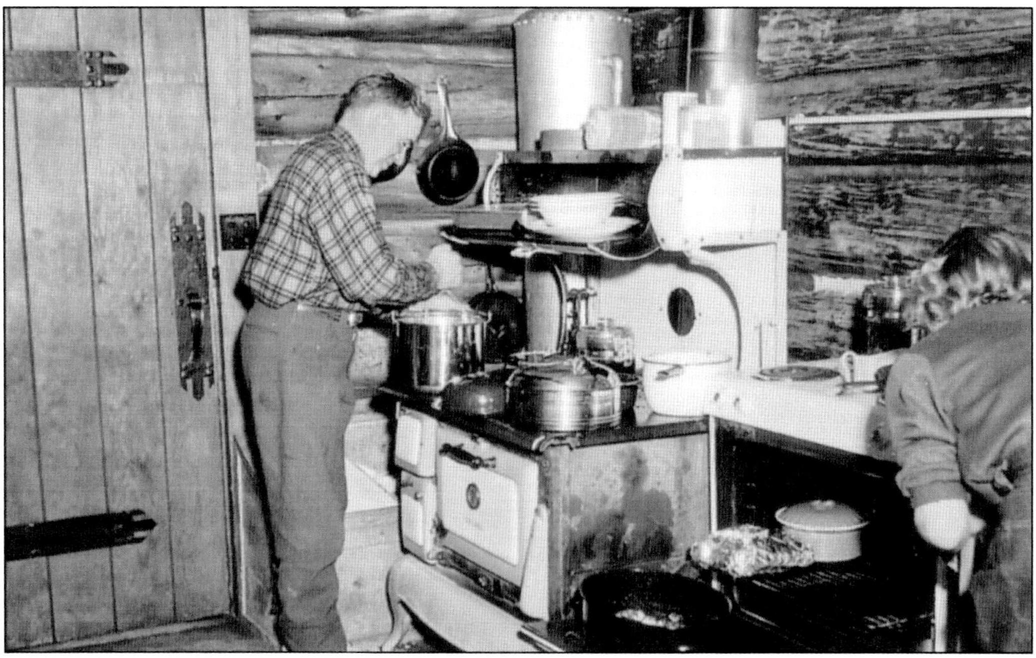

Lone Mountain Ranch Kitchen. Here, the kitchen staff at the dude ranch prepares a dinner for the guests. As this photograph was taken in the late 1950s, reliable electric power was used for the range on the right. Wood stoves were the only option besides an open fire in the early half of the century and still common in the 1950s. (Lone Mountain Ranch.)

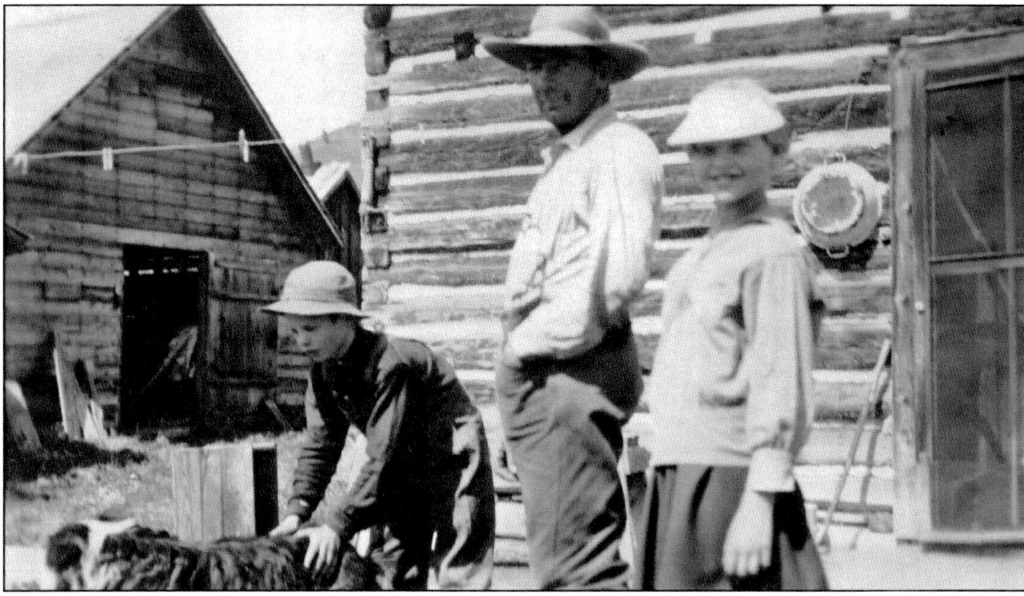

"The Bunch" (Above); David Breneman Ahorse (Below). In November 1918, Annie Breneman's younger brother Duburg Breneman and his wife, Rilla, succumbed to Spanish influenza. Annie's parents took in two of the three orphaned children, David and Glen Louise, pictured here with Emmett at the Crail Ranch, with the understanding that Annie, age 32 at the time, would see to their upbringing. The Brenemans and children were frequent visitors and workers on the Crail Ranch. On most ranches, children grew up working hard at chores to sustain the ranch and the family's subsistence. (Both, HCRC.)

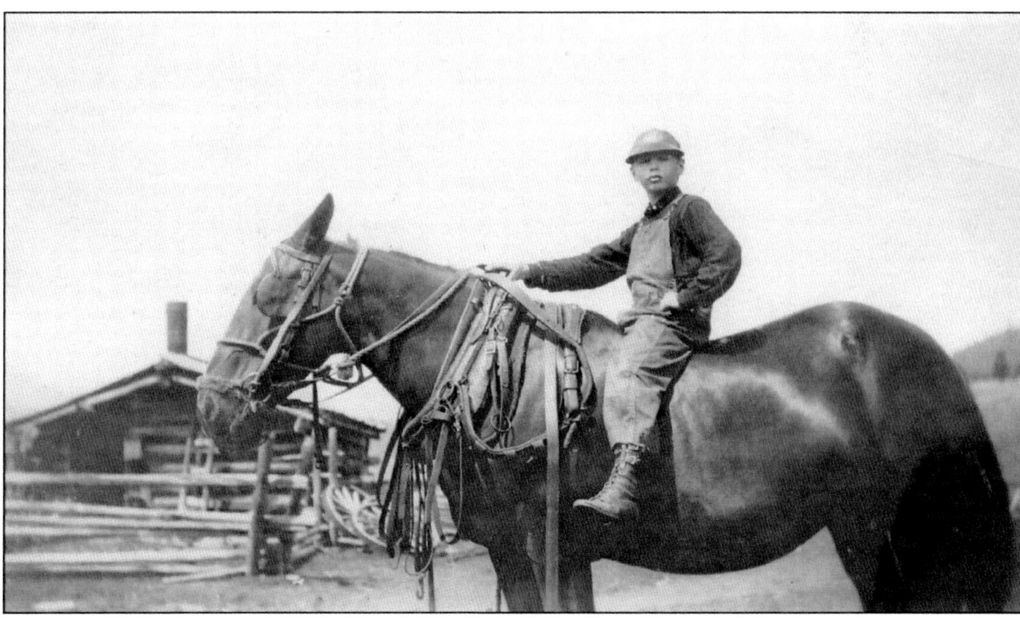

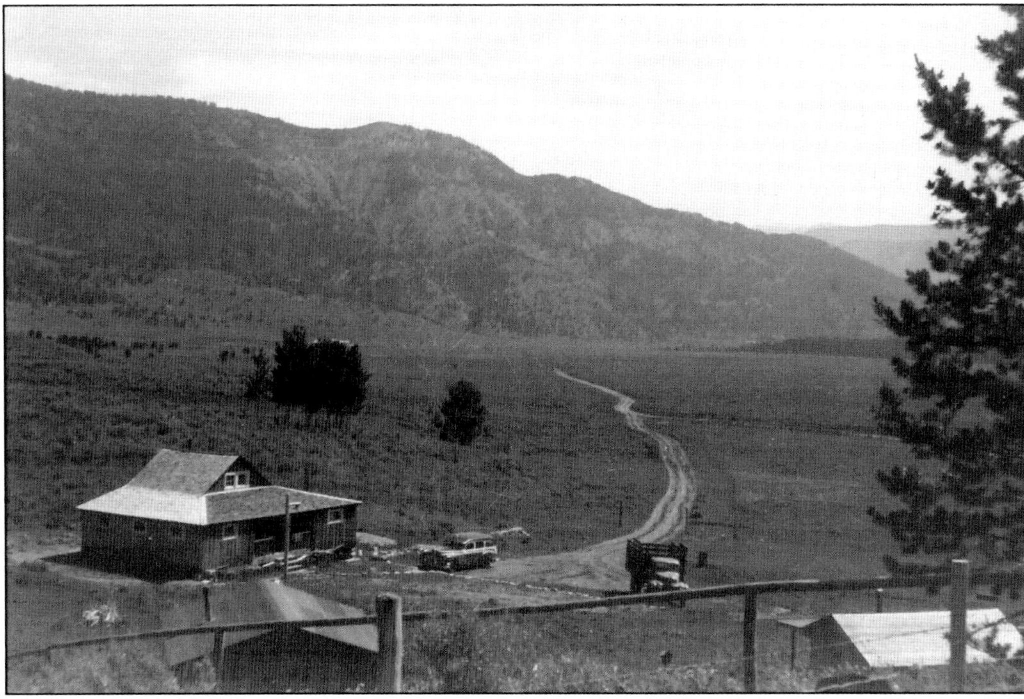

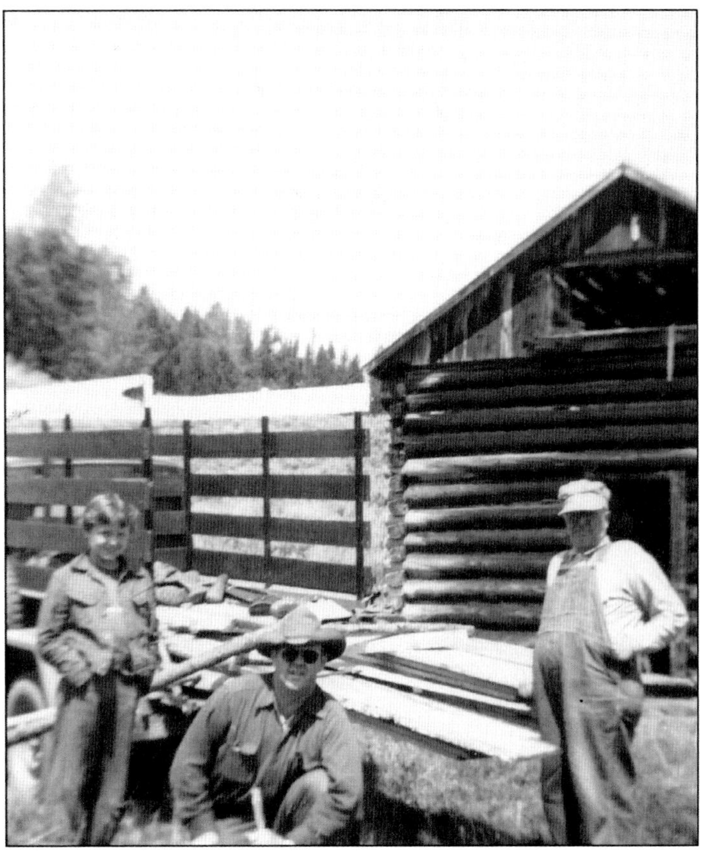

5-K IN EARLY 1950S (ABOVE); MCBRIDES AT THE JOHNSON PLACE (LEFT). Several of the homestead properties changed hands in mid-century as the original pioneer families aged and moved on. In the 1920s, Henry Johnson proved up the quarter section that cornered on the B-K and the Crail property. Ken McBride (at left, center), photographed with daughter Jean and father Everett, bought it from Johnson's widow in 1952 and named it the 5-K. The remodeled home can be seen above with the Crail Ranch in the far distance over the trees. They ran sheep on the ranch for decades and, adapting to the resort, developed the Westfork home and business properties. (Both, McBride family photographs.)

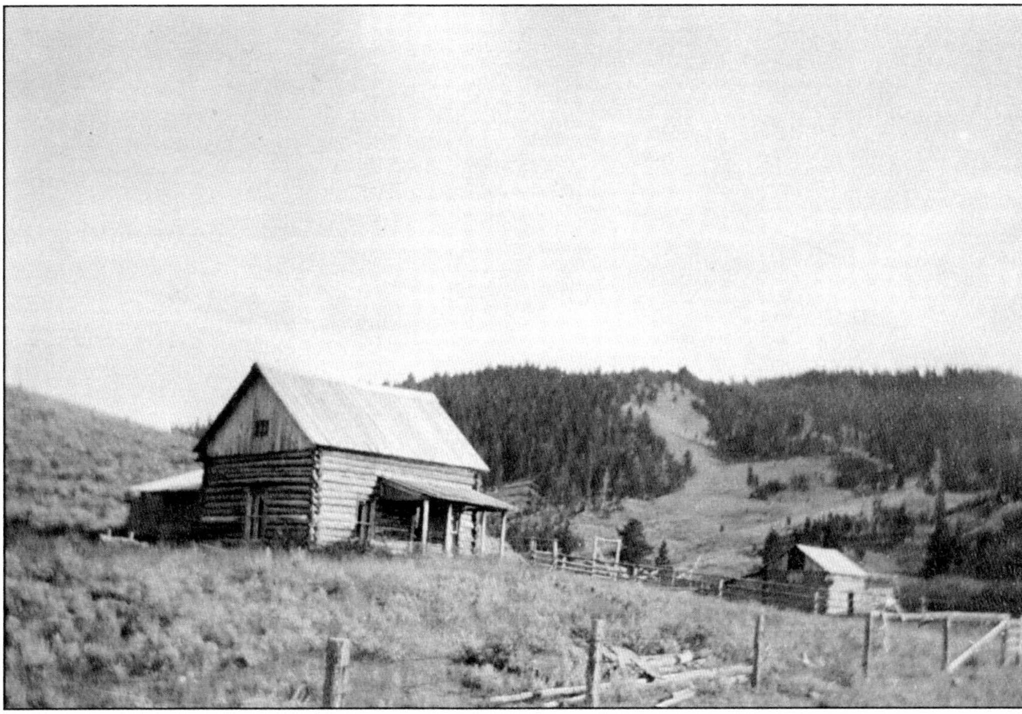

Foley Waters Homestead, 1915 (Above); Markley Cabin, 1960 (Below). These photographs represent the changing character of the Big Sky area. The Waters family had 320 acres on two adjacent homesteads on some of the best hay fields around. However, from illness, poor farming, or other disappointments, they soon disappeared from the scene. Joe and Donna Markley had the summer cabin below on a US Forest Service lease at Deer Creek. As transportation improved, more and more people used the area for seasonal vacation homes. The advent of the ski resort has not changed this pattern. (Both, PM.)

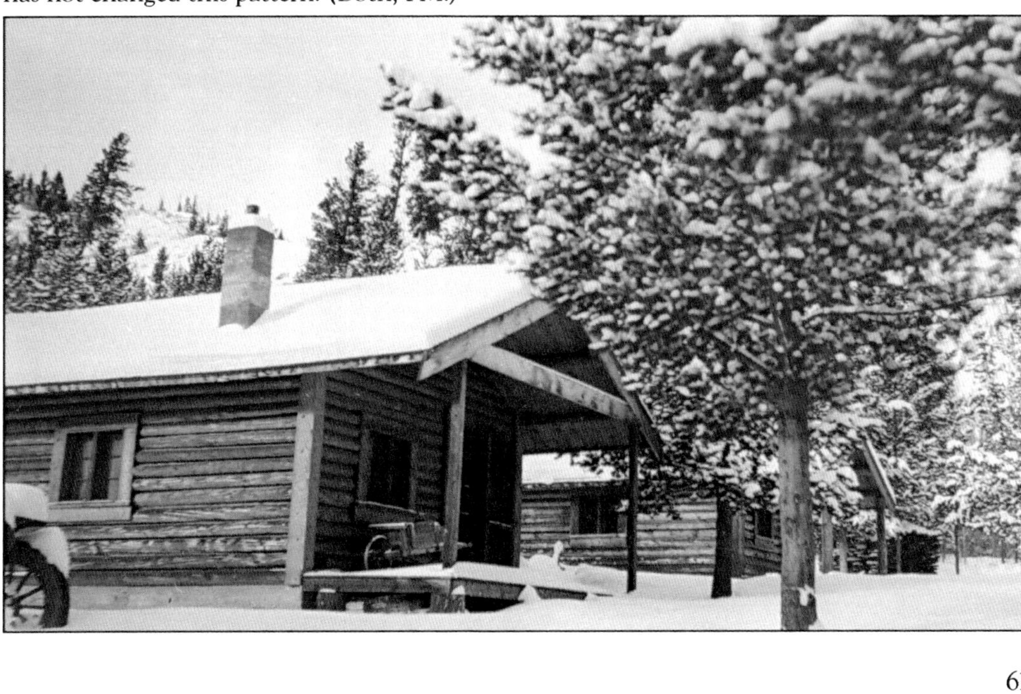

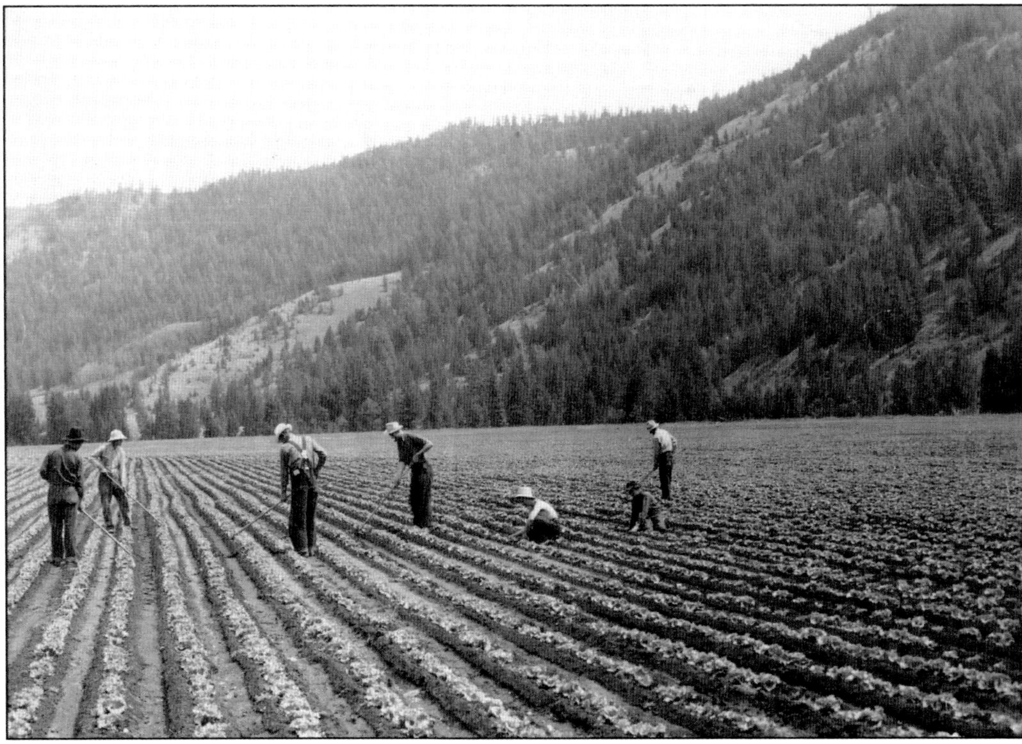

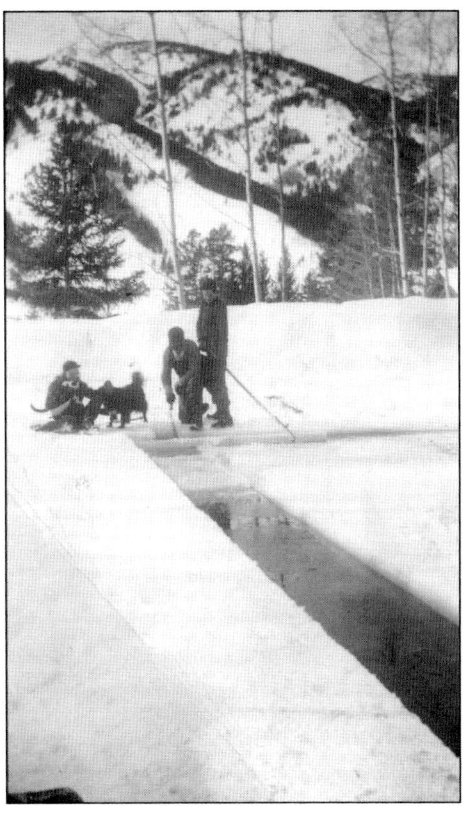

Durnam Lettuce Farm (Above); Durnam Ice Pond (Left). Ed Durnam, a golf professional from Minneapolis, came to the Karst Kamp in 1914 and married Isabelle Karst in 1923. After working for Pete Karst until 1936, he and Isabelle purchased a 30-acre meadow just south of the Karst Cold Springs and homesteaded at Moose Creek. The Durnams raised lettuce for 29 years, irrigating their crop with Gallatin River water and preserving it with river ice. The Gallatin Gateway brand sold at a premium from Bozeman to St. Paul and was shipped in crates made from local timber cut in the Durnam's sawmill. When farming became uneconomical as refrigerated trucking flooded the market with California lettuce, they raised Hereford cattle until Ed's death in 1970. Choice wildlife habitat, this land was returned to the National Forest Service. (Both, S. Anderson.)

Six

Ophir School, the Gold Standard

Education

After holding school during the summer for six years, homesteaders formed a school board and registered the district with the State of Montana. The Ophir School District, established on December 18, 1912, was named for the biblical reference in 1 Kings 10 to Solomon's gold mines. Although prospectors had not found much gold in their mountains, they believed they had, metaphorically, found gold when they established a school district.

The first real schoolhouse, built in 1929, was located east of the Gallatin River, north of Porcupine Creek. More than 20 years later, Ophir trustees erected a teacherage next to the schoolhouse. In 1964, a second school building was constructed west of the Gallatin River on the current site. Today, this facility's small footprint is enveloped by a larger, 60,000-square-foot building.

Ophir remained a K–8 district for 97 years until 2009 when it added a high school, the first Montana district to do so in over 45 years. Renamed Big Sky School District in 2012, the schools themselves retain the historical Ophir names.

Ophir has always been the community's center. The Gallatin Canyon Women's Club (GCWC), begun in 1927, immediately used the schoolhouse for meetings. In fact, the GCWC gifted funding for the new 1964 school, stipulating that the school would have a community meeting room. The Community Library began in 1959 when the Ophir Board announced that the school's library would open to the public.

It is interesting that the Gallatin Canyon area, unlike so many pioneer communities, had no church until 1999. The Soldiers' Chapel was erected as a war memorial but not used for regular services. It was the school that provided the focal point for the community.

In 1910, the area had no name. The US census called it the "Gallatin National Forest." By 1920, "Ophir" became the census precinct name. Although the community would eventually be called "Basin" and then "Big Sky," the school remains the site for all voting. Home of the community library and performing arts center, the school serves as the center of the community.

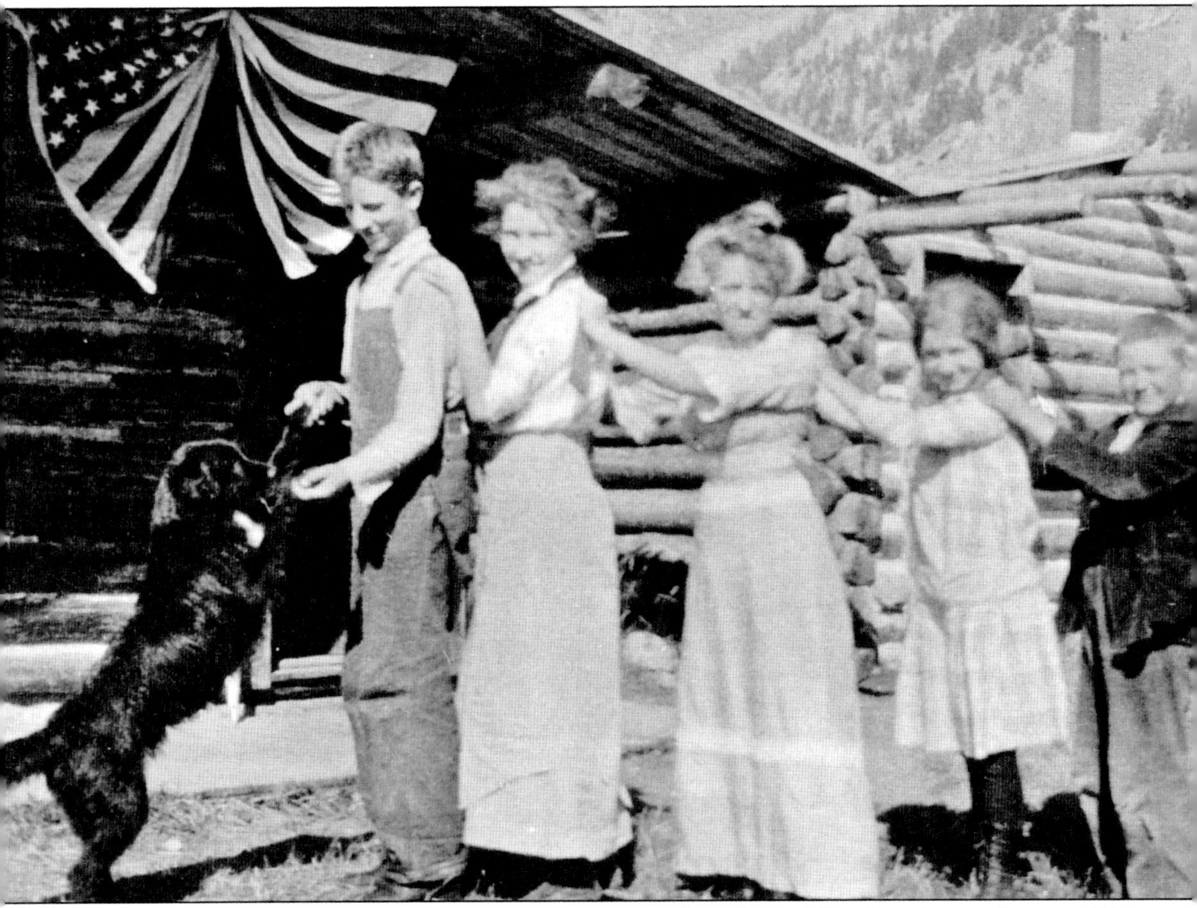

Teacher Kate Cope And Students. Kate Cope stands in the middle of her four students in 1914. Cope's four-month contract paid $280. Pictured from left to right are Charley Michener, Maggie Michener, Kate Cope, Ora Michener, and Evans Kelly. Thomas and Mary Michener were parents to Charley, Maggie, and Ora, and Ora would return nine years later to teach the Ophir students. For 17 years, the school was held in various cabins while the community disputed bonding and the preferred building site. (Ophir School archives.)

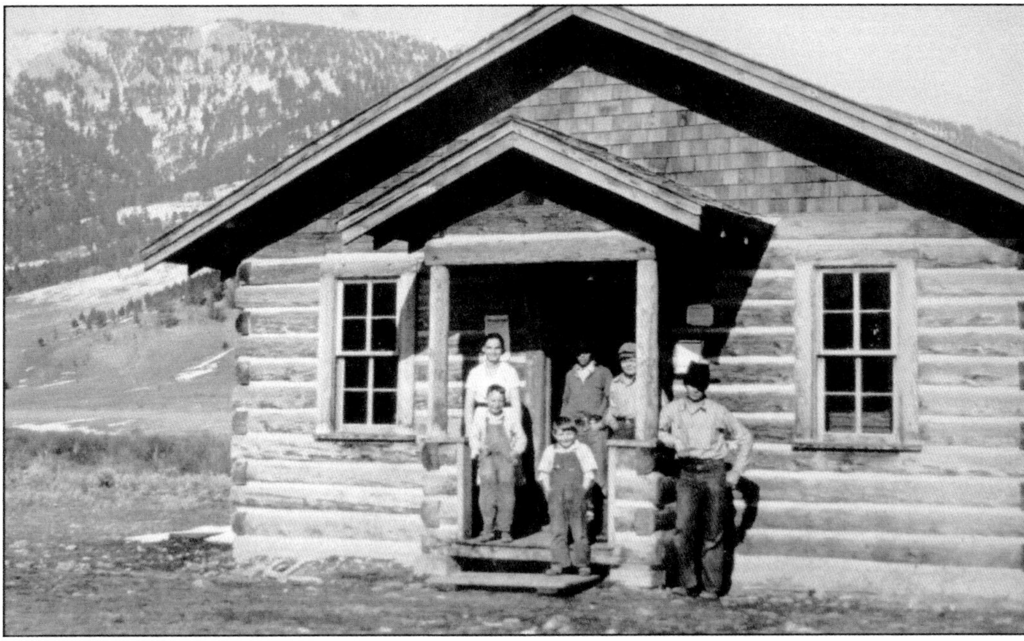

First Ophir Schoolhouse, 1929 (Above); Additions and Outbuildings, 1940s (Below). Under a county threat to disband the district, voters approved schoolhouse construction. The board commissioned Eugene Crail to build a one-room log structure in the "Beaver Creek location." Despite building improvements, school was often moved off-campus, depending on where the majority of students lived. In 1931, school was at the Benhams. With Sara and Jack Durnam the only students in 1943, school was Karst Kamp. In 1924 and 1933, the lack of students forced one-year Ophir closures. The Ophir Board minutes state, "It is not their desire to have school disbanded for two consecutive terms as this allows for the disbanding of the School District." Still today, Montana communities fear consolidation and closure. (Both, Ophir School archives.)

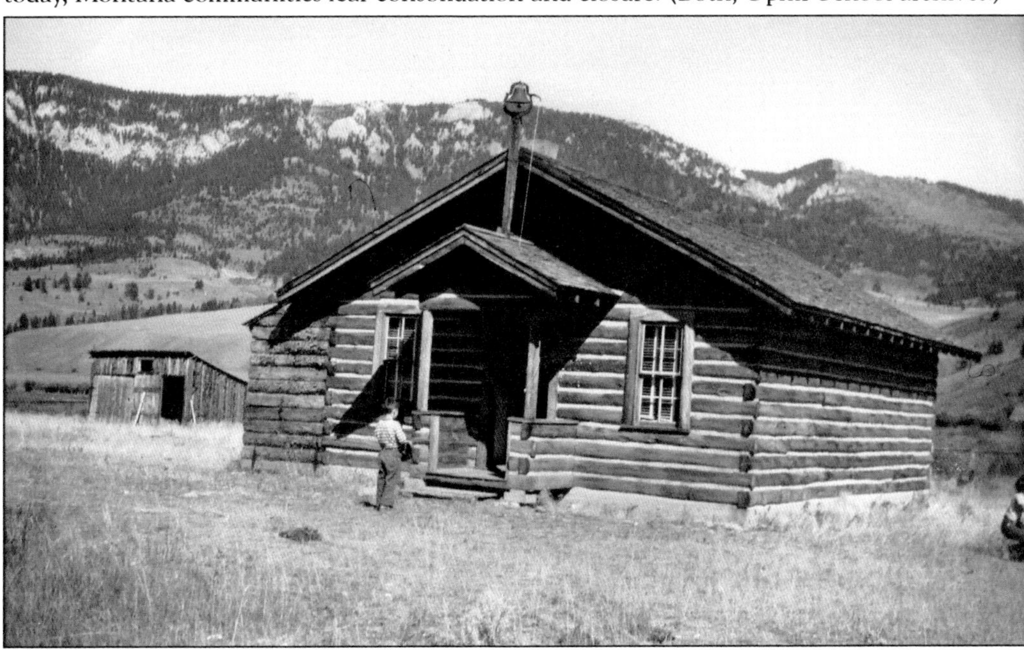

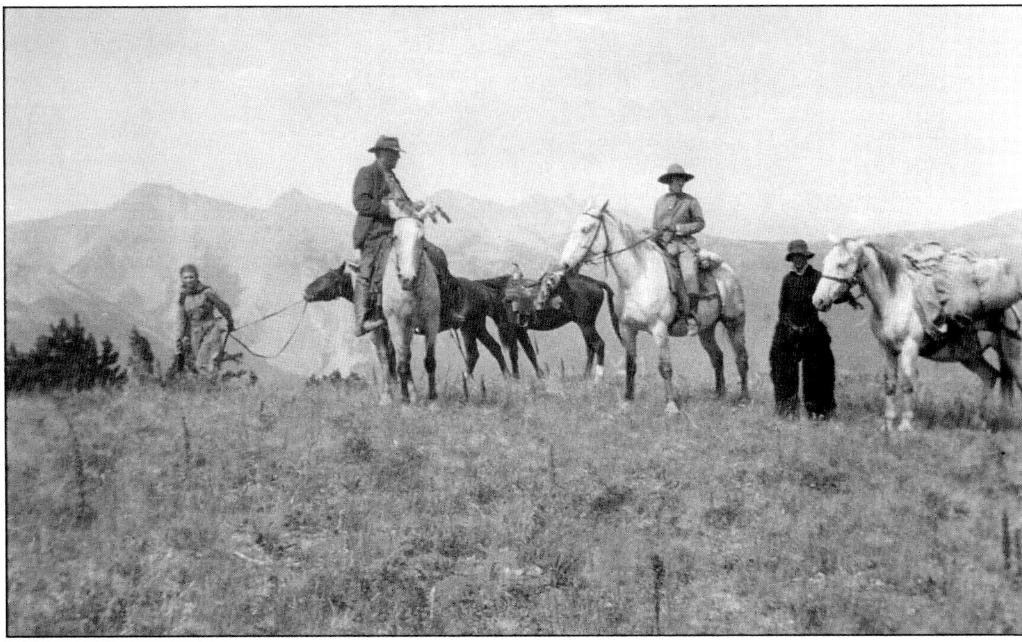

Family of Educators Camping. Royal Burt Lemon, horseman on the left, was educated at Ohio Wesleyan. He moved to the Gallatin Canyon in 1919 with wife Pearl. R.B. taught school, and Pearl and their son George both served on the Ophir Board. Ora Michener Lemon, their daughter-in-law seen here leading a horse, had a three-month teaching contract ($300) in 1923. (PM.)

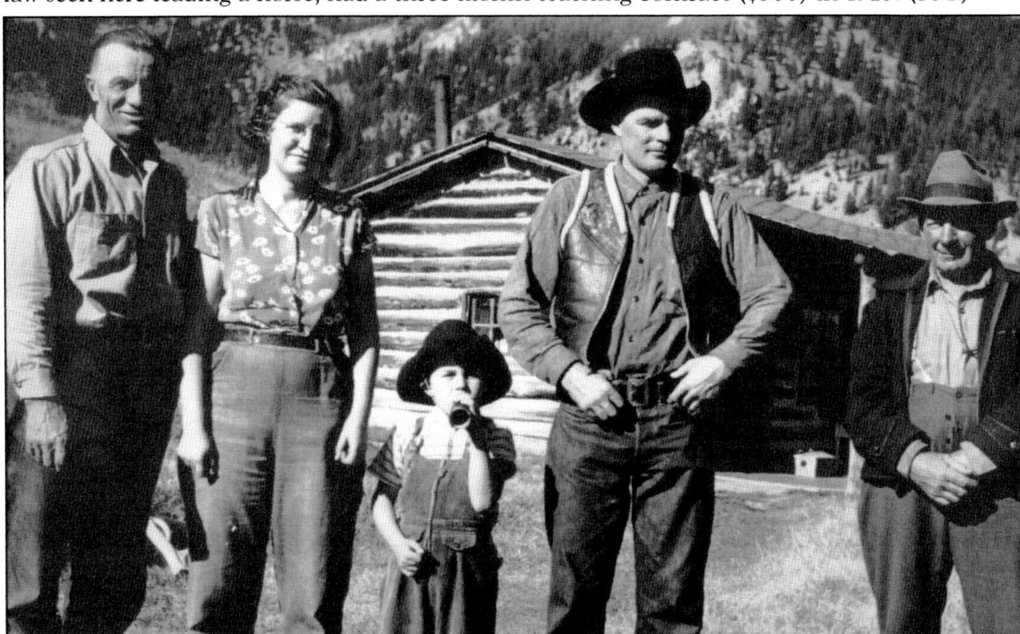

School Champions. Emmett Crail (far right) served as Ophir trustee for 10 years and chair of the board when his brother Eugene built the 1929 schoolhouse. Dorothy Vick (second from left), representative of the Gallatin Canyon Women's Club, urged the board to build a new schoolhouse on the Vick property adjacent to Soldier's Chapel. She stands here with husband Joe (far left) and B-K ranch manager Ed Smith and son. (Ophir School archives.)

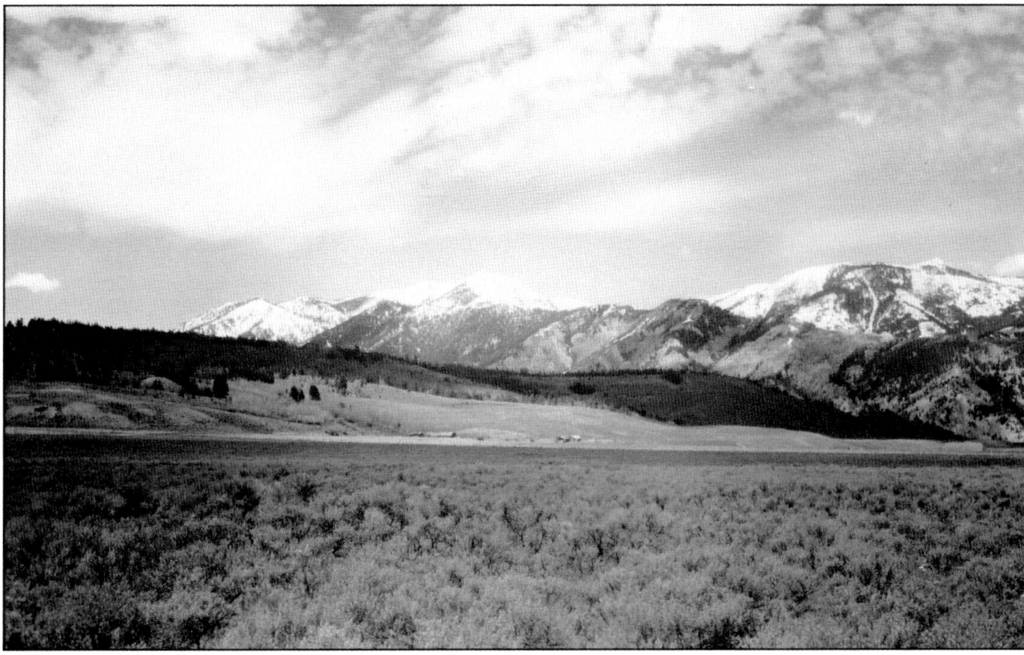

The Stillman Property. After years of discussion, the abandoned Stillman property, across the road from the first schoolhouse, was selected as the site for the new building. The 1929 schoolhouse would eventually be purchased and moved to the Beckman Flats area, 20 miles north of Ophir School. (S. Anderson.)

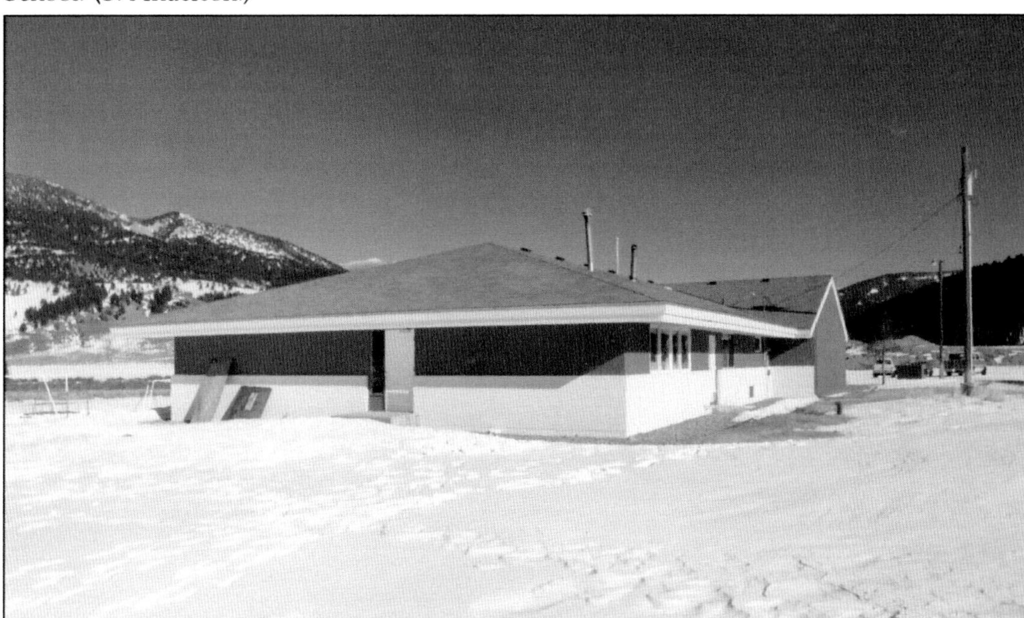

The 1988 Schoolhouse. In 1964, the Ophir Board built a more modern structure on the current site with $29,434. Funding came from the estate of Dr. Caroline McGill, former 320 Ranch owner. McGill donated the money to the Gallatin Canyon Women's Club, stipulating that they use the money for a community project. The GCWC voted in 1961 to dedicate the funds to a new school. (Ophir School archives.)

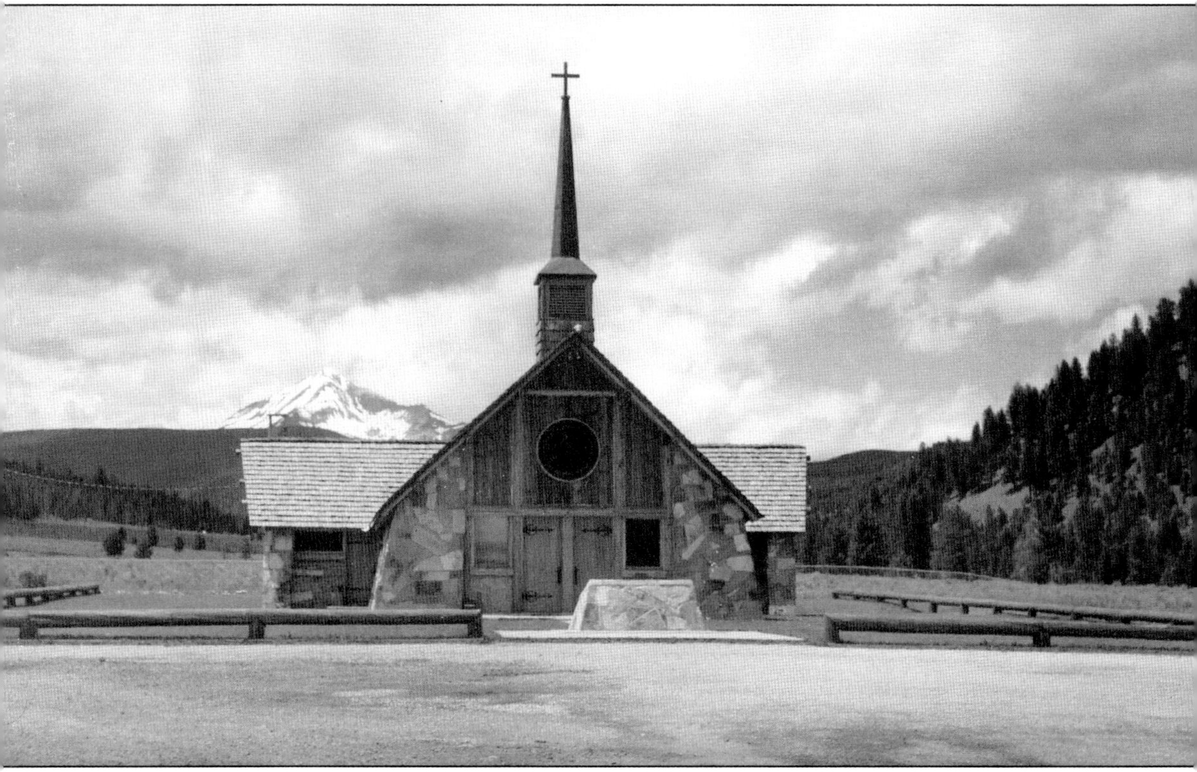

SOLDIERS' CHAPEL. The Soldiers' Chapel was dedicated in October 1955 as a memorial to the war dead of the 163rd Infantry Regiment of the Montana National Guard and to Nelson Story IV, who died in combat in New Guinea. Built and largely paid for by Col. Nelson Story III, who also served in New Guinea, it is open for nondenominational services on Sundays from Memorial Day through Labor Day. Chet Huntley, the founding father of Big Sky Resort, is buried in the nearby cemetery. (PM.)

Seven

"Whoopie Ti-Yi-Yo, Git Along Little Dogie"

Dude Ranching

Herding cattle and tending tourists have many similarities: long hours, difficult and uncomfortable situations, and uncooperative subjects. However, both had another similarity in that dude and cattle ranching proved to be the most successful and long-lasting enterprises in the Big Sky area. American urbanization and nostalgia for the Old West in the early 20th century fueled the desire for this form of vacationing.

Some of the most successful canyon entrepreneurs started directly in the tourist business. Pete Karst began serving travelers down the Gallatin road in 1907, and his Karst Kamp, one of the first dude ranches in Montana, ran successfully for more than 50 years. A January 1906 note indicates collaboration with Tom Michener in the West Fork and Sam Wilson of the Buffalo Horn Ranch (now the 320) to organize dude ranching in the canyon. Cabins were to be rented at $12 per week and horses at $6 per week. Later entrants to the dude ranching business, like Buck and Helen Knight, who started Buck's T-4 in 1946, and the Lemons of the Half Way Inn, now the Rainbow Ranch, catered to the short-term stay.

Social and economic factors led other ranches, particularly those that had been active cattle operations, to open their doors to dudes for extended vacations and the experience of working a ranch. The B-K, now Lone Mountain Ranch, and the 320 Ranch, which started as the Buffalo Horn, were the most lasting and successful of these.

The natural beauty and western environment along the Gallatin made this a most sought-after recreation destination for visitors. Horseback riding and trail rides, ranching, fishing for trout in the Blue Ribbon river, panning for gold, and hunting—all provided the basic diversions for the dudes. Restaurants and bars were a staple, as were the traditional tours of nearby Yellowstone Park. Much like today, the vacationers were always out for something new. Skiing, ski jumping, and snowmobiling were added as well as summer activities like camping, picnics, hiking, and enjoying the plentiful wildlife and flowers of the area.

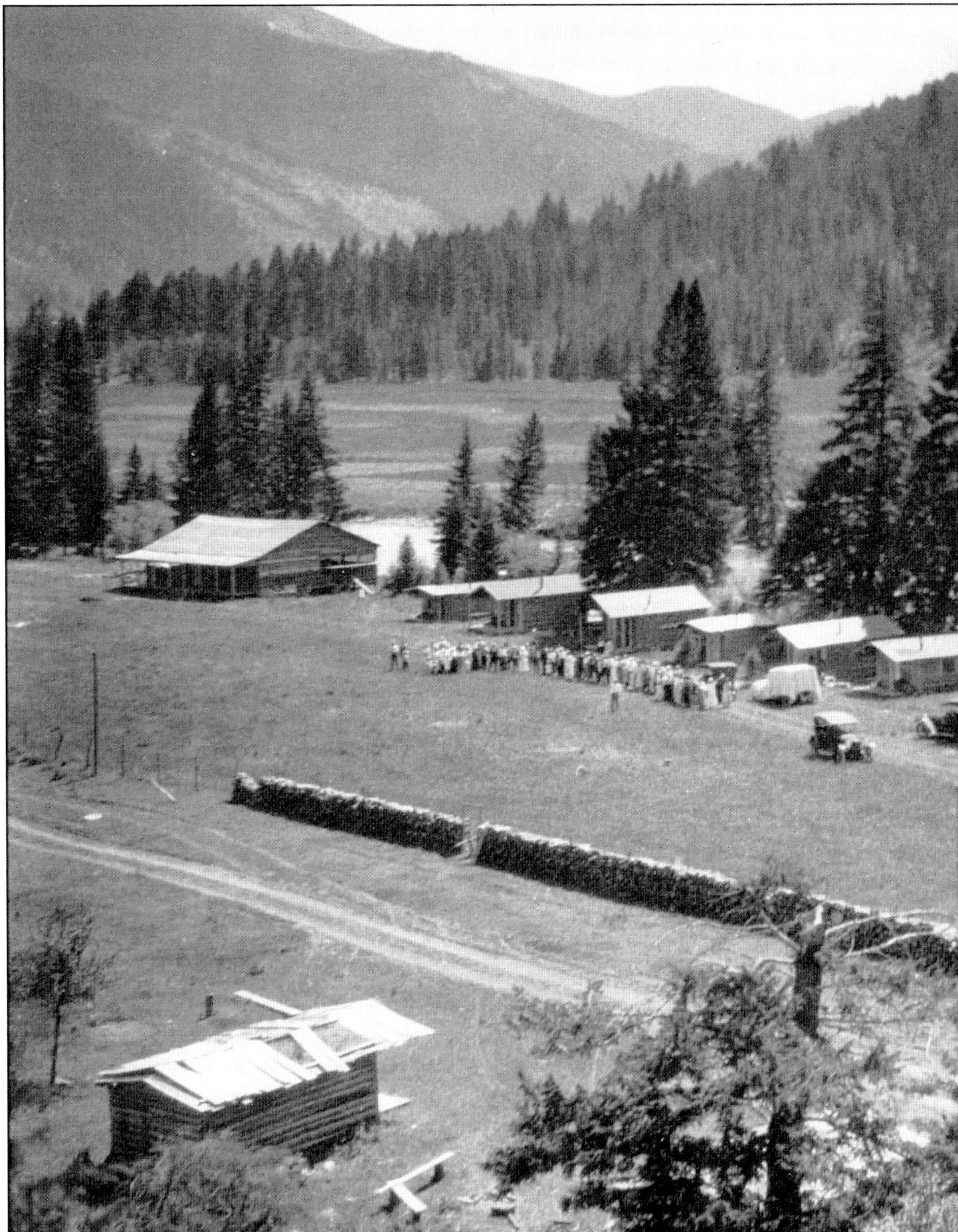

Karst Kamp, 1916. Featuring tours of Yellowstone Park, horse trips, fishing, and big-game hunting, Karst Kamp was quite successful. At its height, there were 56 cabins, a dance hall, swimming pool, curio store and museum, a general store, an ice cream store, an office, and a huge dining

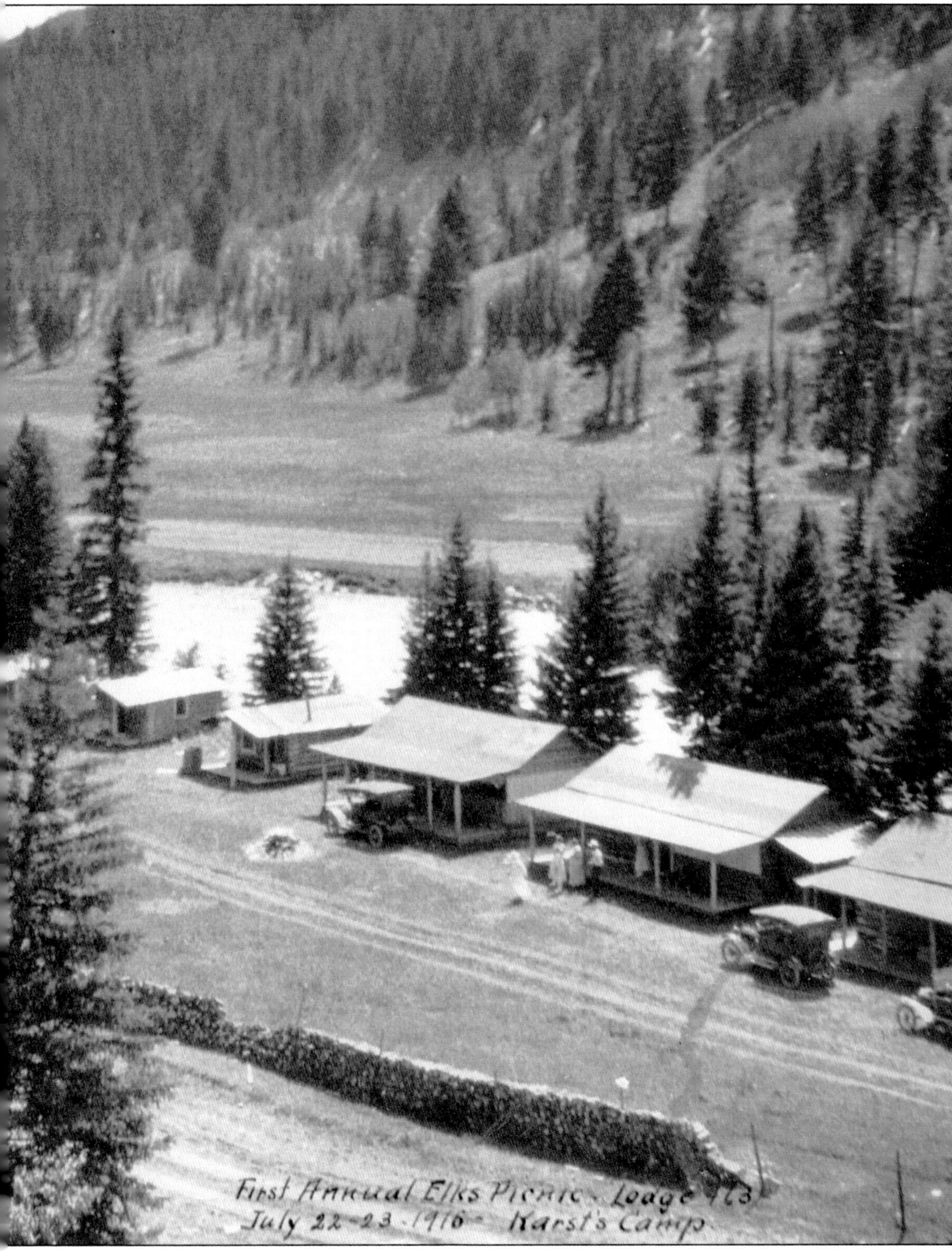

room that was needed to feed the large number of guests. The photograph of an Elks Lodge 963 gathering in July 1916 shows part of the cabin row. Note the start of the piles of cold-weather firewood. (Kevin Kelleher.)

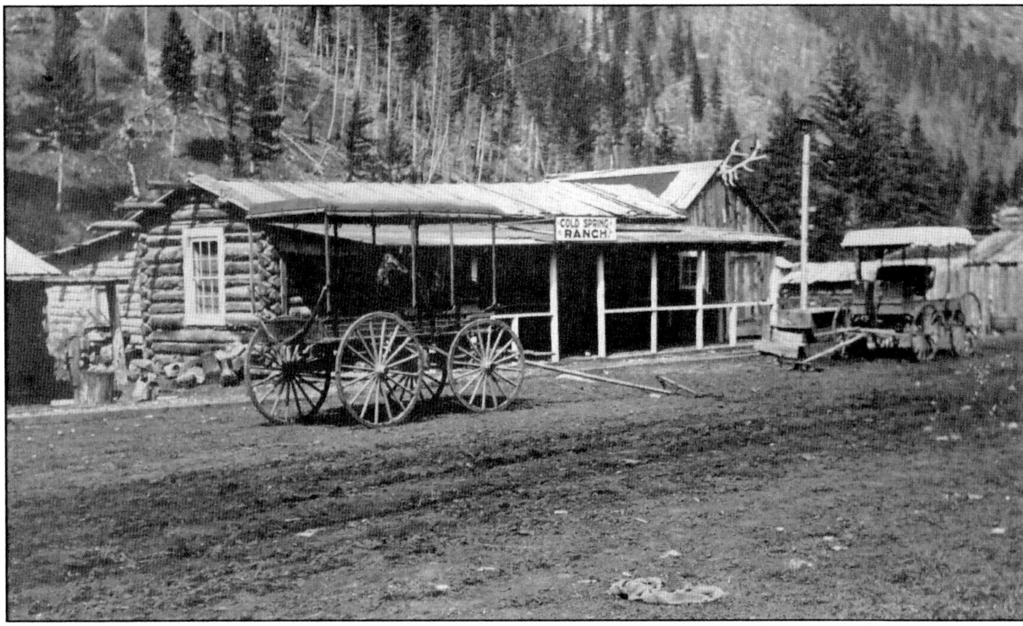

COLD SPRING RANCH c. 1906 (ABOVE); KARST KAMP, 1927 (BELOW). Pete Karst (1875–1966) started in the canyon by carrying mail, freight, and people from Salesville to the Cooper Tie Camp. Since the trip was long and an overnight stop was necessary, Pete acquired the Cold Spring Ranch, pictured above. When the lumber camp folded in 1907, he started dude ranching in earnest. He had 183 guests in 1909, but when the Milwaukee Railroad connected to Gallatin Gateway in 1910 and started promoting "The Gallatin Way to Yellowstone," business really picked up. There were 600 guests that year, and the years following World War I were the "golden age" of dude ranching. (Both, S. Anderson.)

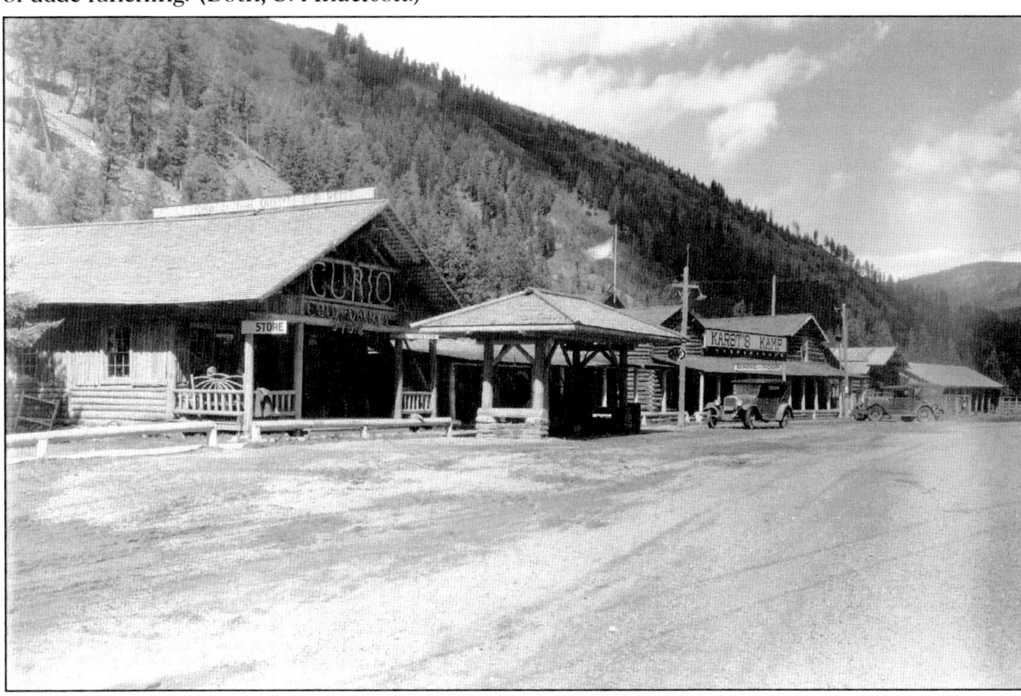

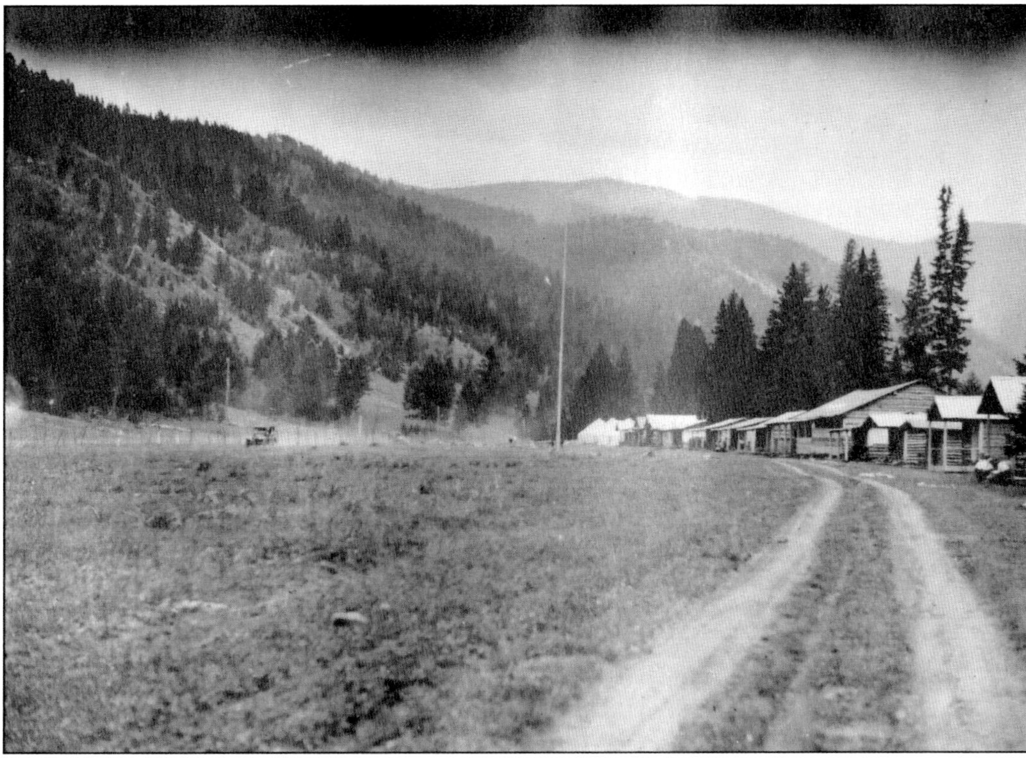

ROAD BY KARST KAMP (ABOVE); DINNER BELL, 1917 (BELOW). At age 75 in 1951, Pete retired and sold the camp to Harold Carlson. It burned to the ground in 1957. (Both, S. Anderson.)

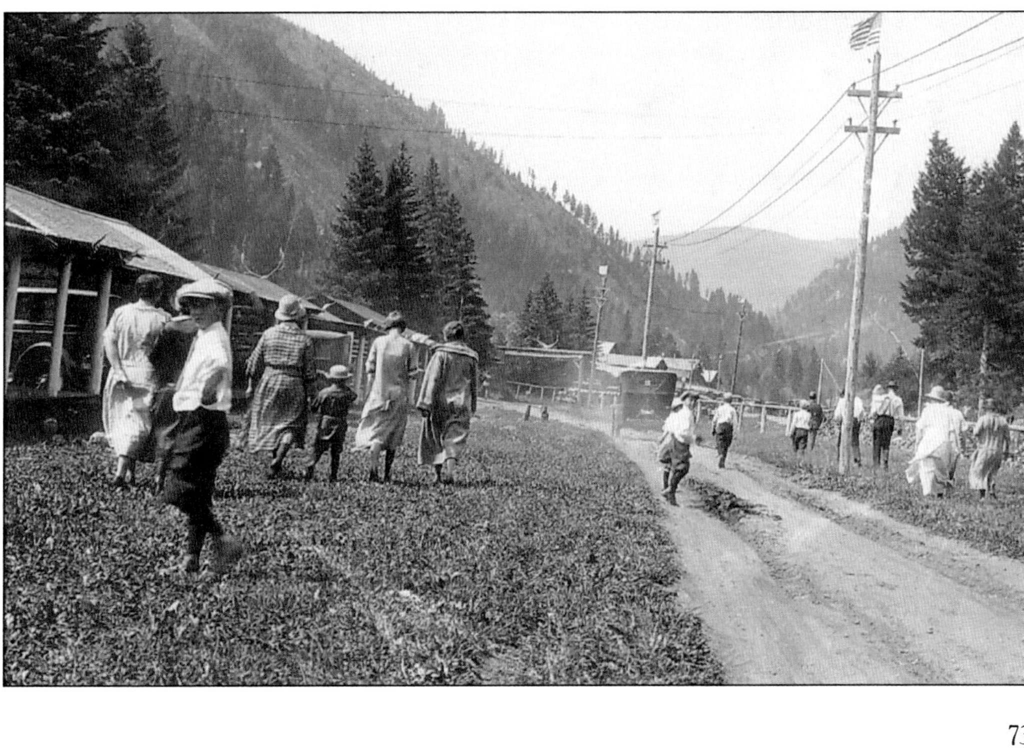

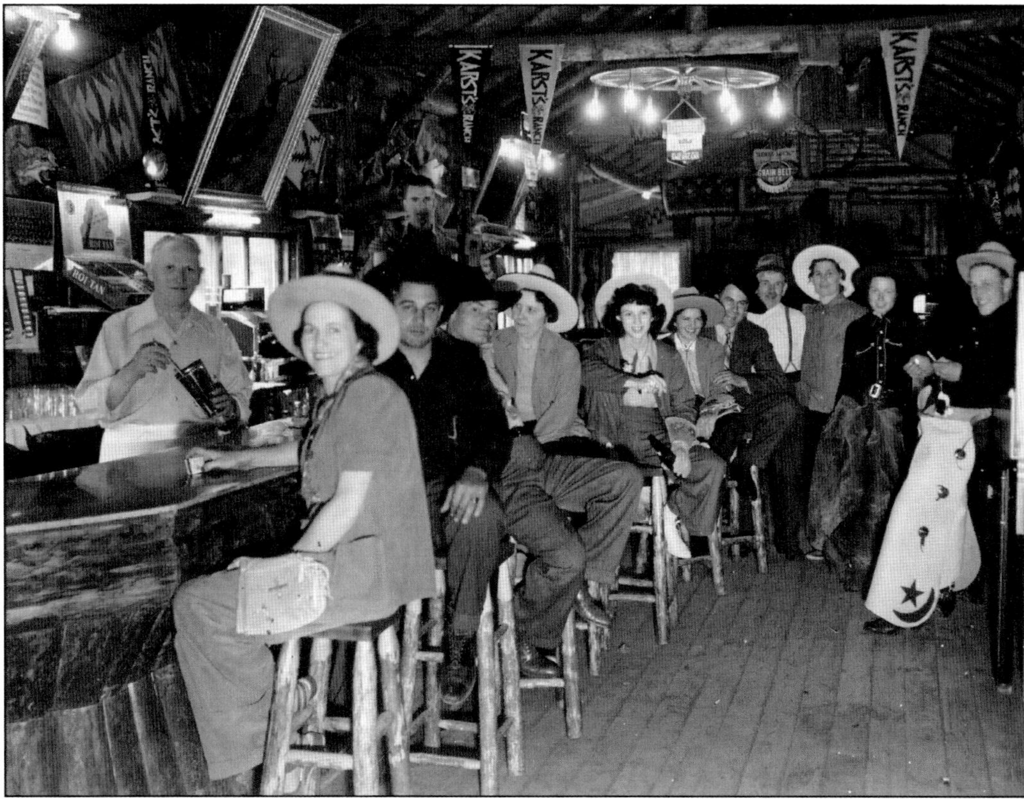

KARST BAR, EARLY 1940S. Longtime bartender John Fechter serves a group of "duded up" partygoers at this convention in the 1940s. In addition to tourists, Karst Kamp served as an overnight site for a variety of local organizations from the Elks and Rotary clubs to the Montana State College football team and conventions like the Montana Cabin Owners Association. (S. Anderson.)

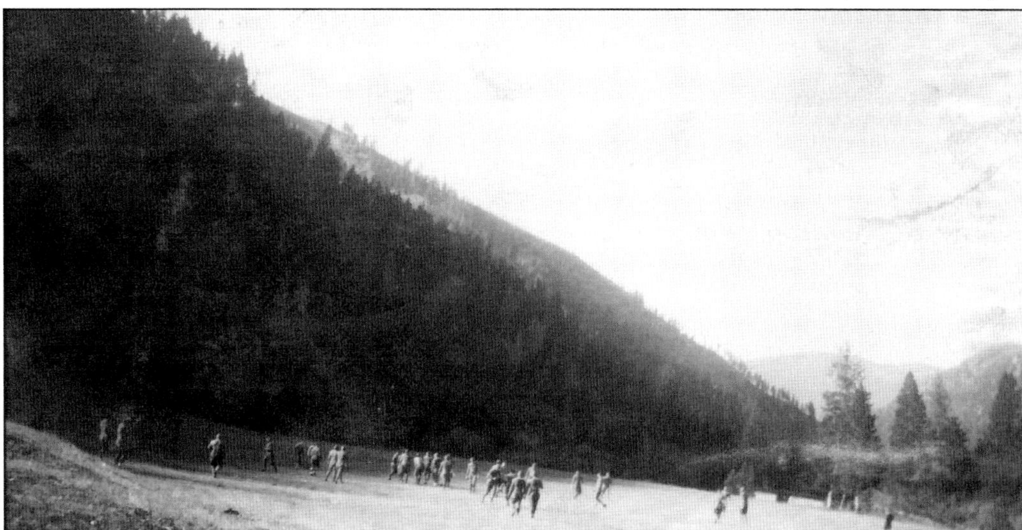

COLLEGE FOOTBALL TEAM. In the early 1930s, the football team from Montana State College practices in the field that became the lettuce farm. (S. Anderson.)

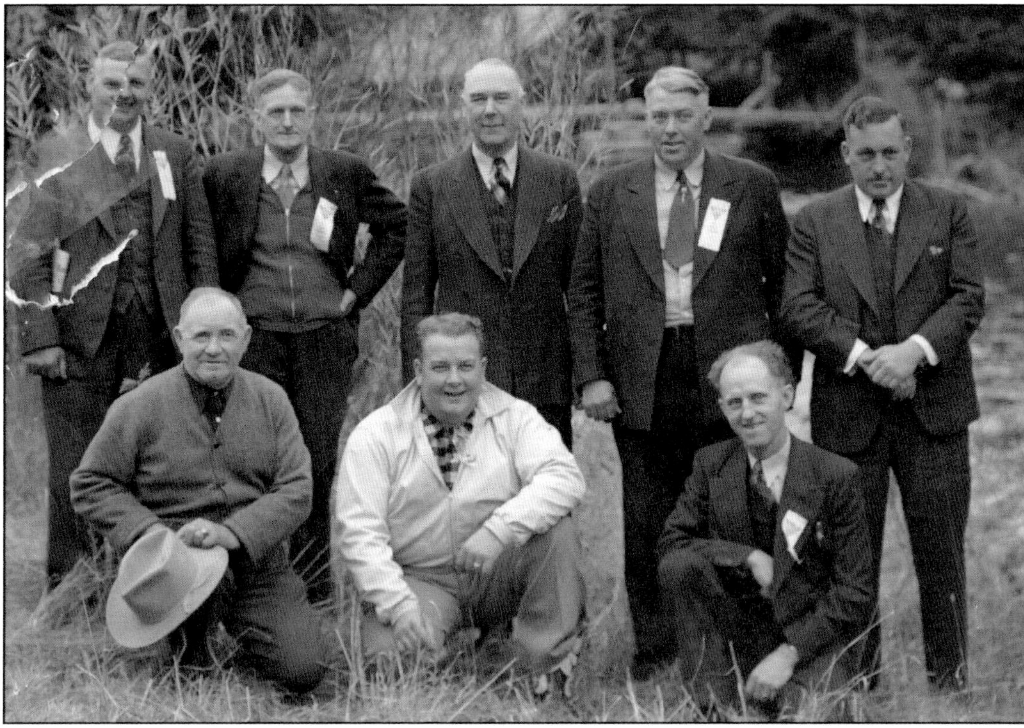

Montana Cabin Owners Association, October 1939. Pete Karst, the host, is in the first row at far left. (S. Anderson.)

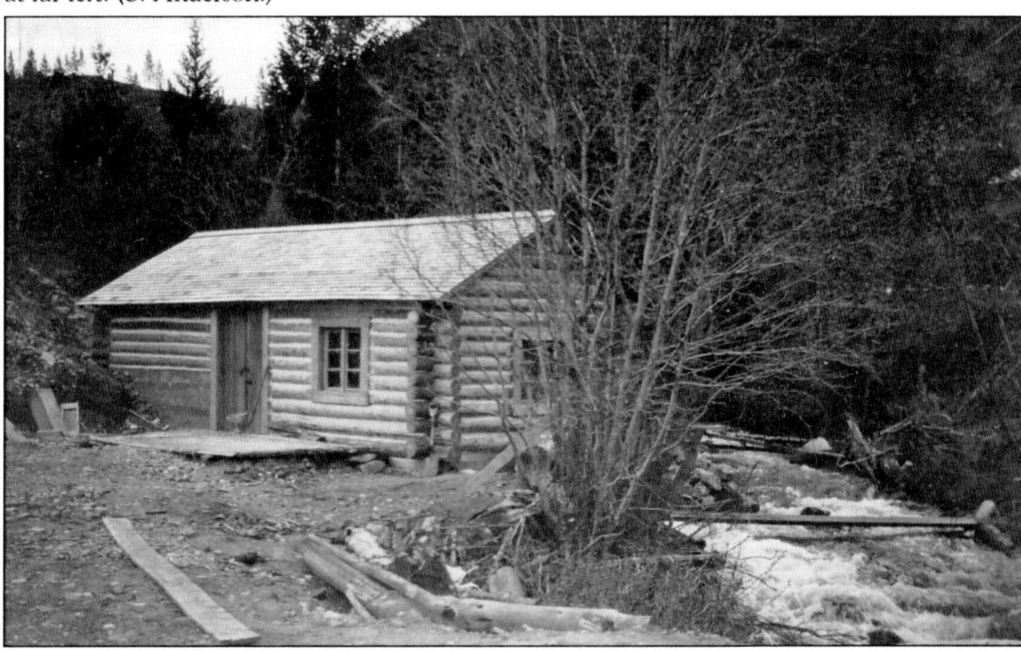

Generator Cabin on Moose Creek. The Rural Electrification Administration (REA) and Montana Power did not bring electricity to the basin and the canyon until 1948. In the meantime, many of the ranches installed generators run by old gasoline engines. Pete Karst built a hydropower generator on Moose Creek in 1922 to supply his ranch's needs. (S. Anderson.)

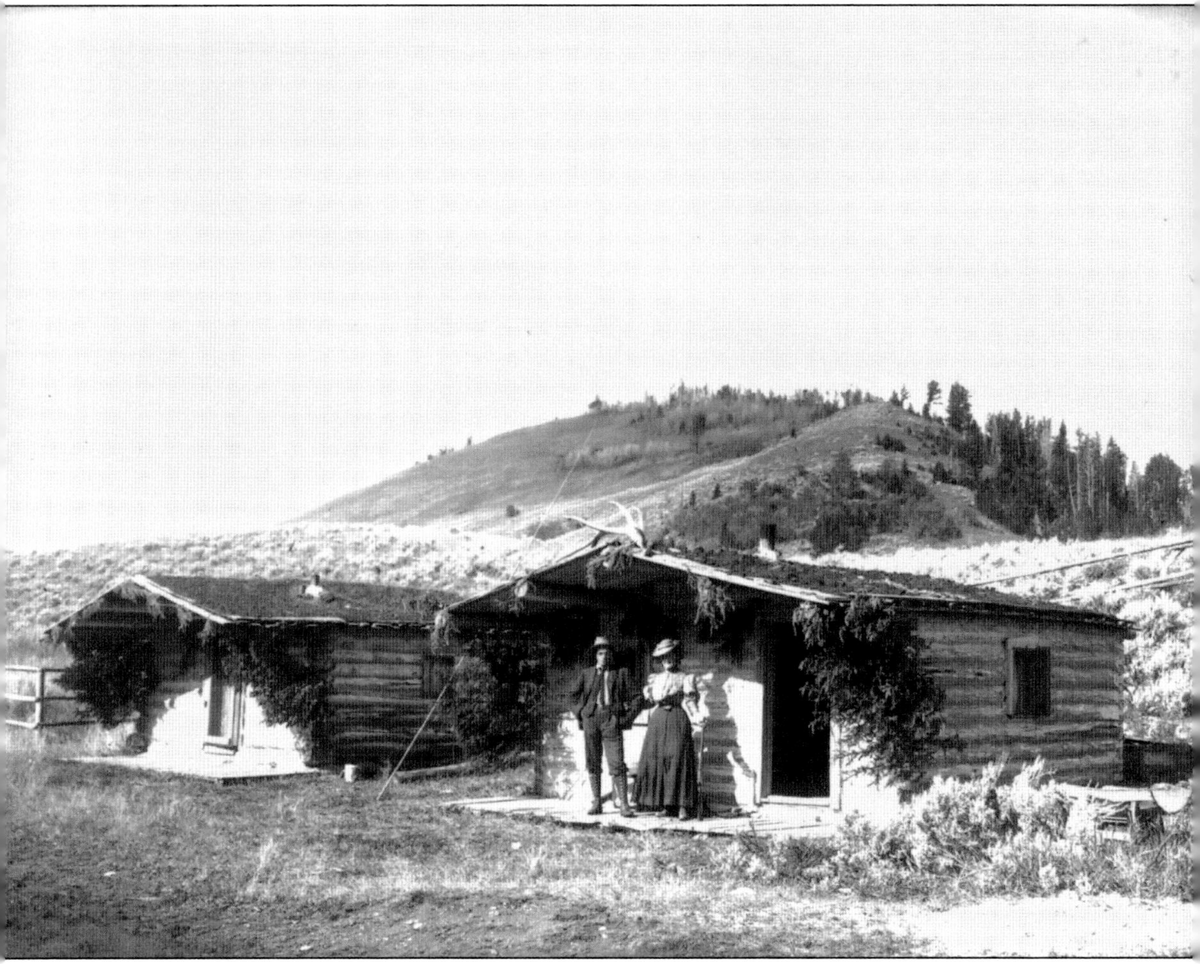

Michener Camp. This photograph of Mr. and Mrs. Achilles Lamme of Bozeman shows the primitive cabins that Tom Michener rented for four to six weeks as dudes helped with the cattle operation. Started in 1907, it was located at the fresh springs where the West Fork enters the Gallatin. When the Hercules Gold Dredging plan folded in 1919, Tom Michener left the area. The homestead and placer mine remained in the family. Tom's mother lived on the site in the 1920s, and his daughter Dorothy and her husband, Joe Vick, returned in 1938 to reopen the dude ranching business. (PM.)

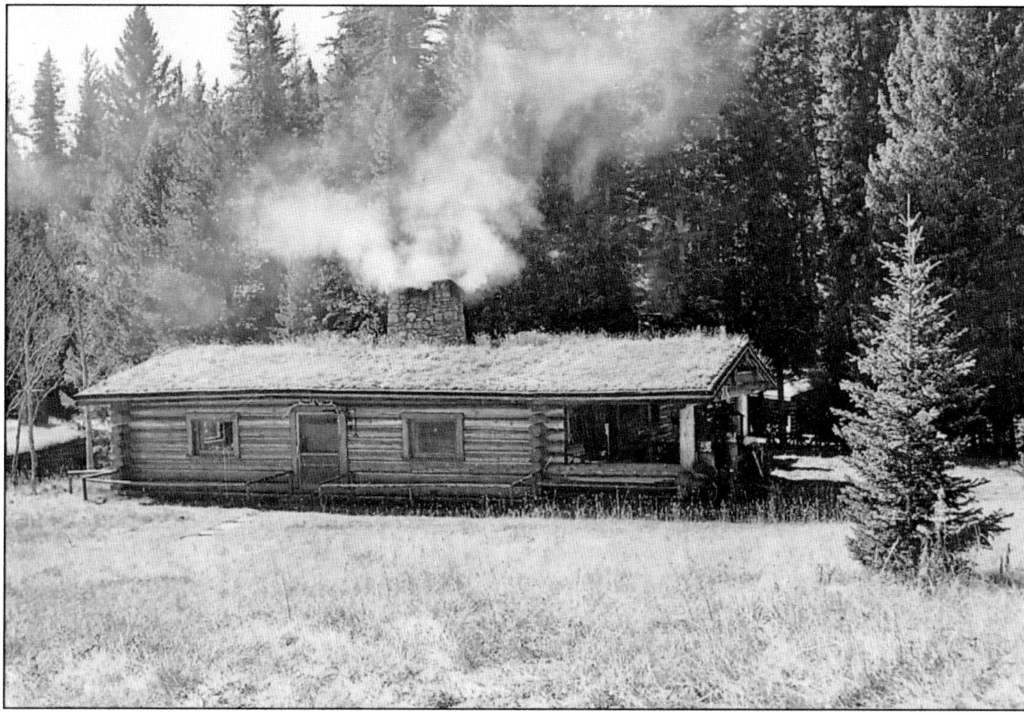

B-K Main Building, 1947 (Above); B-K Cabin (Below). Clarence Lytle homesteaded the area that became the B-K and eventually Lone Mountain Ranch. These original buildings were constructed by their neighbor Eugene Crail, and the ranch was run as a cattle operation. Note the sod roof. Clarence was a bachelor, and upon retirement in 1926, he sold the ranch to Chicago paper mill tycoon J. Fred Butler. (Above, Lone Mountain Ranch; below, HCRC.)

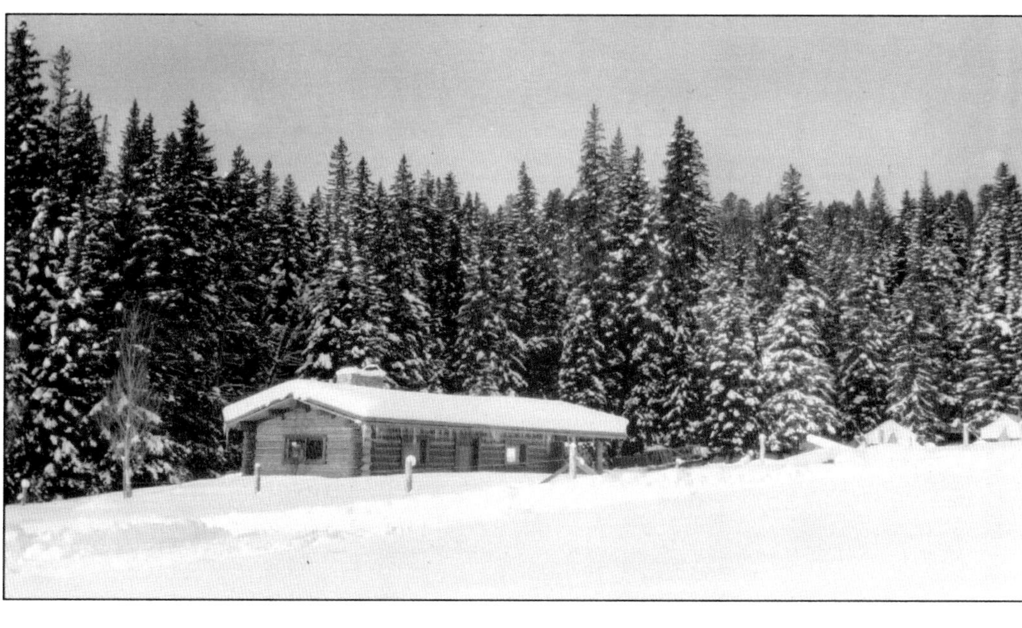

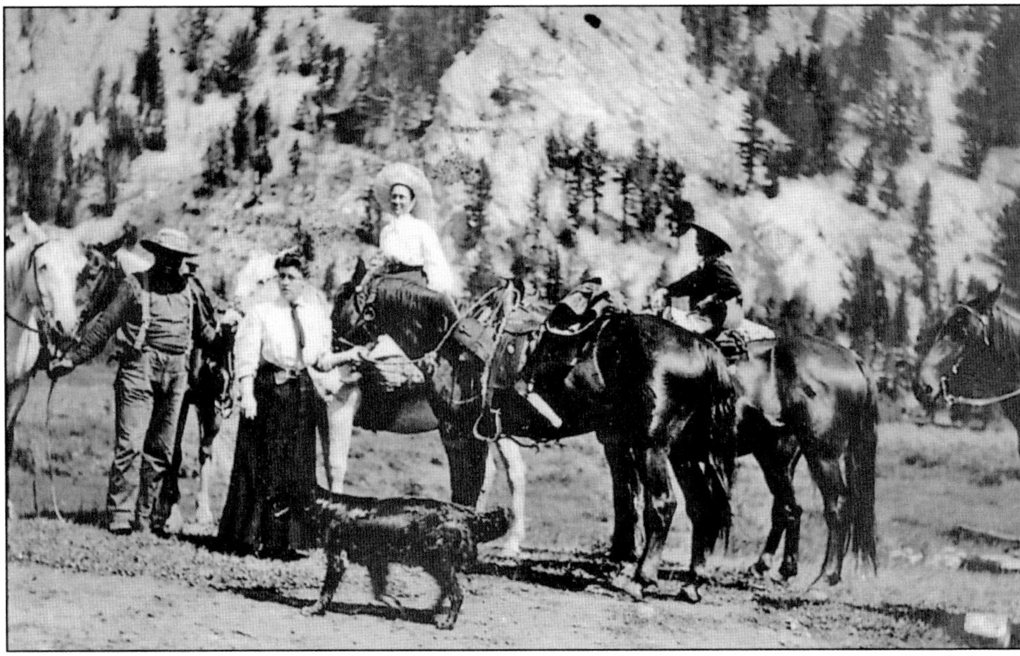

Butler Family on a Ride (Above); B-K Corrals in 1947 (Below). J. Fred Butler, his wife, Lillie, their daughter Florence, son-in-law Don Kilbourne, and grandsons Julius and Paul are seen riding. They named the place the B-K for Butler-Kilbourne and kept it as a private vacation retreat until J. Fred's death. Thereafter, the Kilbournes ran it as a guest ranch and retreat, decorating many of the buildings with Indian artifacts. (Above, PM and Lone Mountain Ranch; below, Lone Mountain Ranch.)

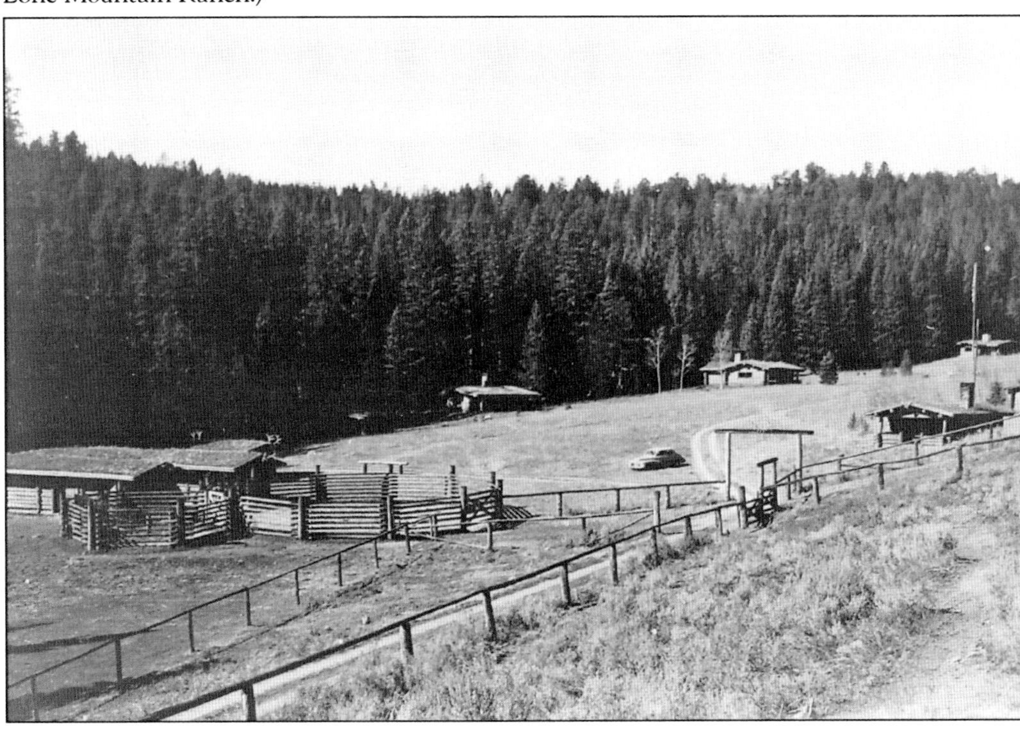

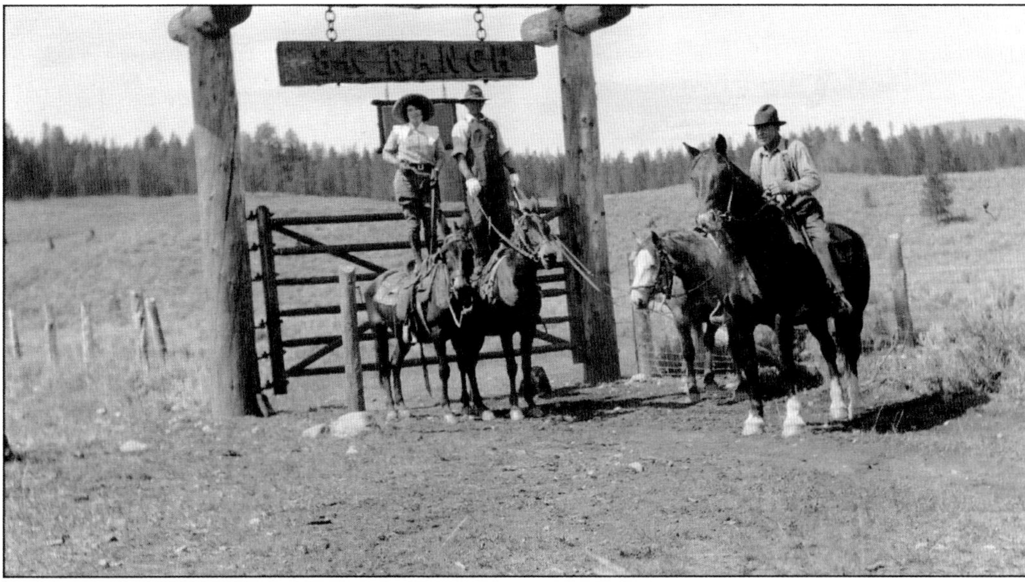

B-K Gate, Emmett Crail and Friends (Above); Ed Smith in B-K Corral (Below). In 1946, Earl and Louise Risser, along with Henrietta Joyce, bought the B-K Ranch. They turned it over to Joyce's nephew Robert Turner, a minister who ran it as a boys' camp to "instill values" into these young men. This experiment was brief, and it returned to guest ranching. With the coming of Rural Electricity Administration (REA) electricity to the area in 1948, the B-K became the first place in Montana with underground electricity. (Above, HCRC; below, Lone Mountain Ranch.)

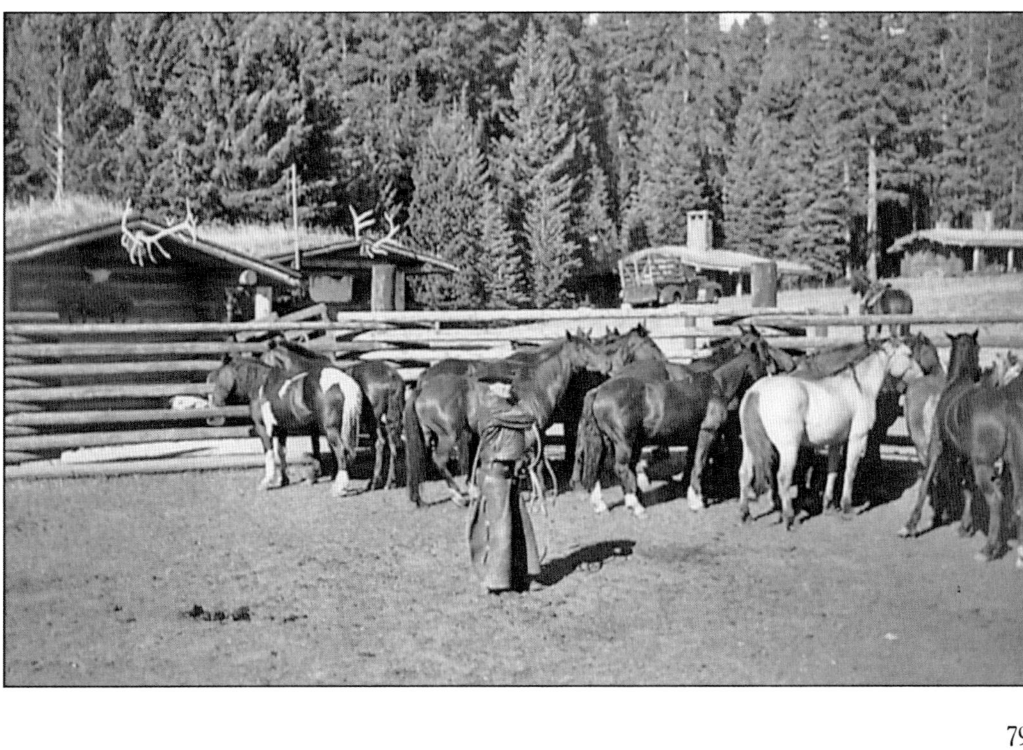

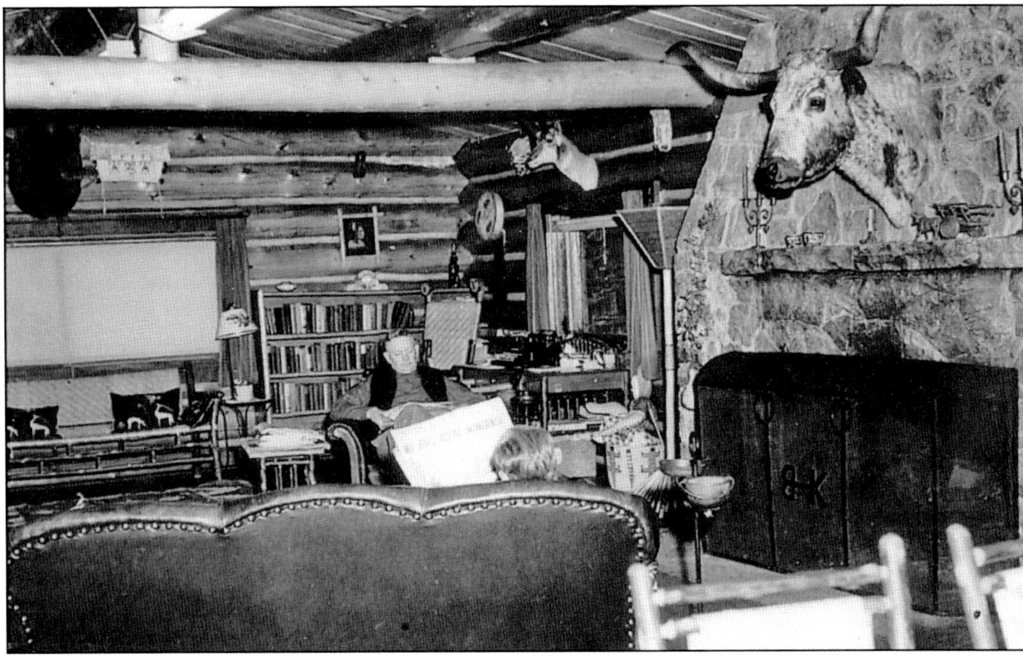

Lone Mountain Ranch Lounge, 1957 (Above); Highway Sign, 1957 (Below). After a brief period as the Corcoran Logging Camp from 1950 to 1955, Jack and Elaine Hume, who bought the Crail Ranch in 1950, added the B-K to make nearly 2,000 acres of holdings. They renamed it Lone Mountain Ranch and carried on guest ranching until 1962. Sam Smeding bought it from them and continued dude ranching until selling to the Chrysler Realty Corporation, which was acquiring property for the Big Sky ski resort. (Both, Lone Mountain Ranch.)

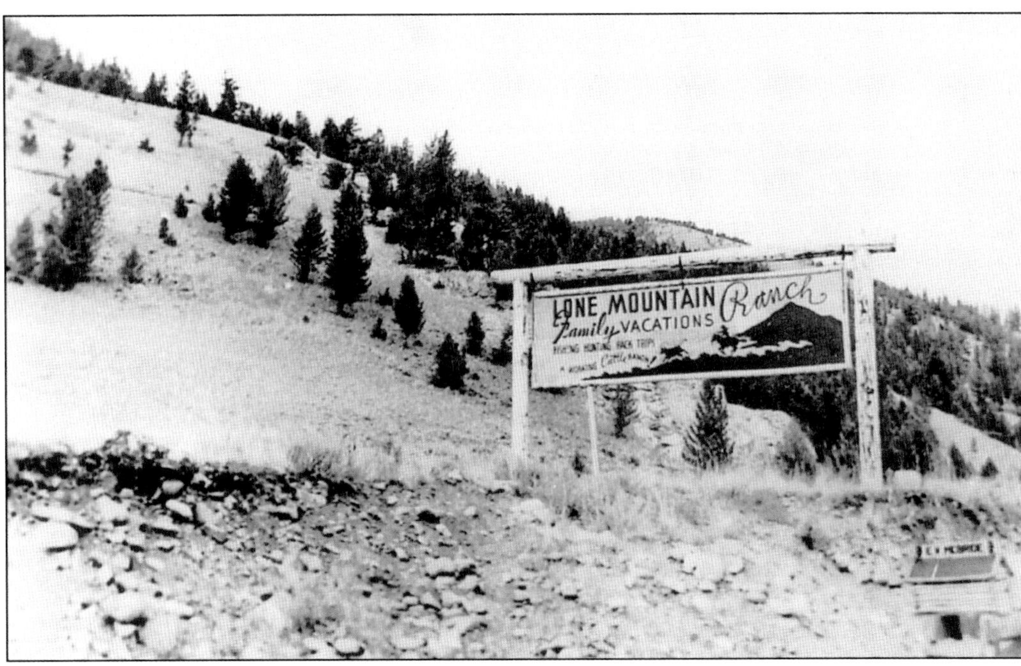

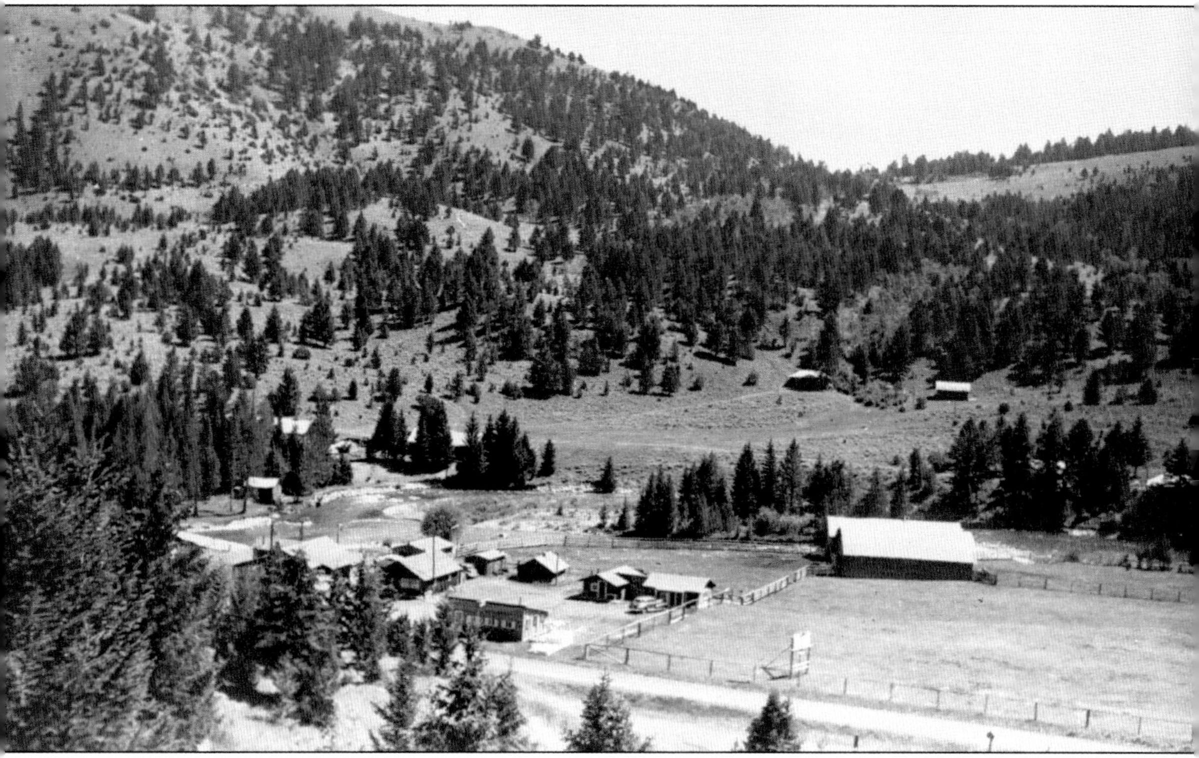

Half Way Inn. The present-day luxurious Rainbow Ranch Lodge stands on property that knows a long tradition of ranching. Herman "Jim" McMullen homesteaded the area in the late 1800s. Lew Bart failed to prove up his homestead there when he served in the Spanish-American War, and his full-time residency was contested by neighbor Bert Stillman. In the early 1900s, as the Dew Drop Inn, it served as a brief respite for weary Yellowstone Park wayfarers riding down from the railroad terminus at Gallatin Gateway. It was sold to the Lemons in 1919 and renamed the Half Way Inn. Lemon Drop Mountain rises in the background of the picture. Named for the shape of the hill and for the Lemon family, it is a favorite hike for present-day locals. (PM.)

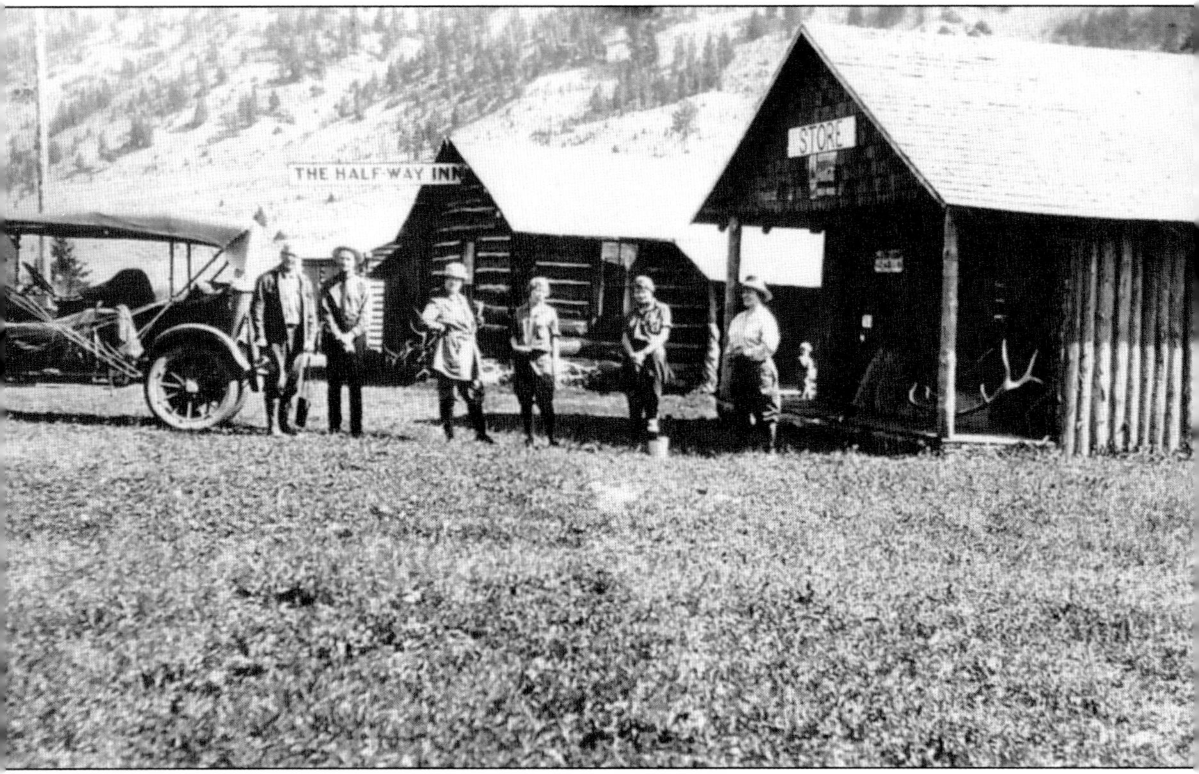

LEMONS' HALF WAY INN, 1920s. In 1919, R.B. and Pearl Lemon relocated their family from Ohio. They ranched and ran a cattle operation and also logged for their steam sawmill. The spread included a blacksmith shop and smokehouse, and the Lemons added lodging amenities to their ranch stock operation. The Half Way Inn was named for its location between Bozeman and Yellowstone National Park, while the Eat Here Café served up home-cooked fare and famous pancakes. Son Stanley later installed a gas station and automobile shop. Ranching ceased after 1946, when the Lemons sold the property. Named the Rainbow Ranch after that sale, the property has since been resold four times. The photograph shows the Lemon family with friends and neighbors shortly after the purchase. Three-year-old George Lemon is seen behind the porch. (Beth Naert.)

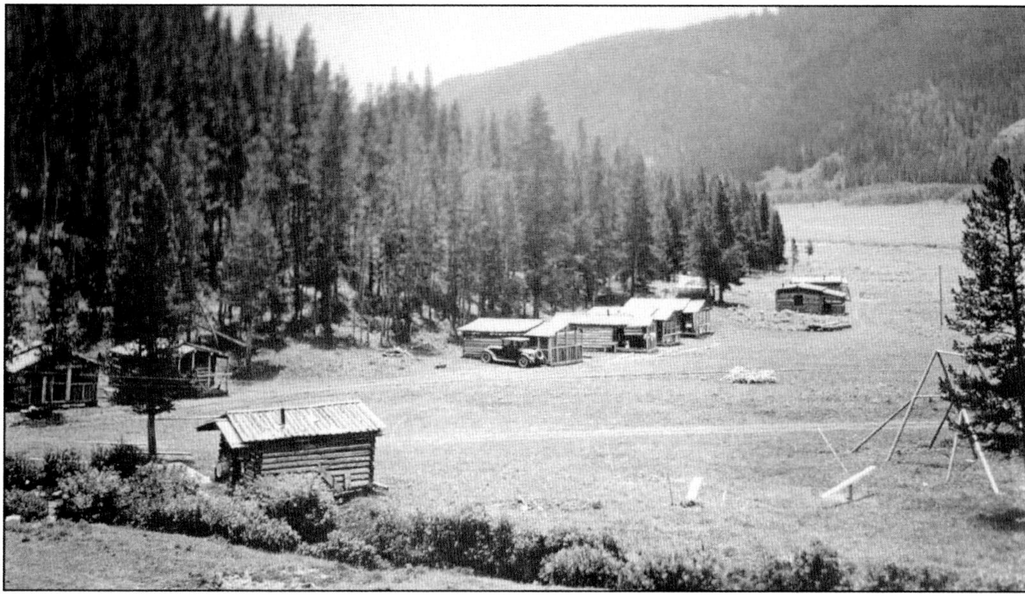

320 Ranch in 1935 (Above); 320 Barn, Jim Goodrich Hitches Horses (Below). The 320 Ranch, started by Sam Wilson as a homestead in 1898, was called the Buffalo Horn Resort. With two adjoining 160-acre parcels, the name eventually changed to the 320 Ranch. Sam died in 1929, but his wife, Josephine, continued on as postmistress for many years and hired ranch managers. Dr. Caroline McGill, a physician from Butte, bought the ranch in 1936 and ran it as a dude ranch and a healthful retreat to nature. She had several managers, but Jim and Patty Goodrich were the most enduring, as they purchased it after the doctor's death in 1959. The 320 Ranch continues to this day as a summer dude ranch and serves skiing guests through the winter. (Above, US Forest Service; below, 320 Ranch.)

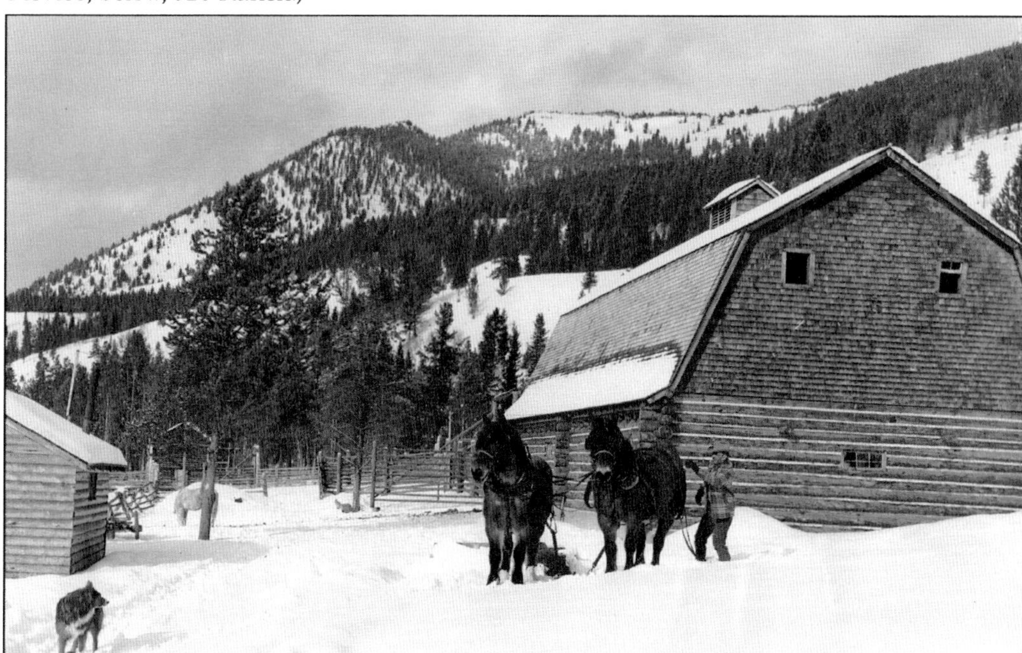

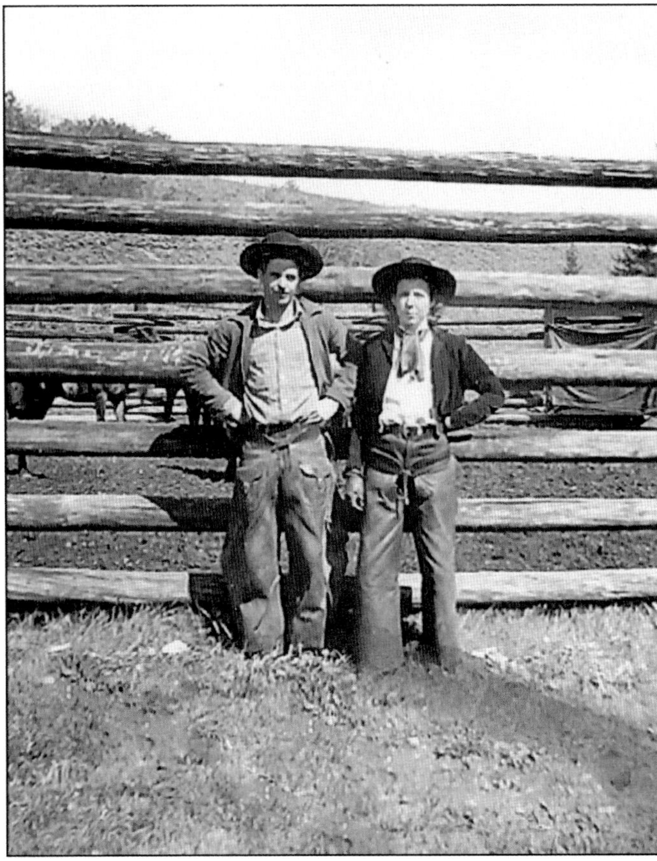

Buck and Helen Knight (Left); Buck's T-4 in 1972 (Below). Buck and Helen Knight are the prime example of dude ranchers of the mid-century. Rather than converting an existing stock ranch or mining claim into a tourist attraction, they built from scratch and created a legacy that has extended to the present. Starting with 10 acres on the old tumbledown Stillman property, they opened a summer and hunting resort, gas station, and motel in 1946. Buck was a renowned hunter, and he was sought after as a guide and outfitter. The paving of the highway in 1952–1953 brought more traffic with a need for a motel, and the place took off. (Left, Beth Naert; below, Buck's T-4.)

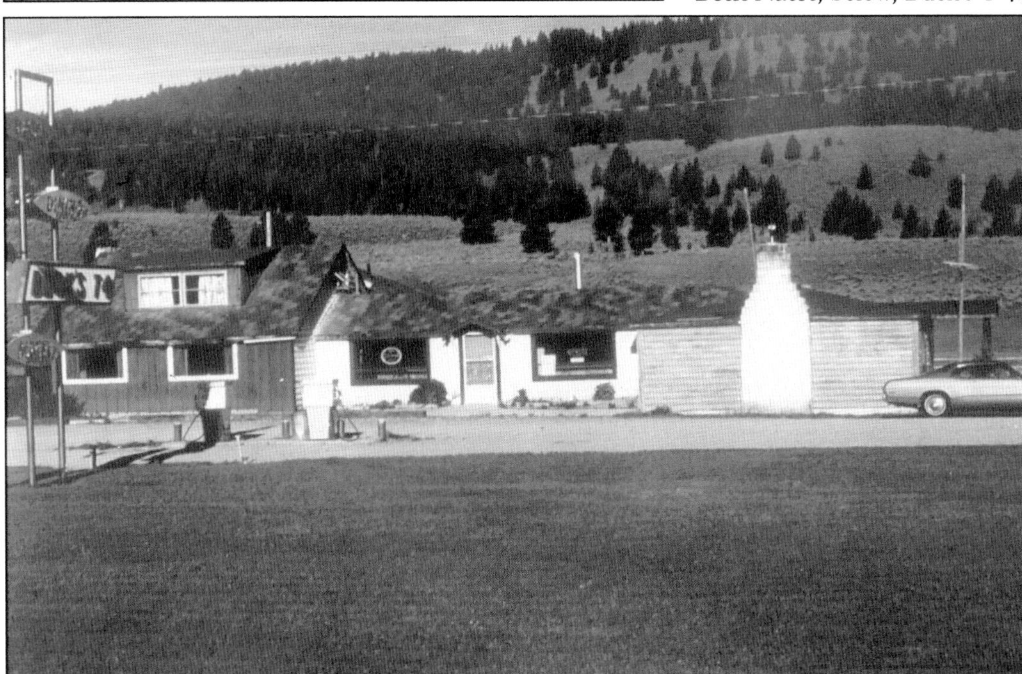

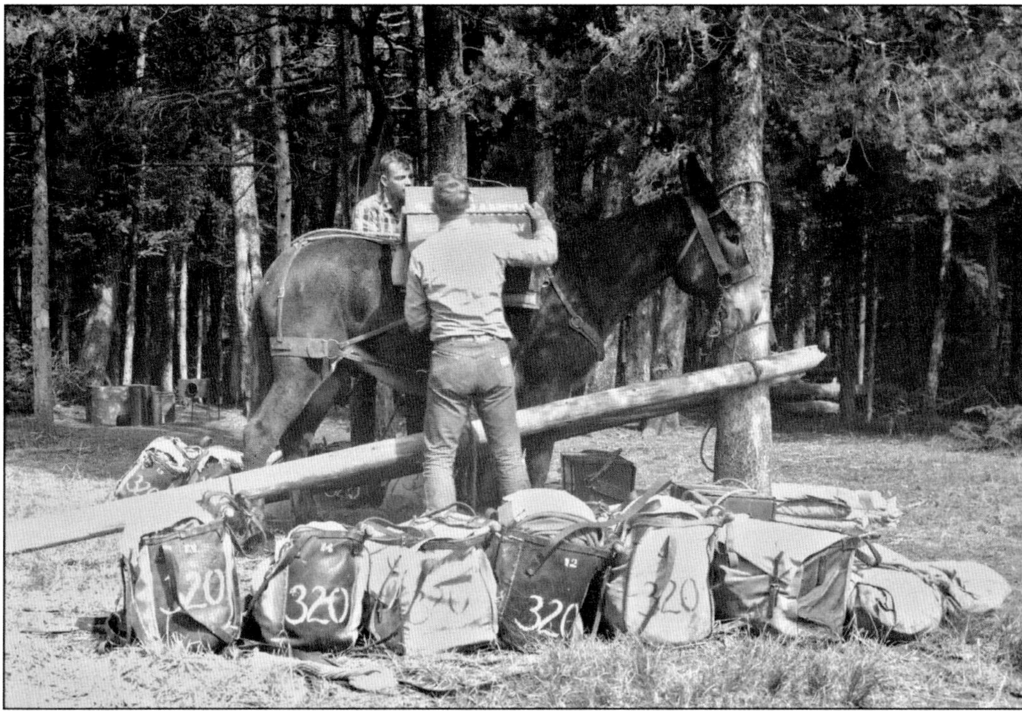

Loading Mules (Above); Pack Trip, c. 1930 (Below). Trail rides, campouts, and cookout picnics were common short recreational trips for the dudes, but the defining moment of the dude's vacation was the overnight pack trip. Patty Goodrich said that the food was kept fresh with frozen chickens but no ice. Pack horses took in a stove, a kitchen box, and a pallet of sleeping bags. Five or six mules could carry everything else. With one dude per horse as well, there was a lot for the wranglers to do. (Above, PM and the 320 Ranch; below, S. Anderson.)

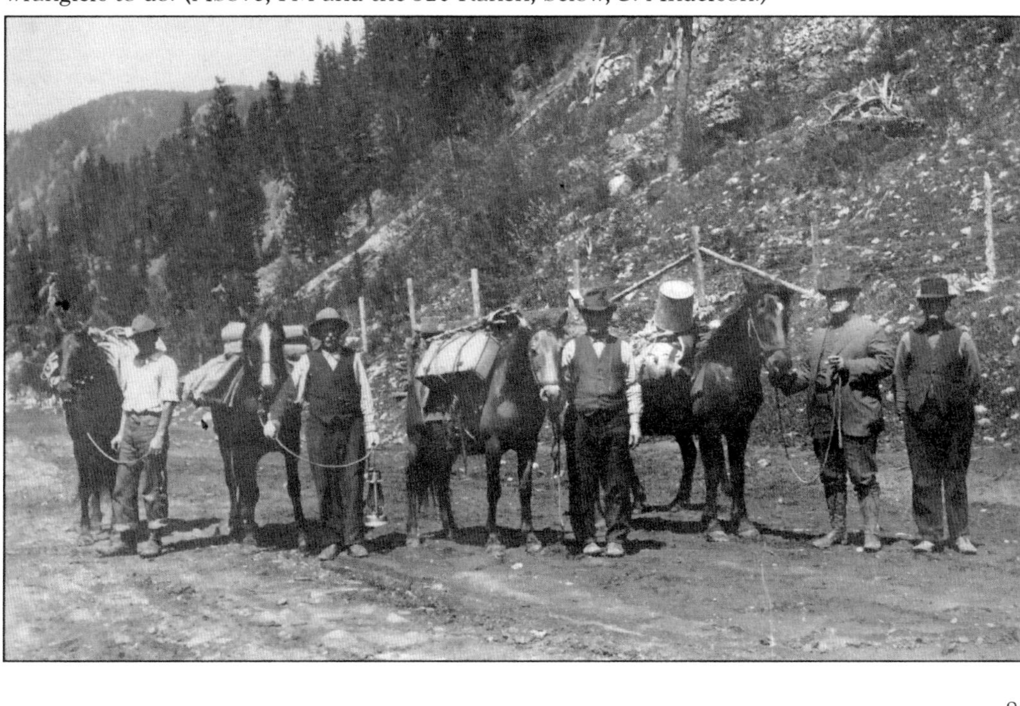

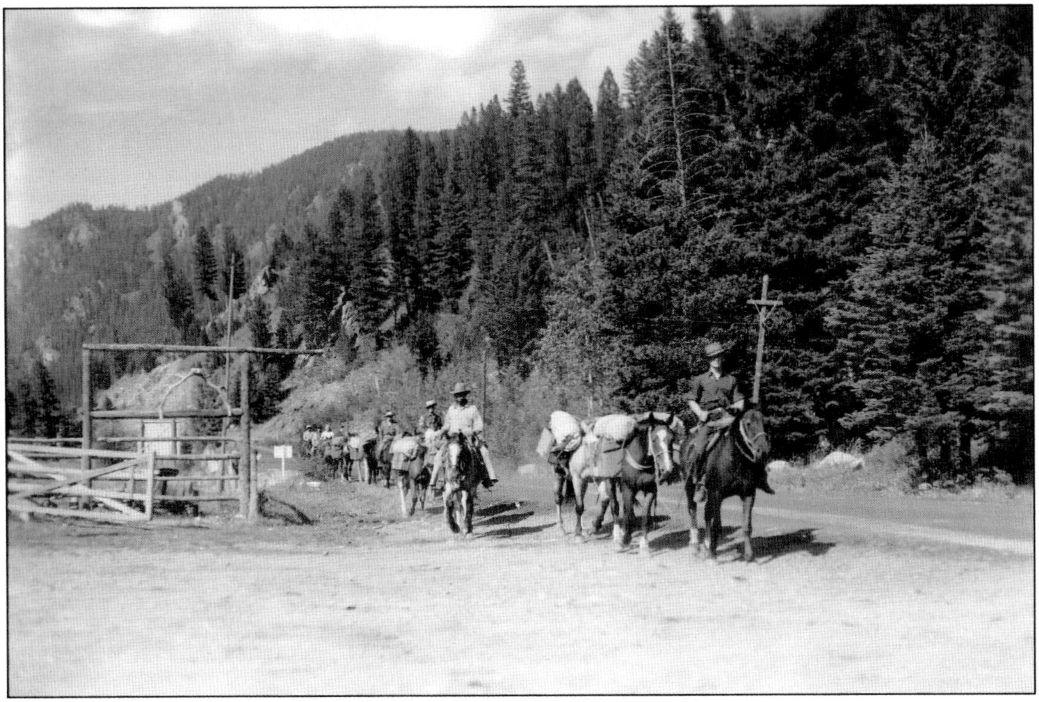

Boy Scouts Return (Above); Trail Ride (Below). In the photograph above, the Boy Scouts return to Karst Kamp after a week in the mountains. The 1950s image below shows a wrangler from the Lone Mountain Ranch leading guests to camp. (Above, S. Anderson; below, Lone Mountain Ranch.)

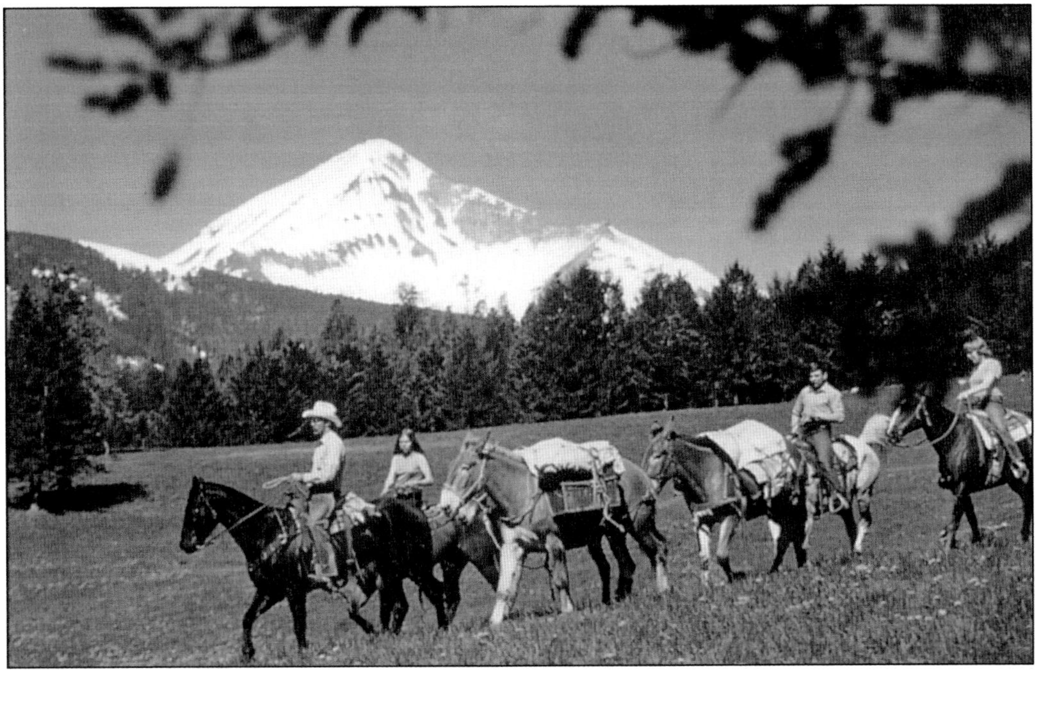

Eight

"Back in the Saddle Again"

Recreation

Despite the hardships of living here, the canyon and basin evolved into a recreation center where tourists came to learn about life in the "Wild West." Trail rides, dances, rodeos, and picnics were an important part of life then as now.

Hunting, initially for meat and then for pleasure, was the first recreational activity in the area, and hunting camps are documented as early as the 1880s. Many dudes, however, were quite happy just to come and see the wealth of wild animals here. Even today, tourists are delighted with sightings of the bighorn sheep herd near the Meadow Village entrance, elk on the golf course, or moose munching bushes outside bedroom windows.

Fishing, too, has had a long and famous history. The Gallatin River was the centerpiece of the Robert Redford film *A River Runs Through It*, and the Blue Ribbon trout fishery designation brings many to cast a fly in its waters.

The canyon road was built to serve visitors to Yellowstone Park where its proximity made Big Sky an early gateway. Now one can see the park in a few hours' drive, but even in the early 20th century when it took days, dude ranches arranged tours, and friends and family visitors were taken to "Colter's Hell."

The Gallatin Canyon and the West Fork Basin are surrounded by the Gallatin National Forest and the Lee Metcalf Wilderness. Hiking and mountaineering, horseback riding, and campouts are as important now as they were when Tom Michener, Sam Wilson, and Pete Karst started herding dudes.

Despite current common lore, winter sports did not start in 1972 with the coming of the resort. There was an active skiing community with backcountry skiing, primitive lifts, and ski jumps well before Big Sky was even conceived. Snowmobiling, too, has been popular in the long winters.

Remote and isolated it may have been, but the pioneers not only had an active social life, they also were able to share and profit from the abundance of recreational opportunities in the great outdoors.

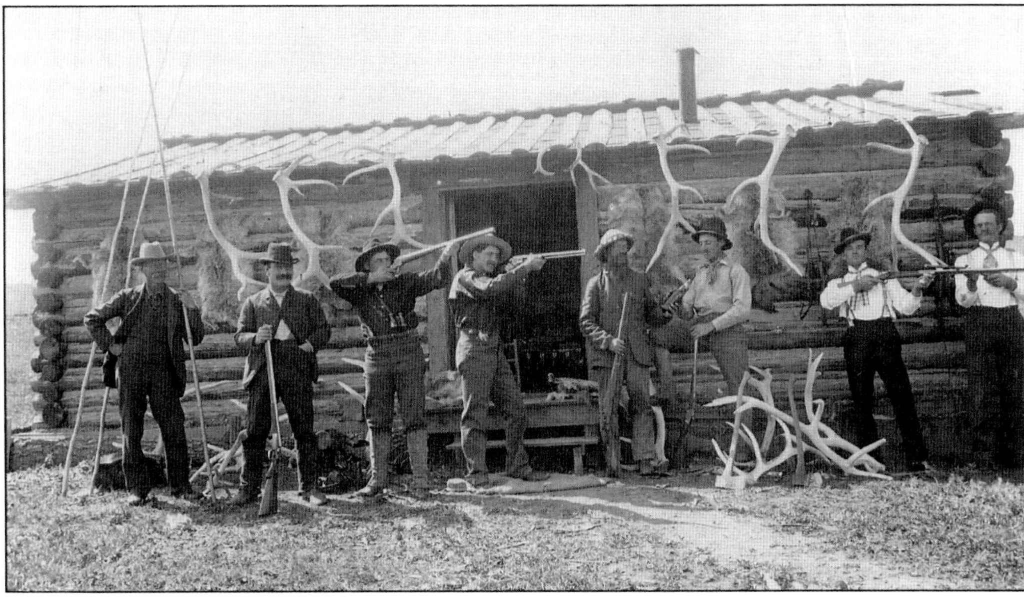

Inabnit Hunting Camp (Above); Tent Camp (Below). Hunting for big game attracted many to the area, as it still does. In the above photograph, William Wright, Sam Pyfer, Henry ?, George Pyfer, Daniel P. Inabnit, Fred Pyfer, Joseph Inabnit, and John R. Inabnit pose in front of the hunting cabin on Goose Creek. Below, Joe Huff and Albert Schlechter rest successfully in camp with deer, elk, and wolf pelts and carcasses hanging. (Above, HCRC; below, PM.)

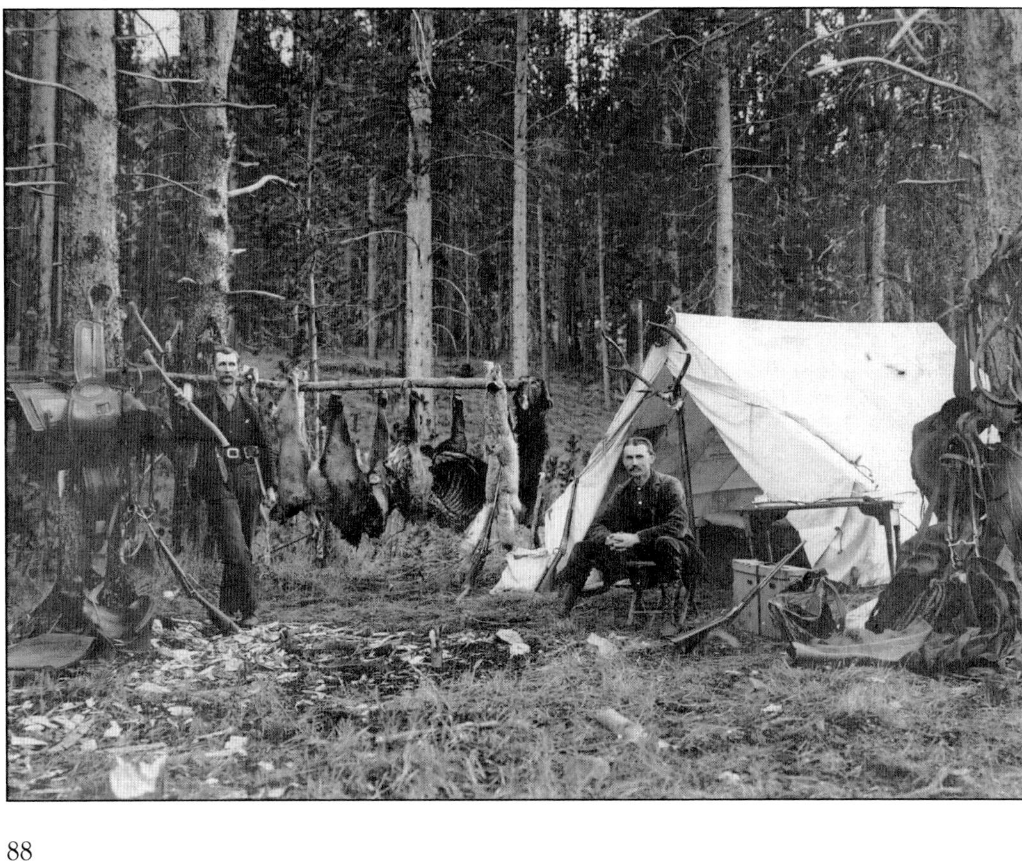

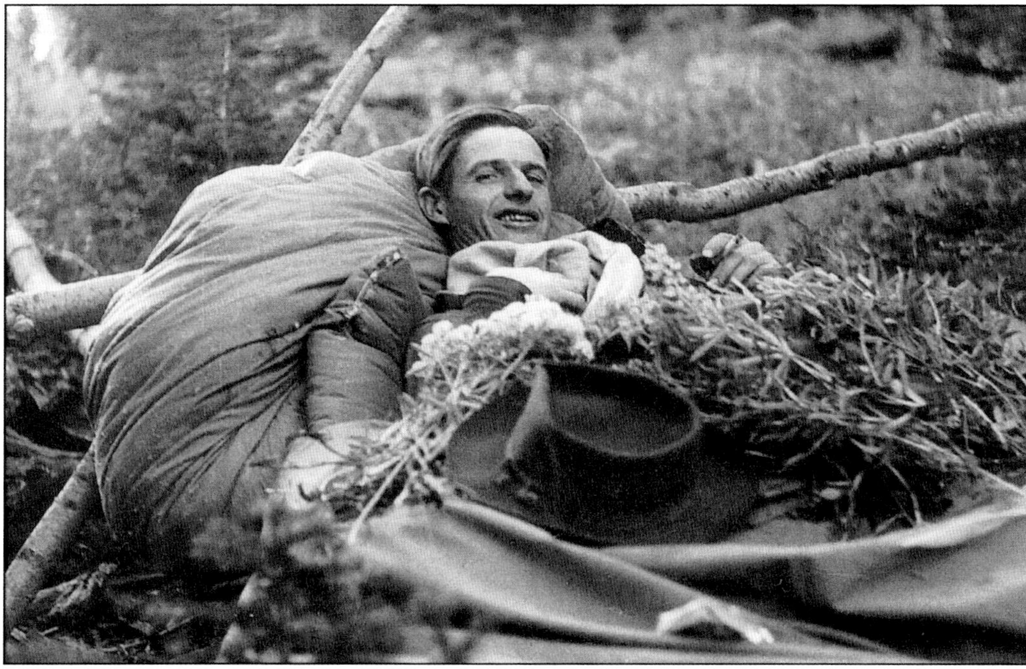

Buck Knight (Above); Wolf Pelts (Below). Buck Knight is pictured above, smiling as always and cozy in his blind. Below, Eugene Crail (left) and A.F. Crail (right) with an unidentified friend show off wolf pelts at the ranch. Deer, elk, and occasionally moose were hunted for meat. Grouse provided a tasty alternative to the farm chickens. Bighorn sheep, mountain goats, black and grizzly bears, mountain lions, wolves, coyotes, and other "varmints" were also hunted in this rich ecosystem. Hunted, trapped, and poisoned to extinction in the Greater Yellowstone Ecosystem by the 1920s, wolves were reintroduced in 1995. The reintroduction has led to divisive opinions about the need for wolves to balance the ecosystem fauna. (Above, Beth Naert; below, HCRC.)

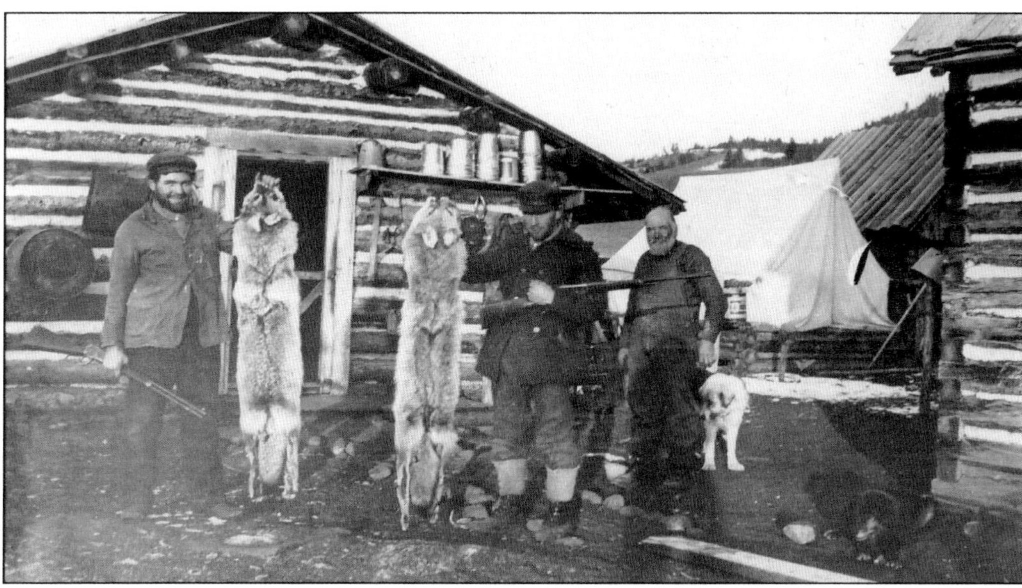

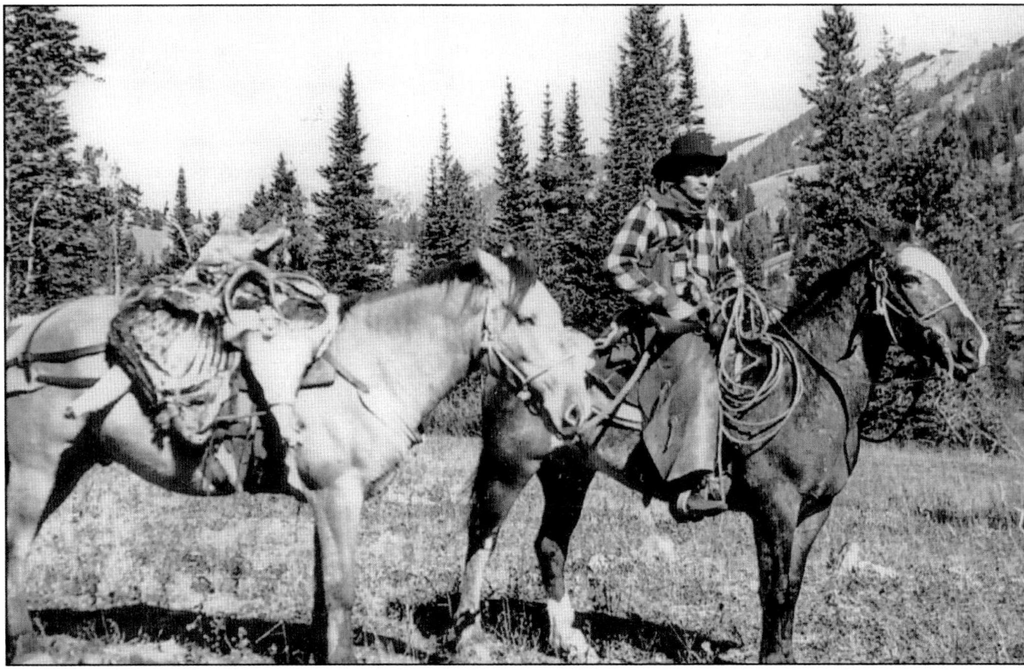

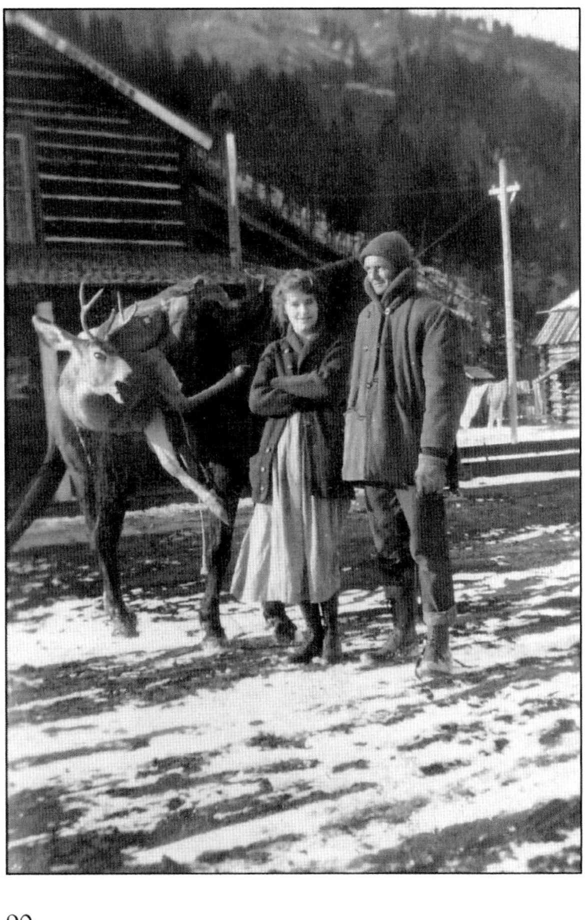

Ed Smith and Deer (Above); Isabelle and Ed Durnam with Deer (Left). Ed Smith, the B-K manager, is seen bringing a harvested deer out of nearby Beehive Basin. In 1930, the Boone and Crockett Montana record moose was taken in that basin, now a favorite hiking destination and the site of upscale housing. Ed Durnam has just returned to Karst Kamp with a deer. Whereas domestic cattle was a "cash crop" for homesteaders, wild game supplemented their diet. During Prohibition, Pete Karst was convicted of selling moonshine and out-of-season elk to a game warden. The understanding Bozeman judge allowed Karst to serve his six months during two winters when the Kamp was closed. (Above, Lone Mountain Ranch; left, S. Anderson.)

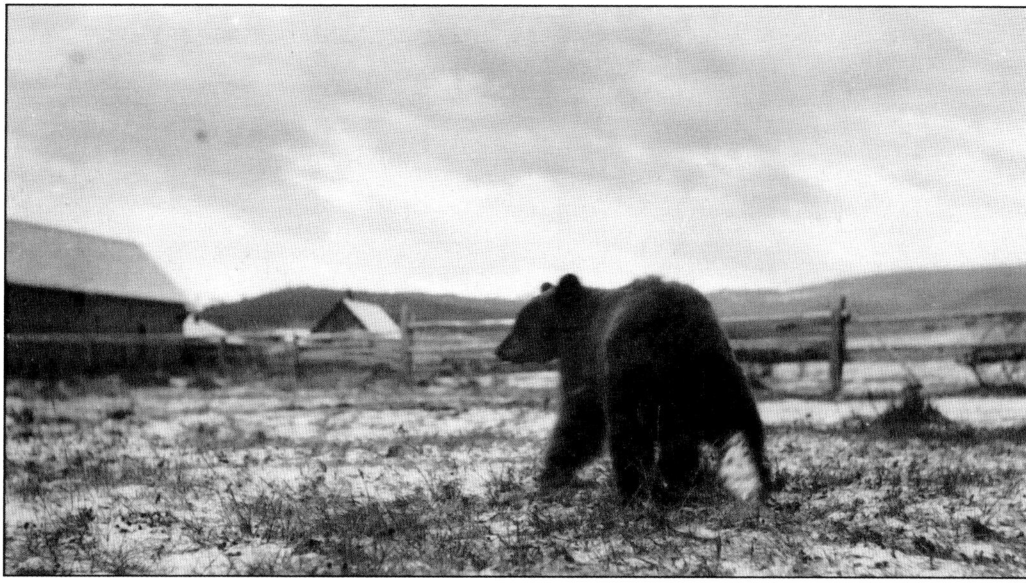

Black Bear (Above); Bull Elk (Below). These two scenes from the Crail Ranch show wild animals "grazing" the property. The photographs were taken in what is now the middle of the Meadow Village of Big Sky. Even today, moose, elk, and the occasional garbage-raiding bear are found foraging throughout town. (Both, HCRC.)

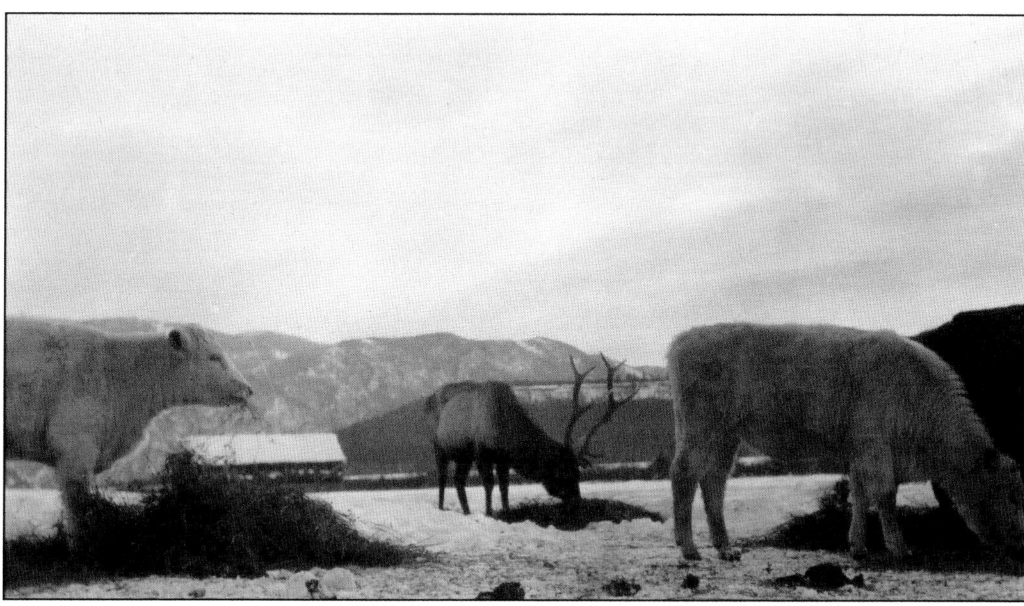

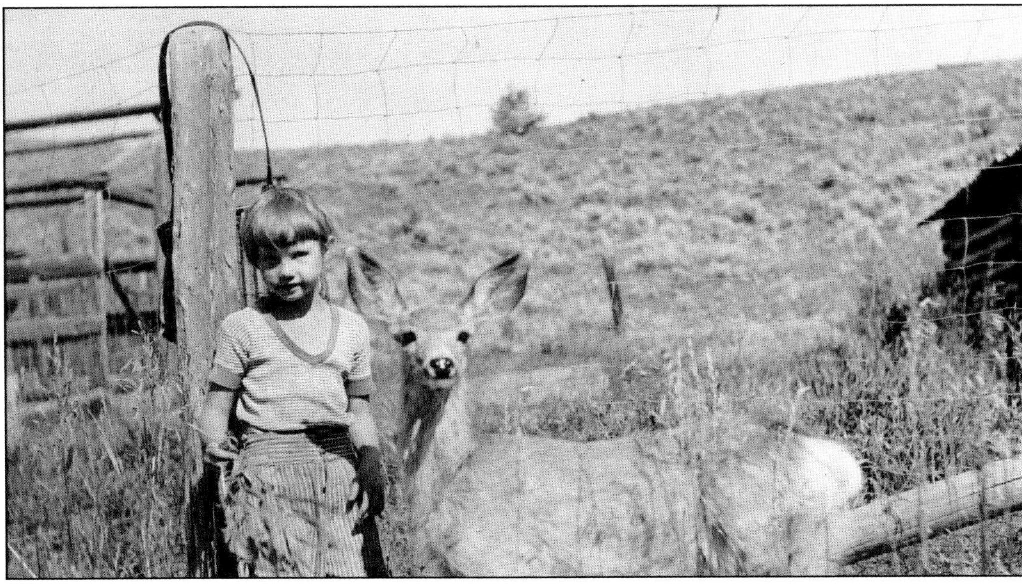

GLEN LOUISE BRENEMAN AND DEER (ABOVE); ISABELLE DURNAM AND DEER (BELOW). Not all the critters were entirely wild. (Above, HCRC, below, S. Anderson.)

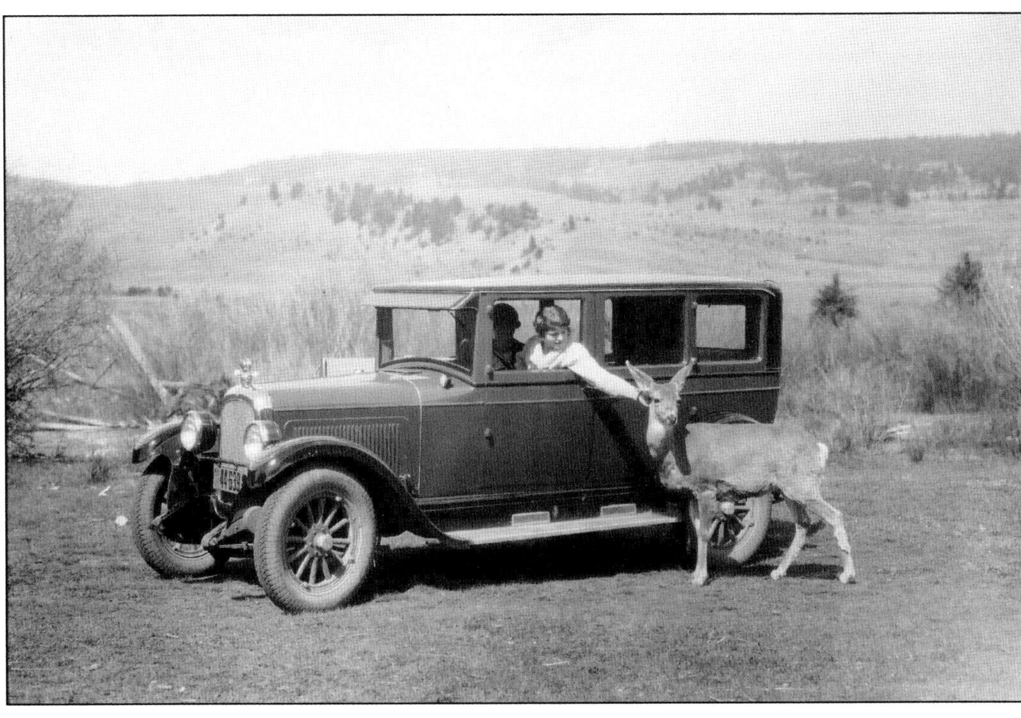

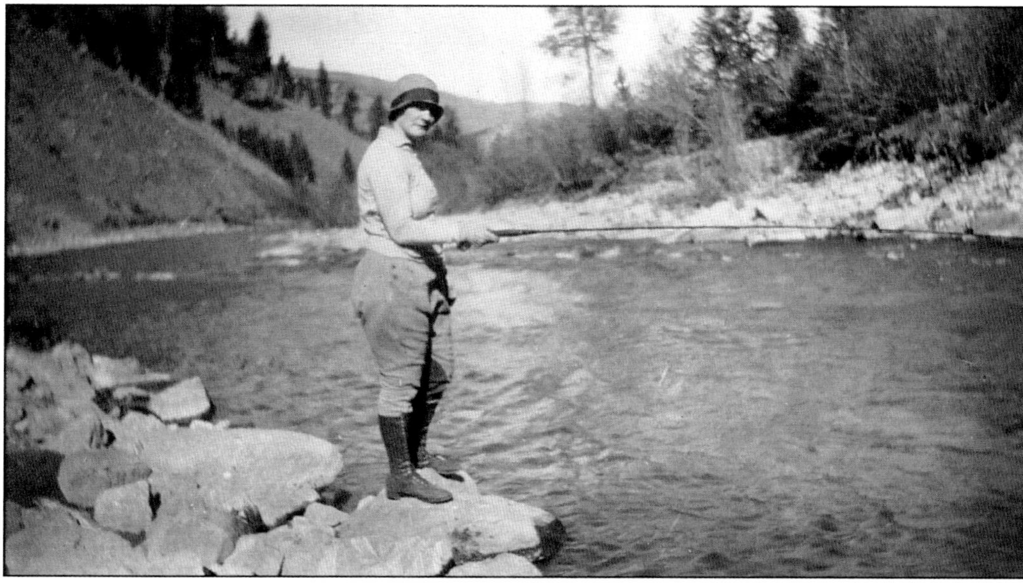

FISHING THE GALLATIN (ABOVE); FISHING ULLERY'S LAKE (BELOW). In the above photograph, an unidentified friend of the Crails is fly-fishing on the pristine Gallatin River. Below, Emmett Crail and a friend raft out on Jack Creek (now the private Ullery's) Lake in search of the big one. Fishing was very popular with locals, friends, and tourists just as it is today. Popular movies have spawned tourism and a boom industry for outfitters, flytiers, and outdoorwear. (Both, HCRC.)

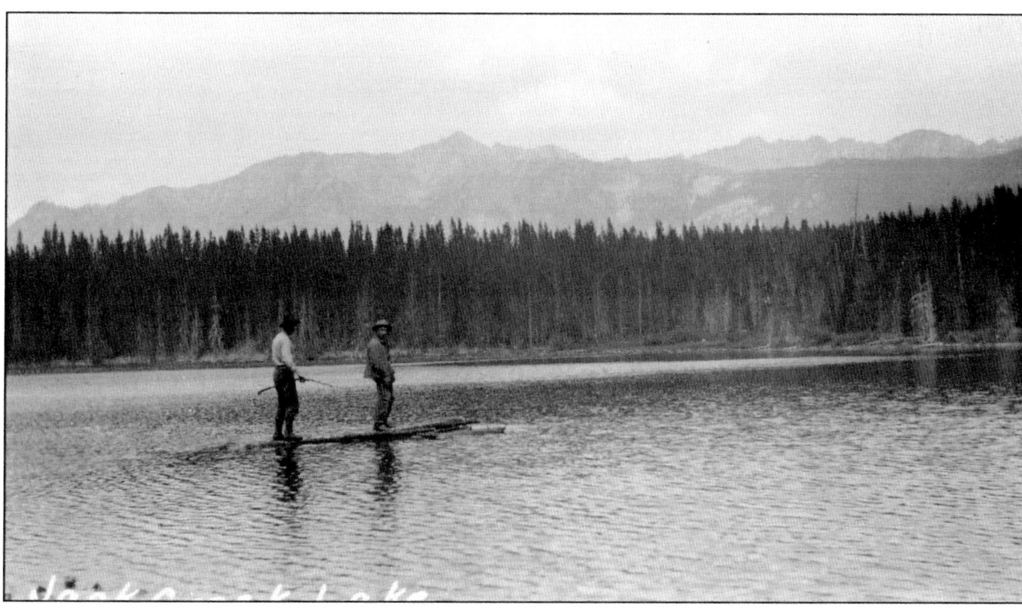

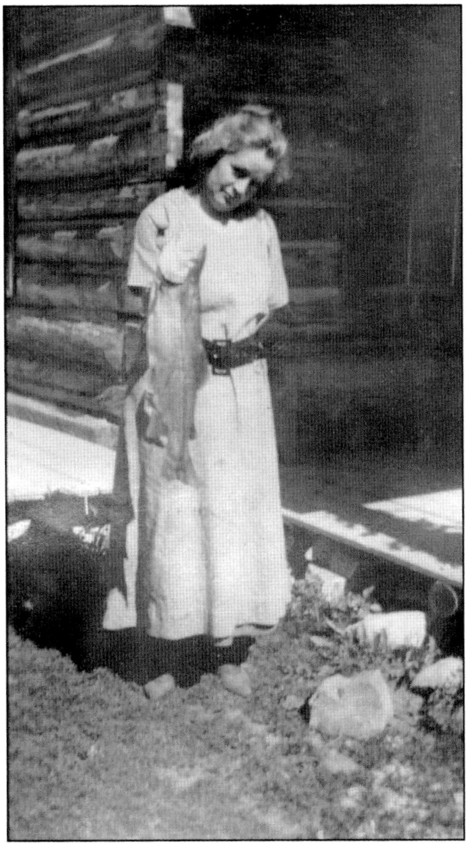

Jennie Karst (Left); Karst Guest (Below). Jennie Karst is seen with a five-and-a-half-pound rainbow trout while a happy guest brings back a mess of fish. The Gallatin River and its tributaries are home to the rare and native Westslope cutthroat trout. Introduced rainbow and brown have become quite numerous and have led to the Gallatin designation as a Blue Ribbon trout stream, much prized by fishermen. (Both, S. Anderson.)

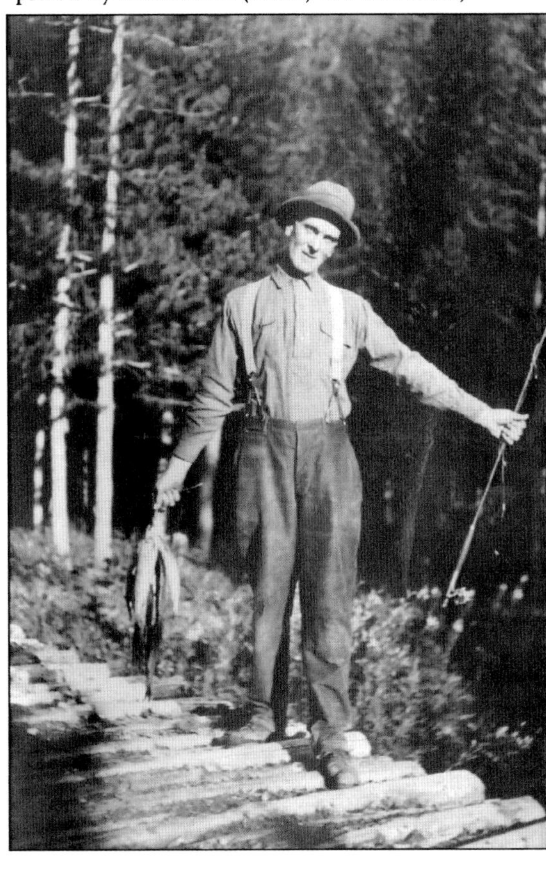

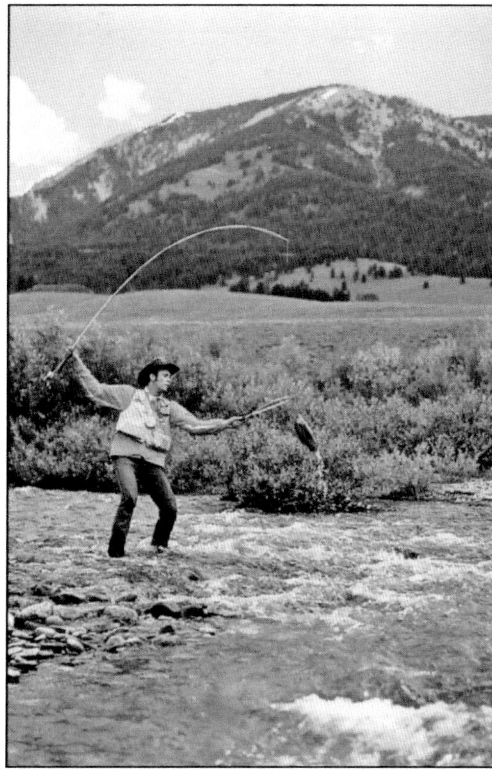

Fishing the West Fork (Right); Freddy Pessl's Trout Pond (Below). Not limited to the Gallatin, there was and continues to be excellent fishing throughout the area. High mountain lakes, small creeks and streams, or privately stocked ponds all held a wealth of sport that still lures avid and novice fishermen alike. This tourist fishing the West Fork is in the middle of what is now the golf course. He would need to duck errant drives at that spot today. Fred Pessl had a home up Beaver Creek with his own trout pond. Fishing is enjoyable however it is done. (Right, Lone Mountain Ranch; below, the Pessl family.)

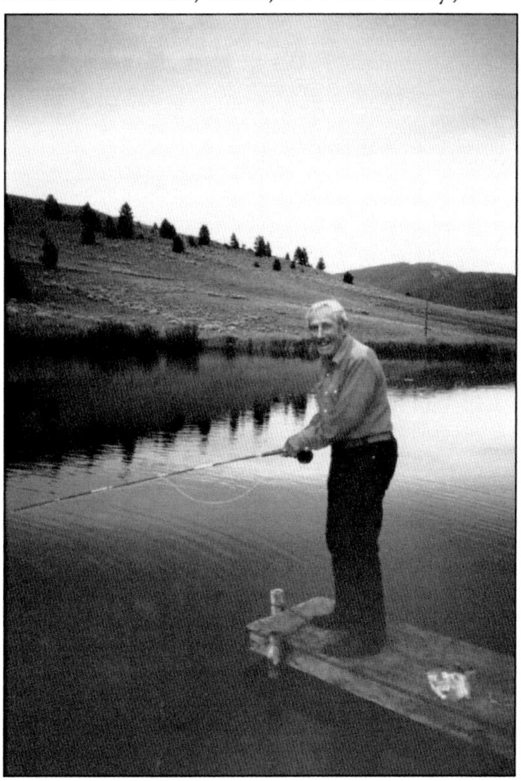

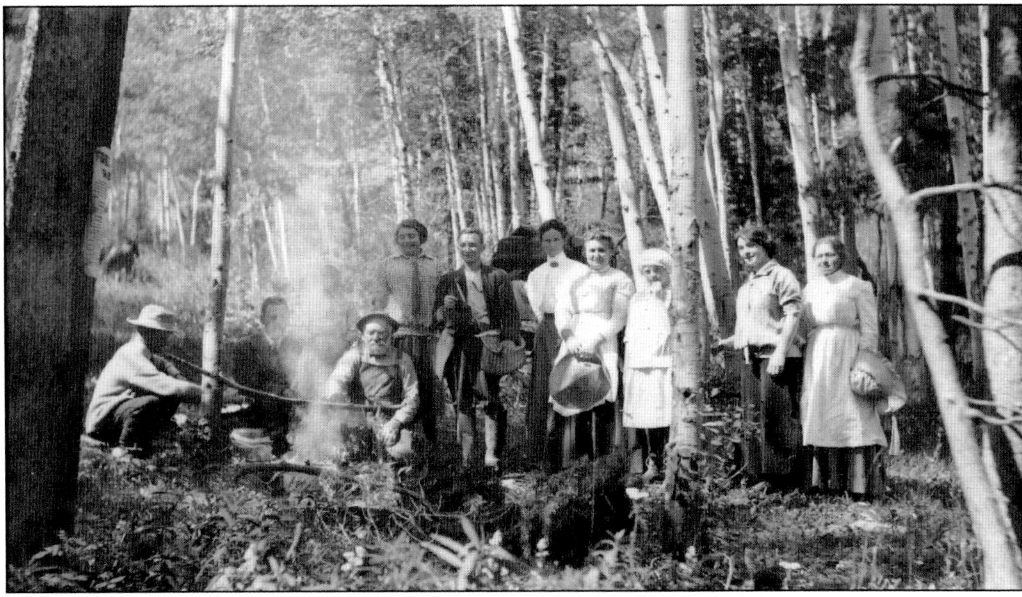

Crail Picnic (Above); Durnam Picnic (Below). Even on remote frontier ranches, people would get together for social fun. In the above photograph, taken around 1912, A.F. Crail is at the fire, Lilian and Emmett are behind him, and his wife, Sallie, is on the far right bringing six friends to a picnic in the aspens. Below, Ruby Cross (left), Isabelle and Ed Durnam (center), and their friend Leah (right) enjoy a little fishing and outdoor fun on the Gallatin in 1919. Even today, Big Sky, with its amazing beauty and natural resources, provides innumerable spots for picnics. Just don't feed the bears! (Above, HCRC; below, S. Anderson.)

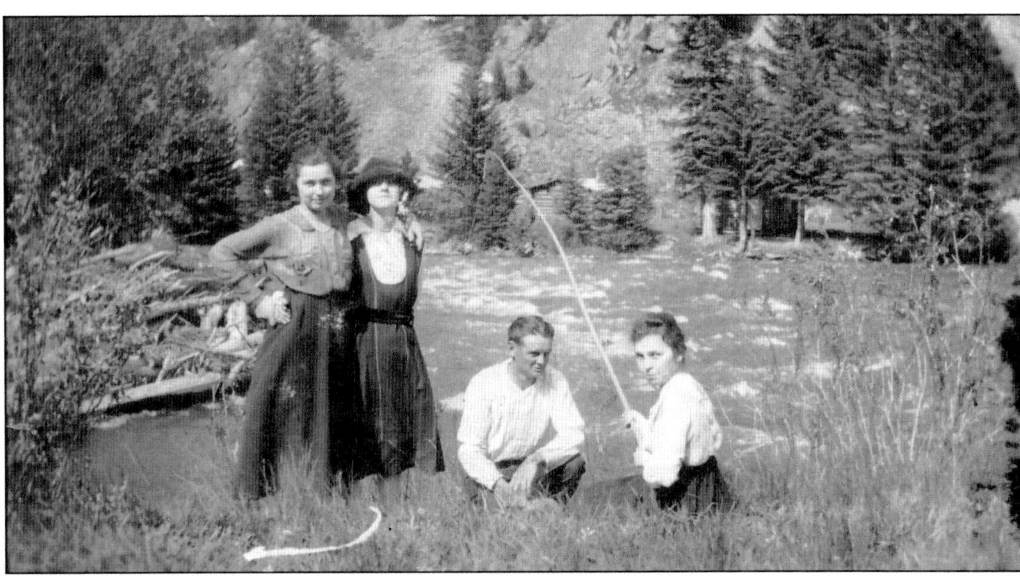

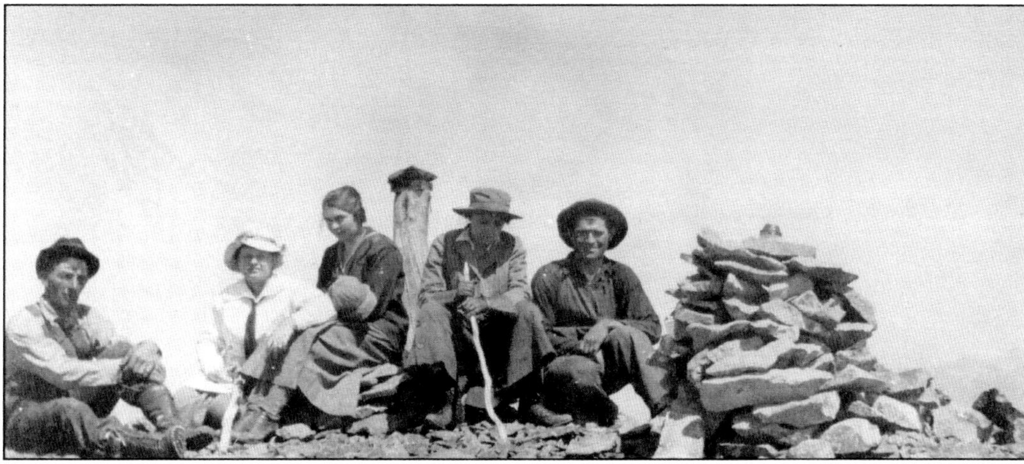

The Lone Mountain Trek (Above); Ousel Falls (Below). Lilian Crail (center) and unidentified friends have just ascended Lone Mountain. Although not a technical climb, the top of this 11,166-foot mountain is scree riddled. Only the hardy endure the trek to the top of Lone Mountain. Those who do, earn the right to add a rock to the cairn, continuing the trail-marking practice that transcends time and continents. Ousel Falls was a short three miles from the Crail Ranch on the South Fork of the West Fork. It is now a community park and popular year-round hiking trail. Whereas the Lone Mountain climb is moderate to difficult, the Ousel Falls trail is quite easy. Whether hiked in 1912 or 2012, both trails lead to spectacular yet different rewards at their end points. (Both, HCRC.)

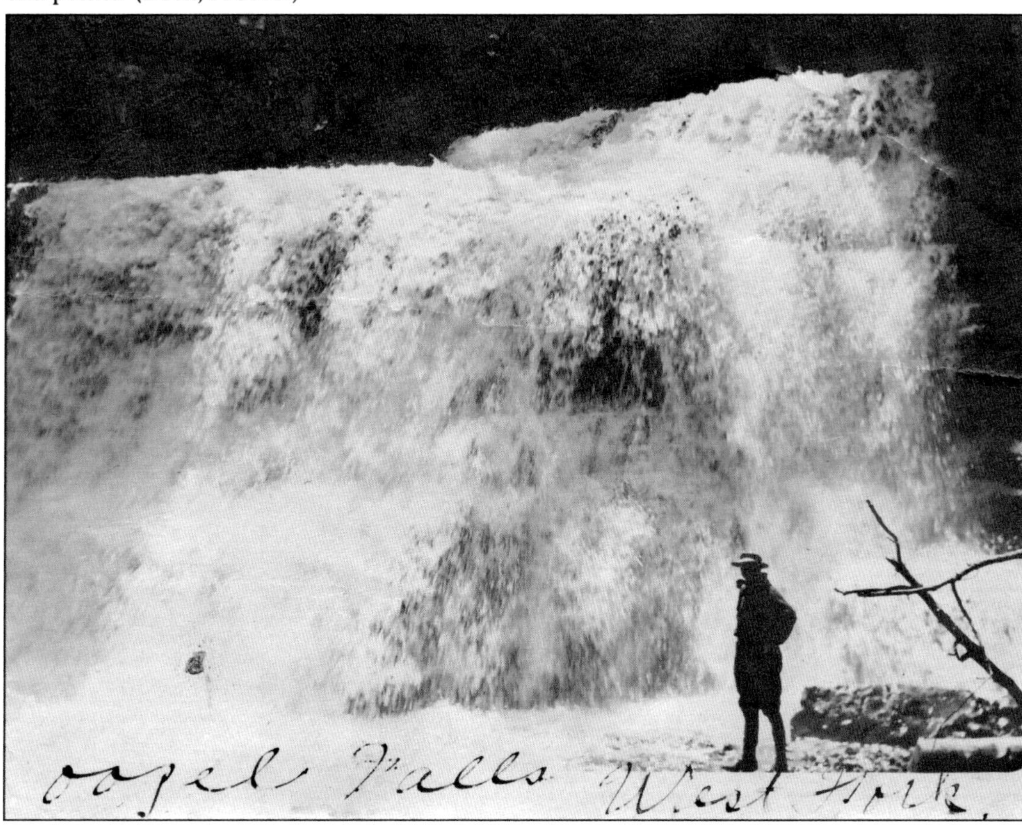

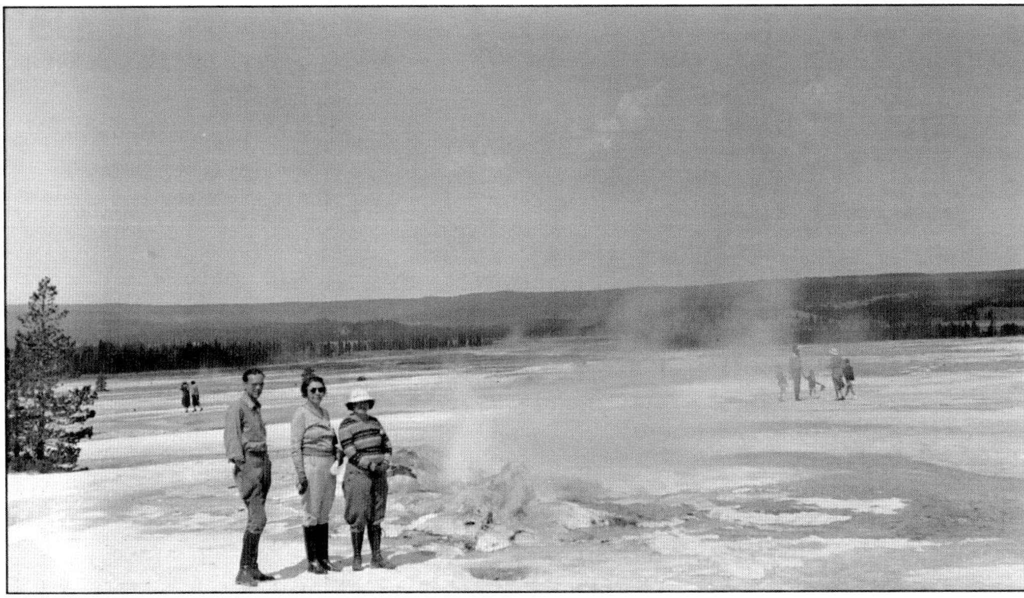

In Yellowstone (Above); at Old Faithful (Below). Yellowstone's geysers have amazed, intrigued, and confounded many for thousands of years. Yellowstone Park, America's first national park, was a popular destination to take both tourists and friends, just as it is today. Here, Lilian Crail (center) and two unidentified friends get close to a geyser in the Norris Geyser Basin. Below, the Erwins and Wilsons watch Old Faithful erupt. Note the jackets, hats, and high heels that were essential garb for tourists in the 1930s. (Above, S. Anderson; below, Bill Erwin.)

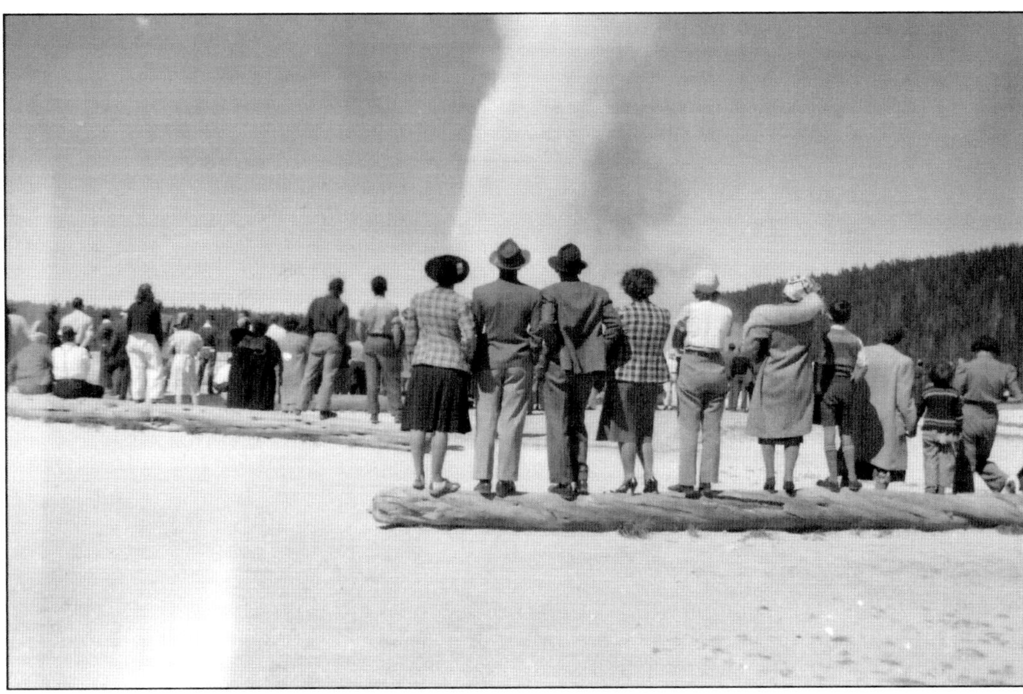

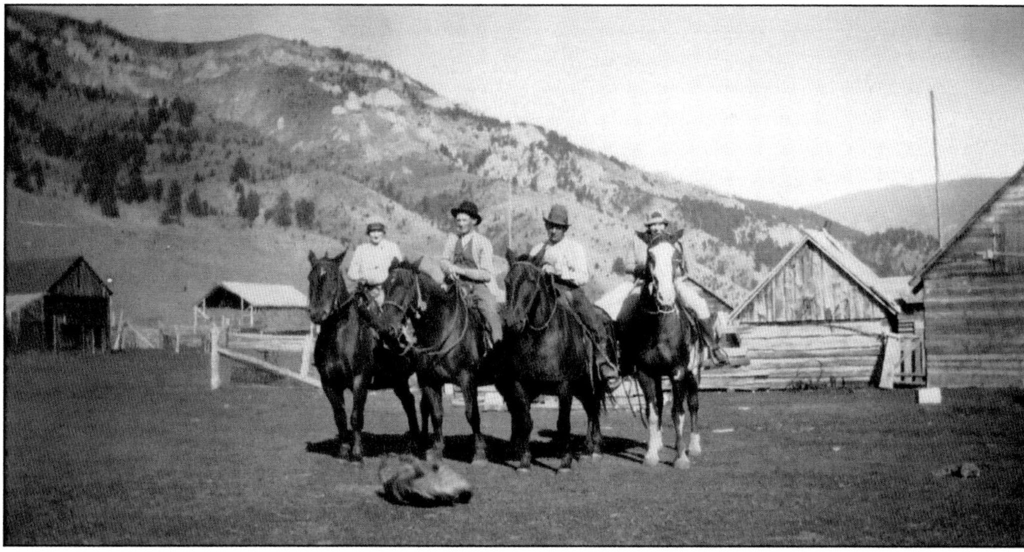

Riding at the Crail Ranch (Above); Slim Pickins and his Trick Horse (Below). Horses were a way of life on the frontier. Not only did they provide transportation, they also were a source of enjoyment. In the photograph above, Emmett and Lilian Crail (right) and two unidentified friends head out from the ranch for a pleasure ride. Many horses, trained for tricks, came to the local rodeos or to entertain at the dude ranches. Wild West shows that traveled throughout the country, such as Buffalo Bill Cody's in the early 1900s, brought visitors to this area who expected to see not only the real Wild West, but also the Wild West as it had been portrayed in the circuses. (Above, HCRC; below, PM.)

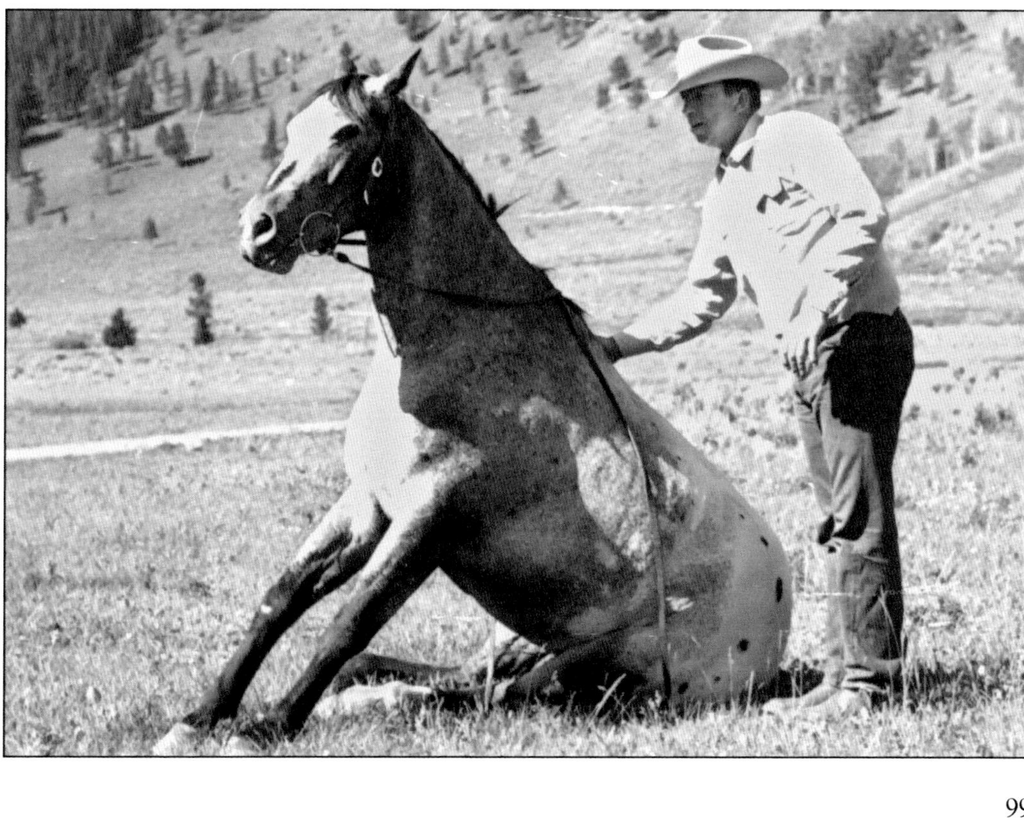

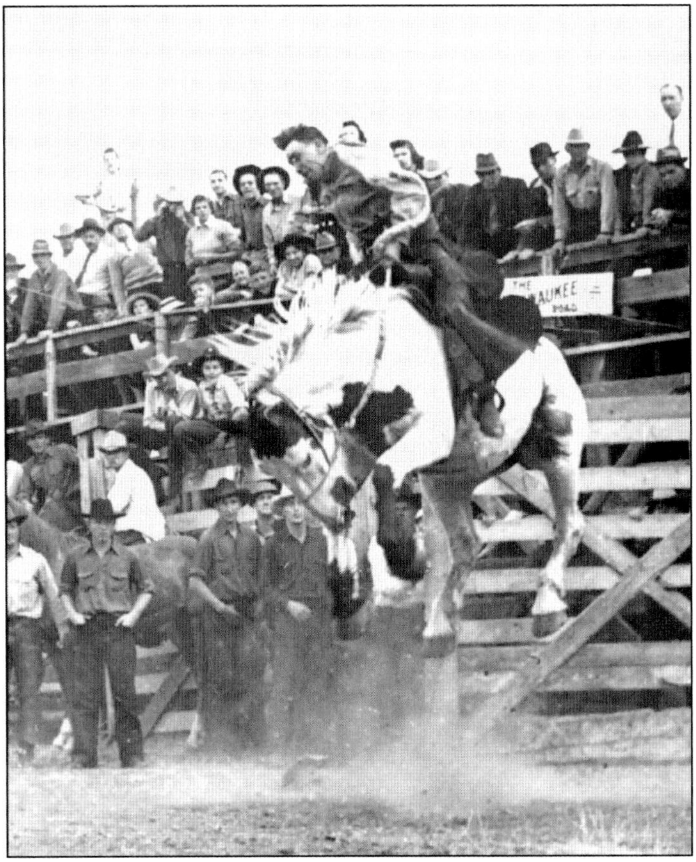

Bucking Horse Ride (Left); Bull Riding (Below). Rodeo competition showcased the skills and prowess that a cowboy needed to cope with daily life. Calf roping, team roping, bulldogging, and bronc riding were part of work. Bull riding was for macho. These photographs are from local rodeos in the mid-1950s, but the Fourth of July Rodeo at the 320 Ranch continued until 2007. It has recently been replaced by professional events. (Left, PM; below, Beth Naert.)

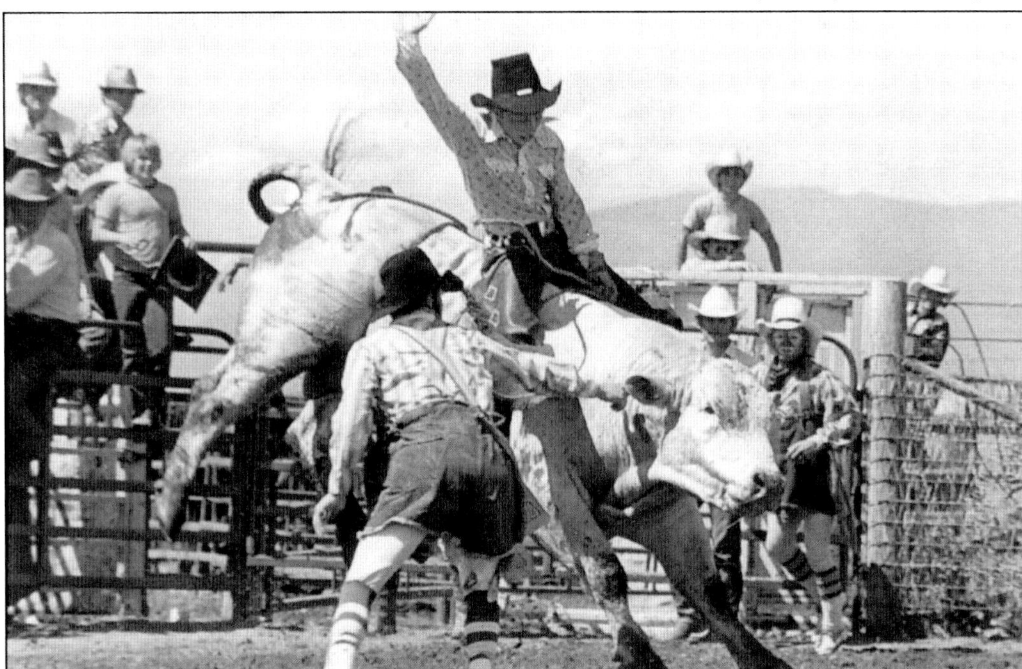

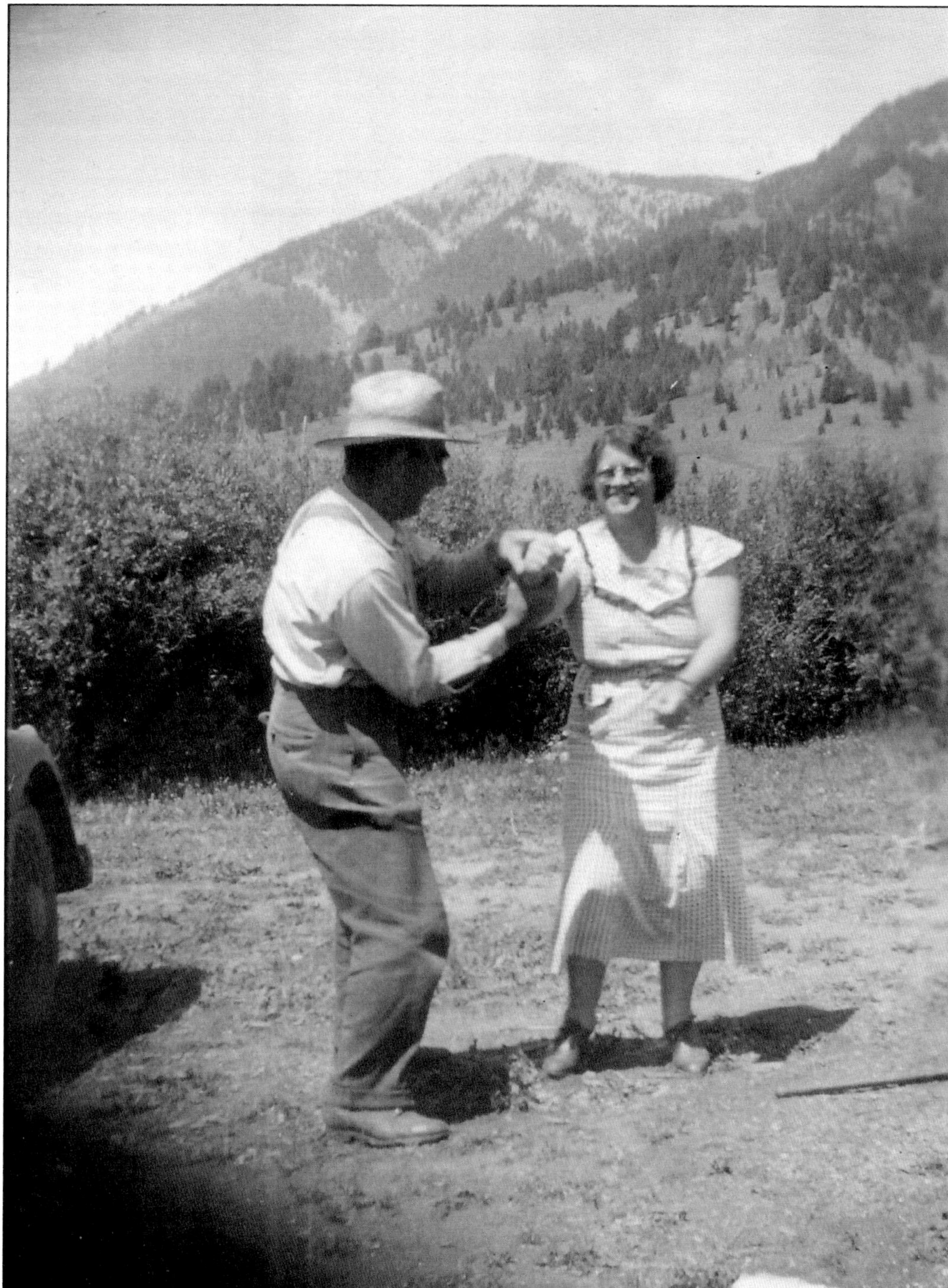

Emmett and His Sweetheart Annie. Dancing is a universal pastime across ages and cultures. Here, Emmett Crail and his intended, Annie Breneman, enjoy time out from their hard ranch work for a little swing in the yard of the ranch. The joy of the moment is captured on their faces. (HCRC.)

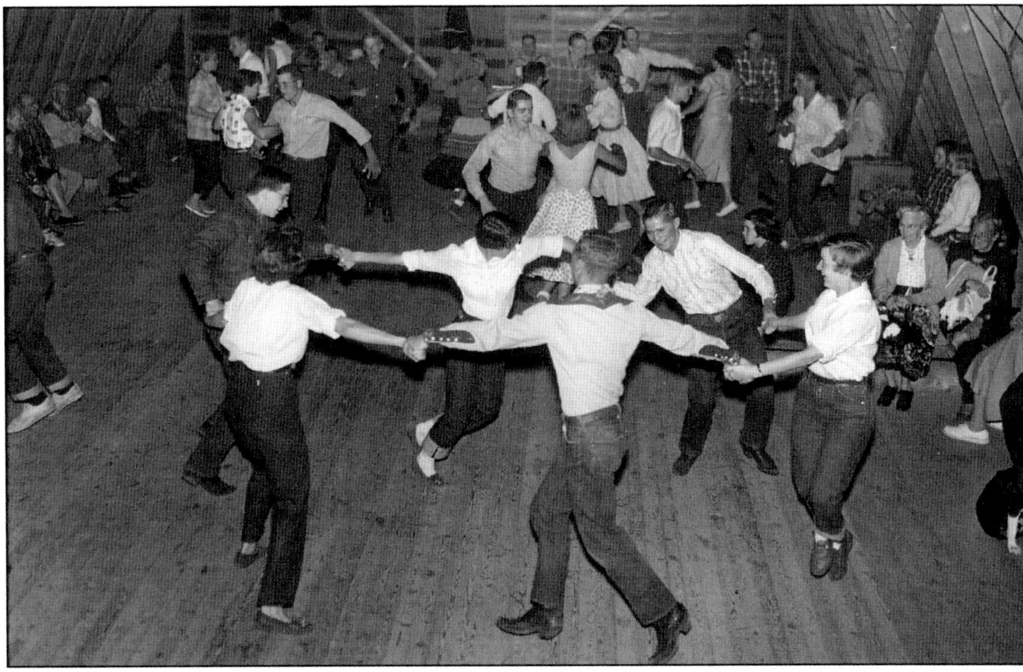

THE BARN DANCE (ABOVE); SLOW DANCING (BELOW). Fast-forward a quarter of a century to the "barn dance" to grab a partner and do-si-do. At this 1952 barn dance at the 320 Ranch, guests and locals mix in the fun. Traditional square-dancing was real Americana, but slow, modern dancing was a better way to end an evening with one's sweetheart. (Both, PM.)

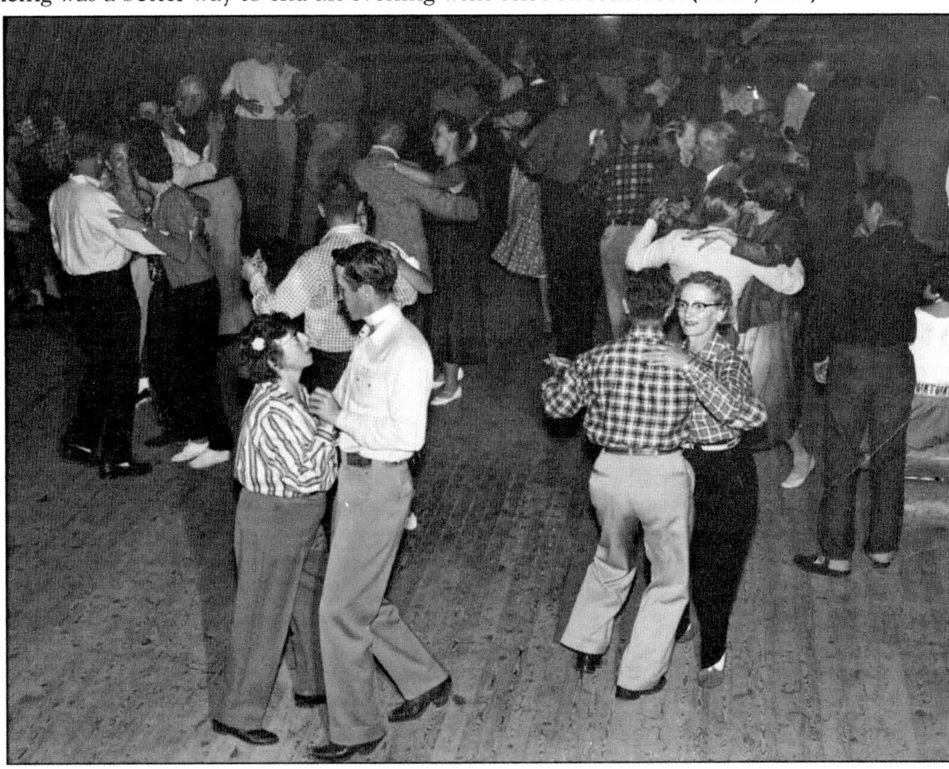

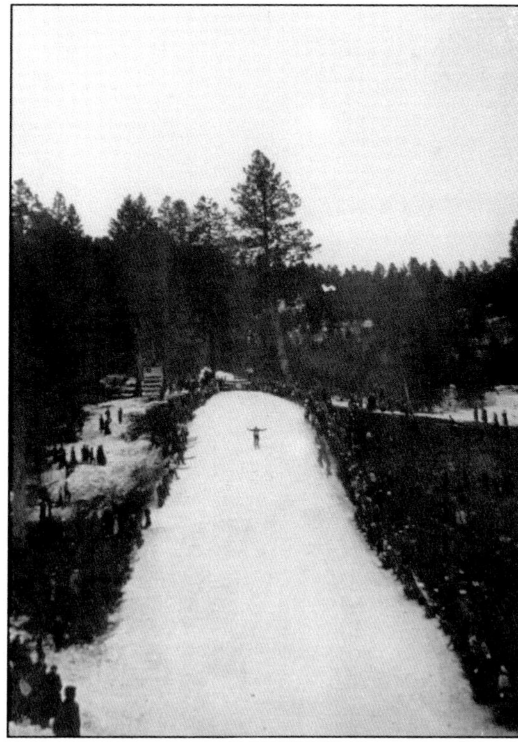

Karst Hill (Right); Ski Jumping (Below). Pete Karst, ever one to find an attraction, built a ski jump on the west side of the river, across from his Kamp. In 1938, the Montana State Ski Jumping Championship was held here. In spite of bitter cold weather, thousands of spectators showed up to watch the competition. (Right, Bill Erwin; below, S. Anderson.)

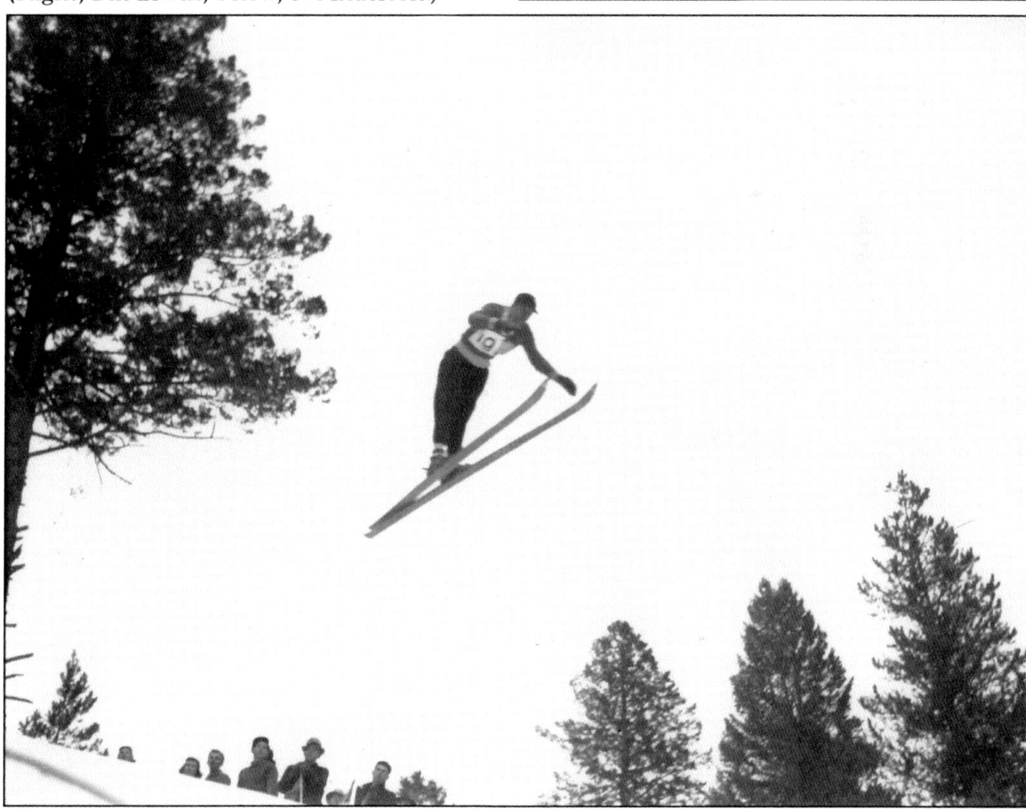

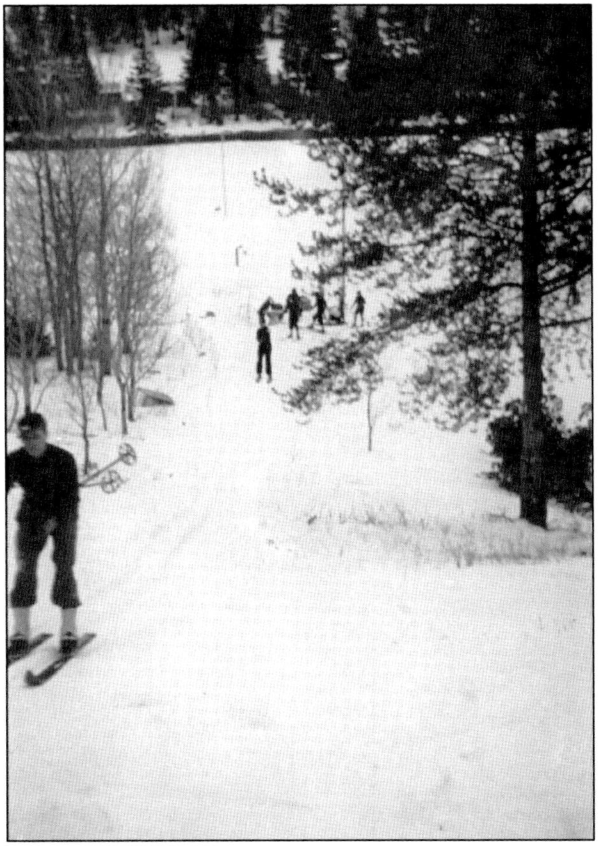

Karst Ski Tow (Left); Ski Styles, 1950 (Below). From a cable he found in an abandoned mine, Pete Karst built this ski tow on a hill near the ski jump. It operated for many years for the entertainment of locals and visitors. There was a long history of skiing in the canyon, and it is obvious that skiing did not just come to Big Sky with the resort in 1972. Just as today at the ski resorts, fashion and fun were on display at Karst's hill by Punk Holm, Emma Lou Erwin, Hazel Wilson, and Helen Pratt. (Both, Bill Erwin.)

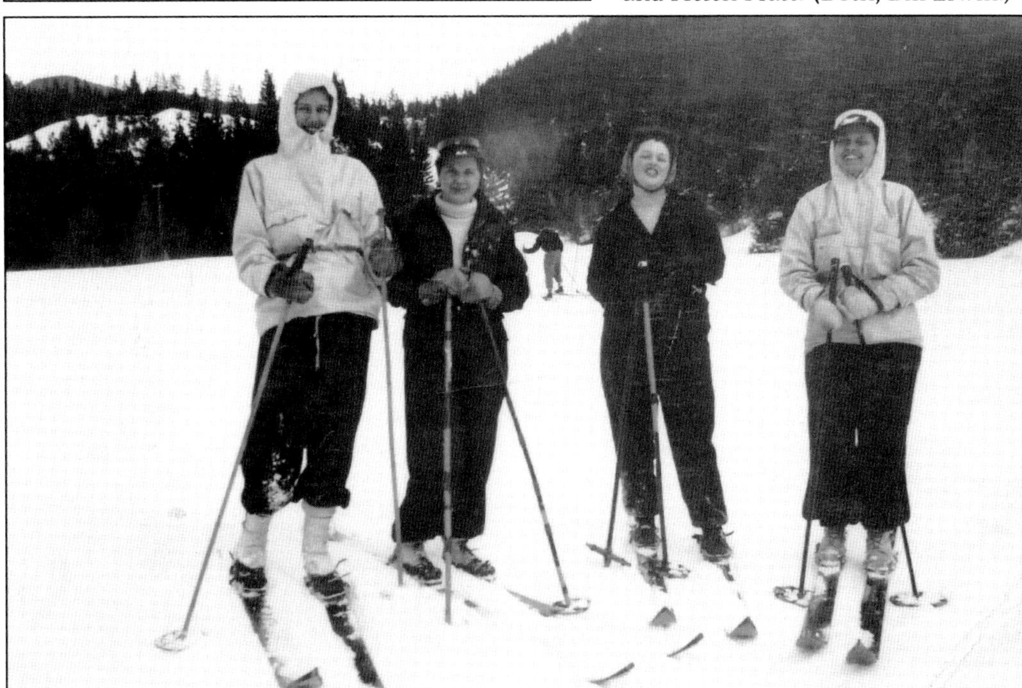

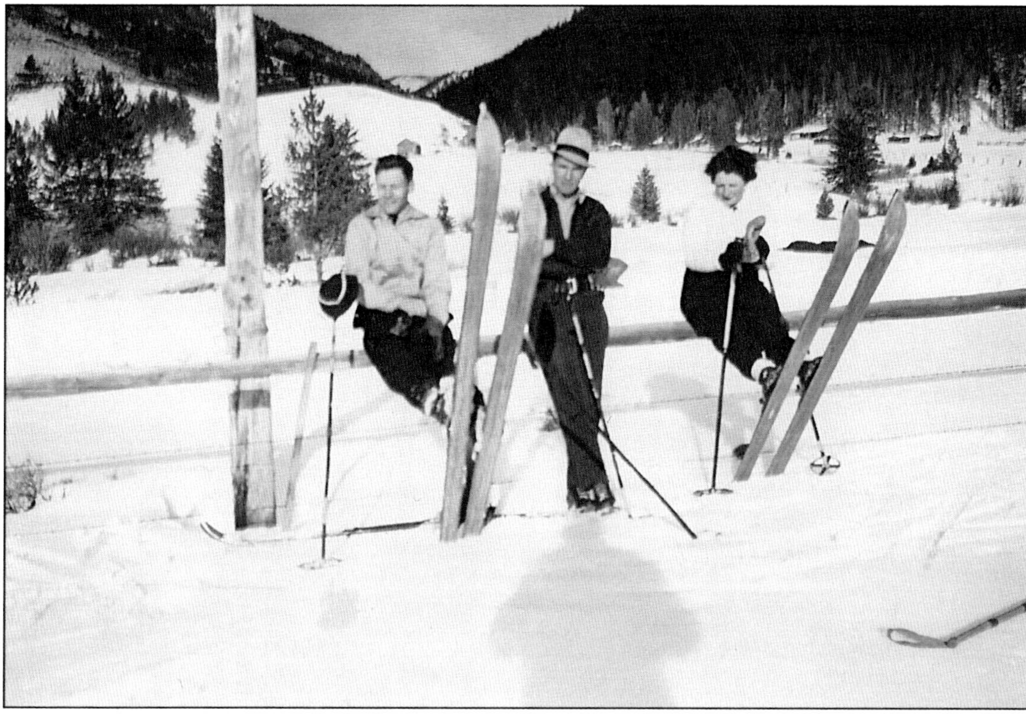

Skiers on the Fence. Howard Erwin rests on the fence with Clint and Hazel Wilson. Sam Wilson, who died in 1929, started the 320 Ranch, seen in the background. His descendants still live in the Big Sky area. It would appear that a fedora and vest were the fashion with the wooden skis. (Bill Erwin.)

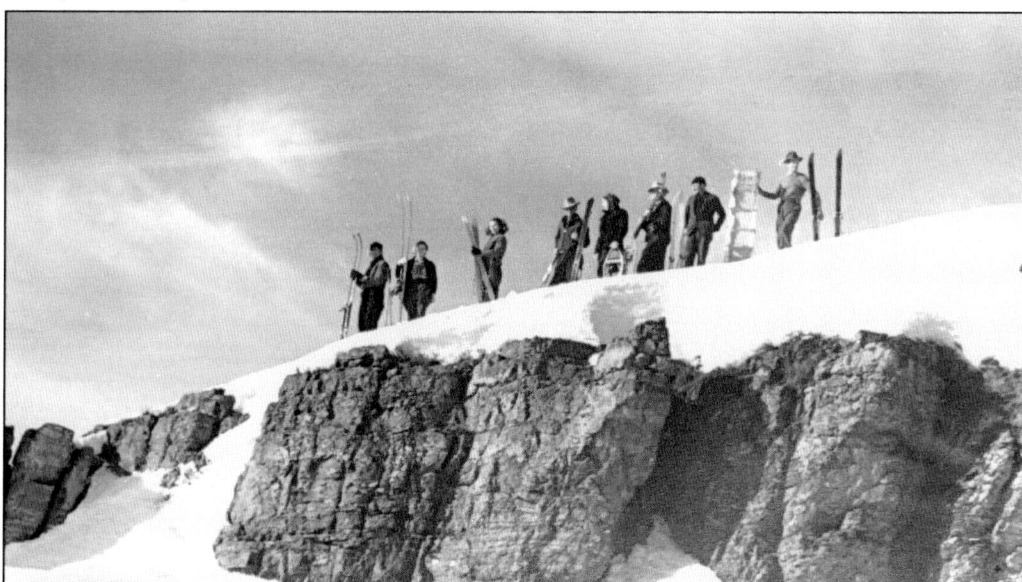

Trekking on Skis. The 320 Ranch has catered to winter visitors and outdoor enthusiasts since the mid-20th century. The trails in the Gallatin and Madison Mountains flanking the Gallatin River valley as well as nearby Yellowstone Park provide an excellent backcountry skiing experience. This photograph shows a trek up Buffalo Horn trail above the 320 Ranch. (PM.)

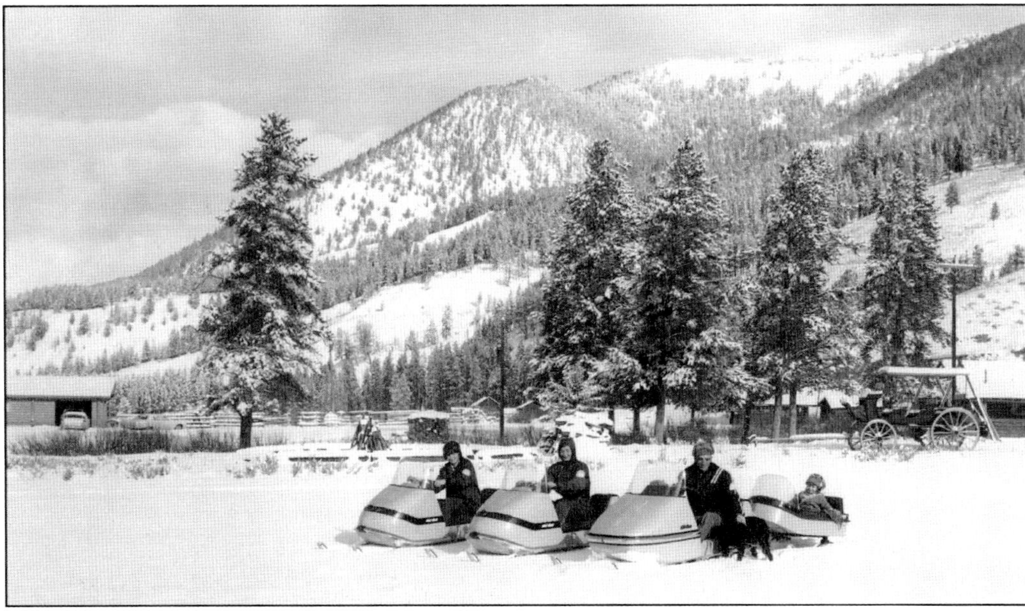

The Goodrich Family on Snowmobiles (Above); the Inaugural Tour of Big Sky (Below). Neighboring West Yellowstone calls itself "The Snowmobile Capital of the World." It is no wonder that snowmobiles have proved popular in the Gallatin Canyon as well. The Goodrich family—Gail, Patty, Jim, and Carrie—owned the 320 Ranch during the 1960s and promoted the sport. In the photograph below, Edna Jacobson, Boots Terrell, Sam Jacobson, and Lee Terrell start the inaugural Tour of Big Sky. This long snowmobile trail south of Big Sky is maintained by the State of Montana through gasoline and resort tax funds. (Above, PM; below, PM and Bill Browning of the Montana Chamber of Commerce, Helena.)

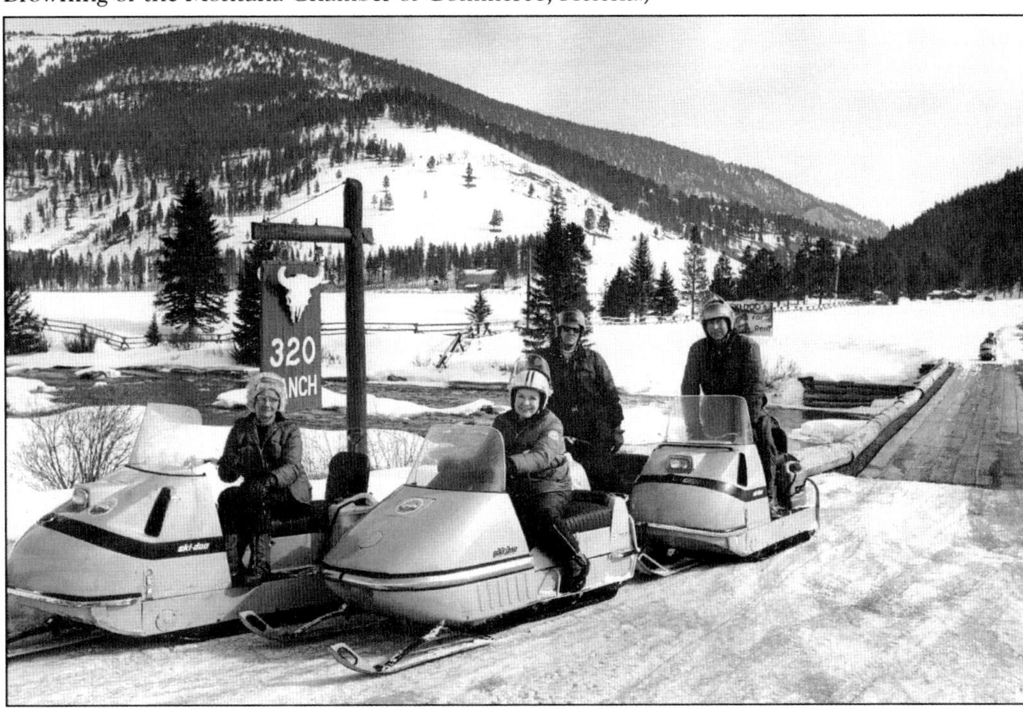

Nine

"Happy Trails"
The People

The high limestone cliffs of the Gallatin Valley, Lone Mountain looming over the West Fork Basin, the Spanish Peaks Wilderness to the north, and the Madison and Gallatin Mountain Ranges to the south give this area an alpine quality much loved by photographers and tourists. Beautiful as it has been—it could be Switzerland or Colorado—it was the people living here that gave it character.

The first residents were primarily transplants from the Midwest, but some were from European countries. All arrived determined to improve their lives. Most respected the landscape and its resources; a few were opportunists.

The records show a healthy and active social life among the community residents; some even married. Sara Durnam Anderson's parents met and married here, as did Ora Michener and Stanley Lemon and William Lytle and Pearl Lockhart . . . and the next generation was born.

The private social lives of common people are rarely documented. Some are shown in chapter eight, and there are oral histories and interviews such as Sara Durnam Anderson's fond memories of Buck and Helen Knight spending every Sunday with her parents and Pete and Nellie Karst.

With the school as the focus of the community, residents were part of the fabric that was 20th-century America. They lived and died, prospered or failed, and made the basin their home.

The lack of documentation or photographic record resulted in the omission of some interesting individuals. In some cases the search for living relatives proved fruitless. But there is no doubt that this was a community of relatives and relationships. It was a community of real pioneers, real Montanans, real people.

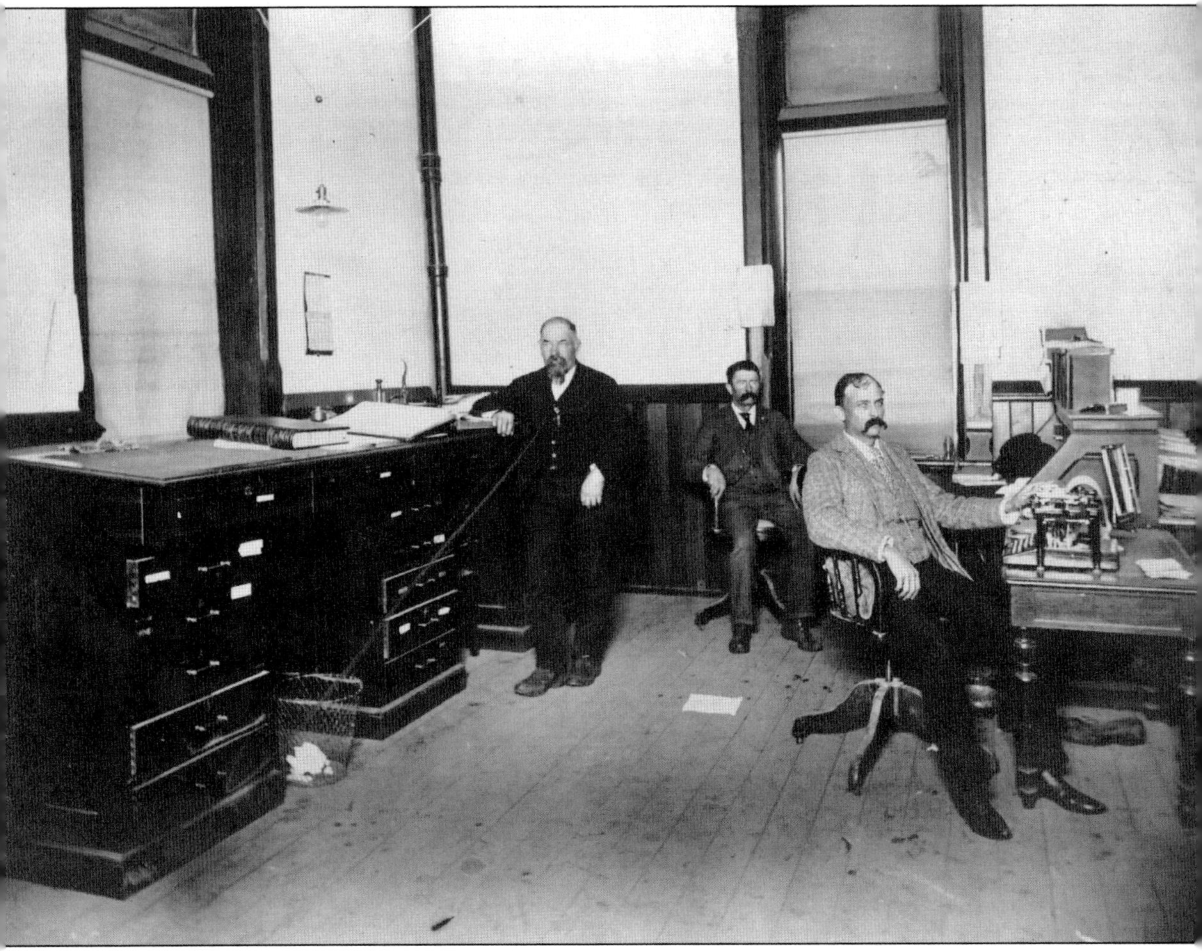

AUGUSTUS FRANKLIN CRAIL. A.F. "Frank" Crail, seen here near the file cabinets, was elected to the clerkship of the Ninth Judicial District in Gallatin County between 1896 and 1900. He ran on the Democratic ticket against a Republican endorsed by the short-lived Populist Party. After his four years in the position, Crail's adventurous spirit drove him through the Gallatin Canyon into the meadowlands where he and others established a small ranching community, a toehold settlement in an otherwise wild yet wonderful environment. Crail was a civic-minded individual who kept current by reading printed materials such as the *Husbandman,* which was filled with news of the day for ranchers. He displayed a keen interest in economics and politics, attending political conventions and once stating that he wished Montana would remain a territory rather than become a state. (HCRC.)

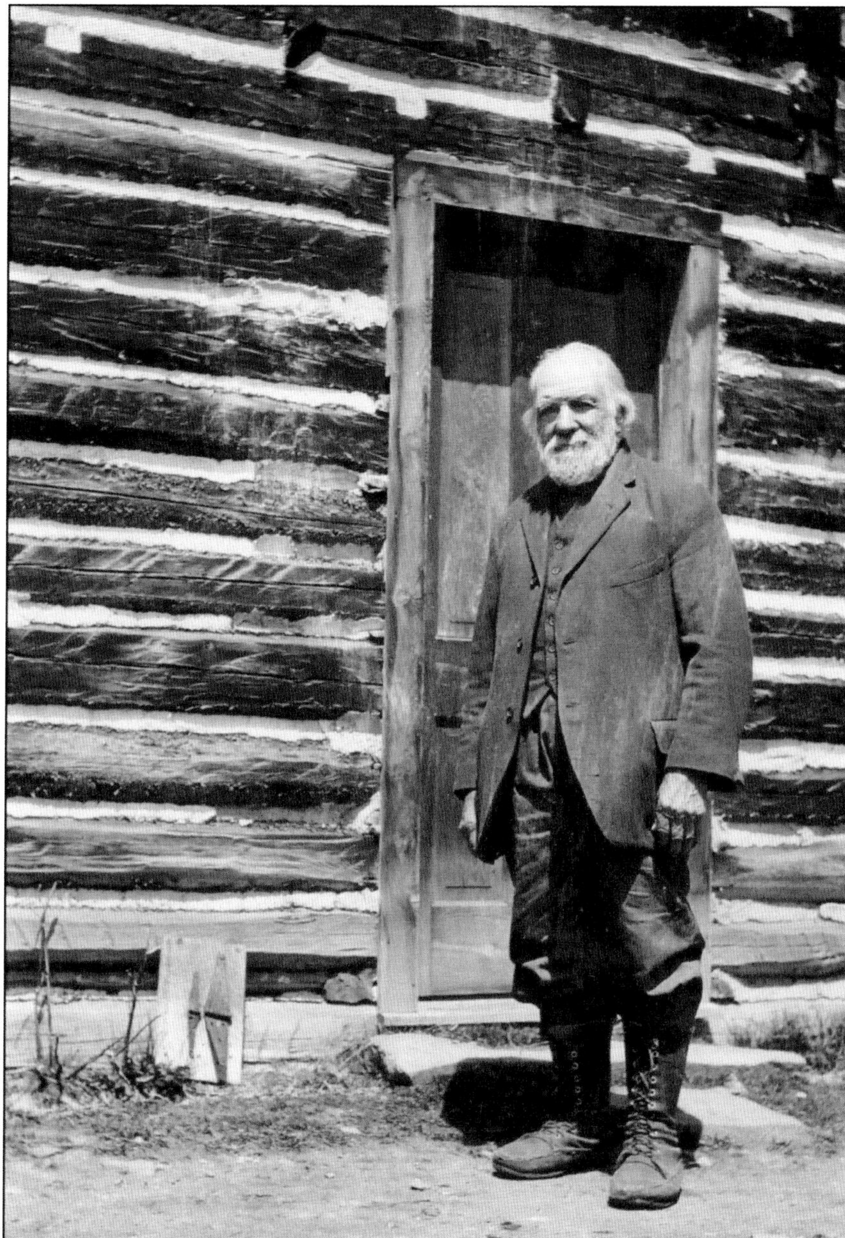

Crail in the 1920s. Frank Crail was born in Indiana in 1842, and at 23, he traveled to the Missouri frontier and joined a wagon train bound for Miles City in the Montana Territory. By 1868, Crail was working at a quartz mining camp about 30 miles from Helena. In 1871, he and two partners claimed a section of land in the Springhill area on the western slope of the Bridger Mountains. Crail hauled much of his produce himself to markets outside of the Gallatin Valley. Before the Northern Pacific arrived in Bozeman in 1883, Crail had decided that he could no longer hold on as a rancher. In the spring of 1875, he leased his land and began freighting between Fort Benton and Miles City, which he did for three years. At age 44, he married Missourian Sallie Creek, who was 22 years old at the time. Over the next 10 years, they had three children. Crail died in 1924. (HCRC.)

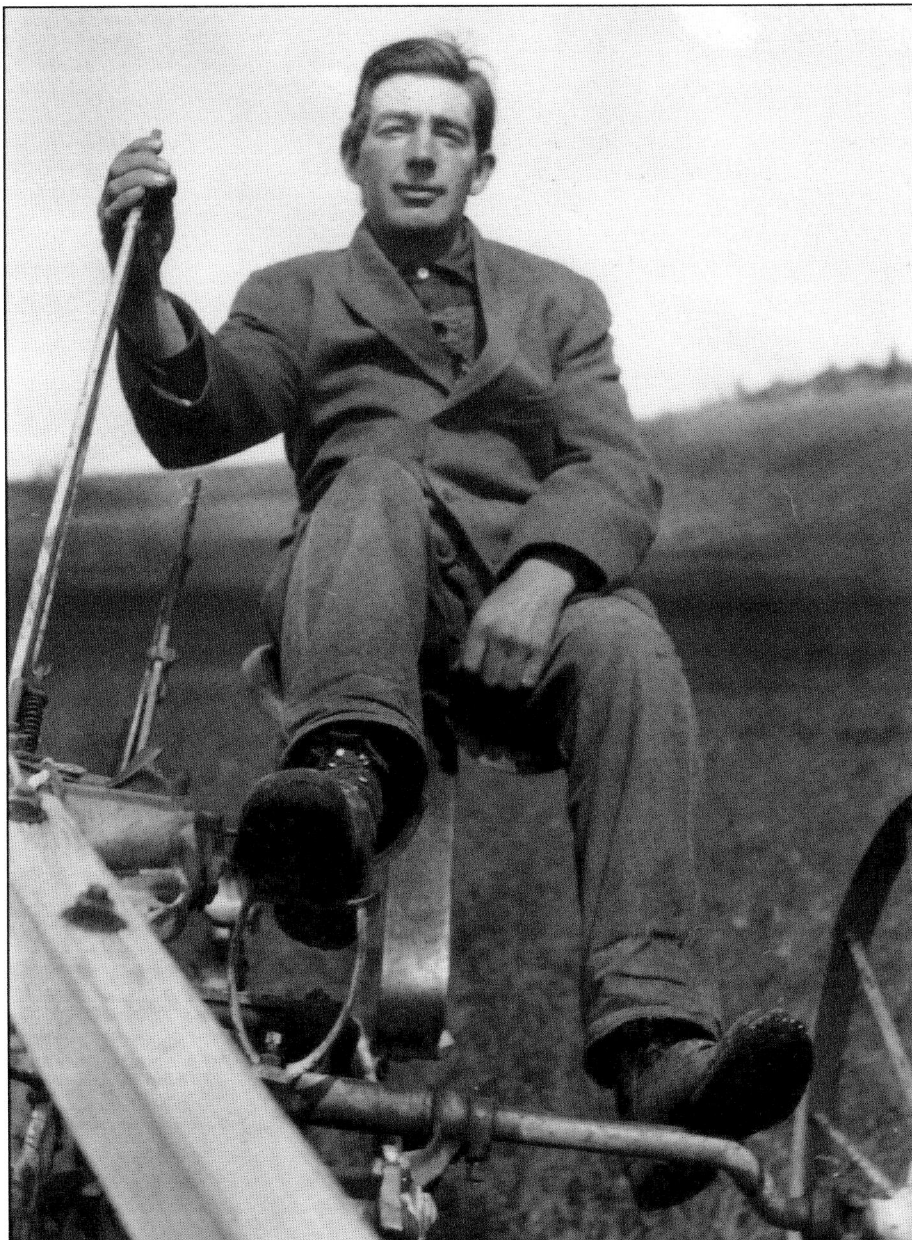

EMMETT CRAIL. When Emmett's brother Eugene joined the World War II production effort on the West Coast, he left the ranch for good. Although his sister Lilian returned often for visits, she never again lived on the ranch. It was Emmett who stayed and worked the ranch for a half century. True to Crail blood, Emmett was civic-minded. Although childless, he began serving on the Ophir School Board in 1923. In 1925, he was elected chair. Board minutes tell a tale of Emmett the peacemaker when families squabbled about the location of the school, which generally depended on the location of children. Under Emmett's chairmanship, the district averted dissolution by passing a bond and building a permanent schoolhouse. Emmett lavished attention on Annie Breneman's niece and nephew, who were often on the ranch. They appear in many pictures with Emmett, working, hiking, and riding. (HCRC.)

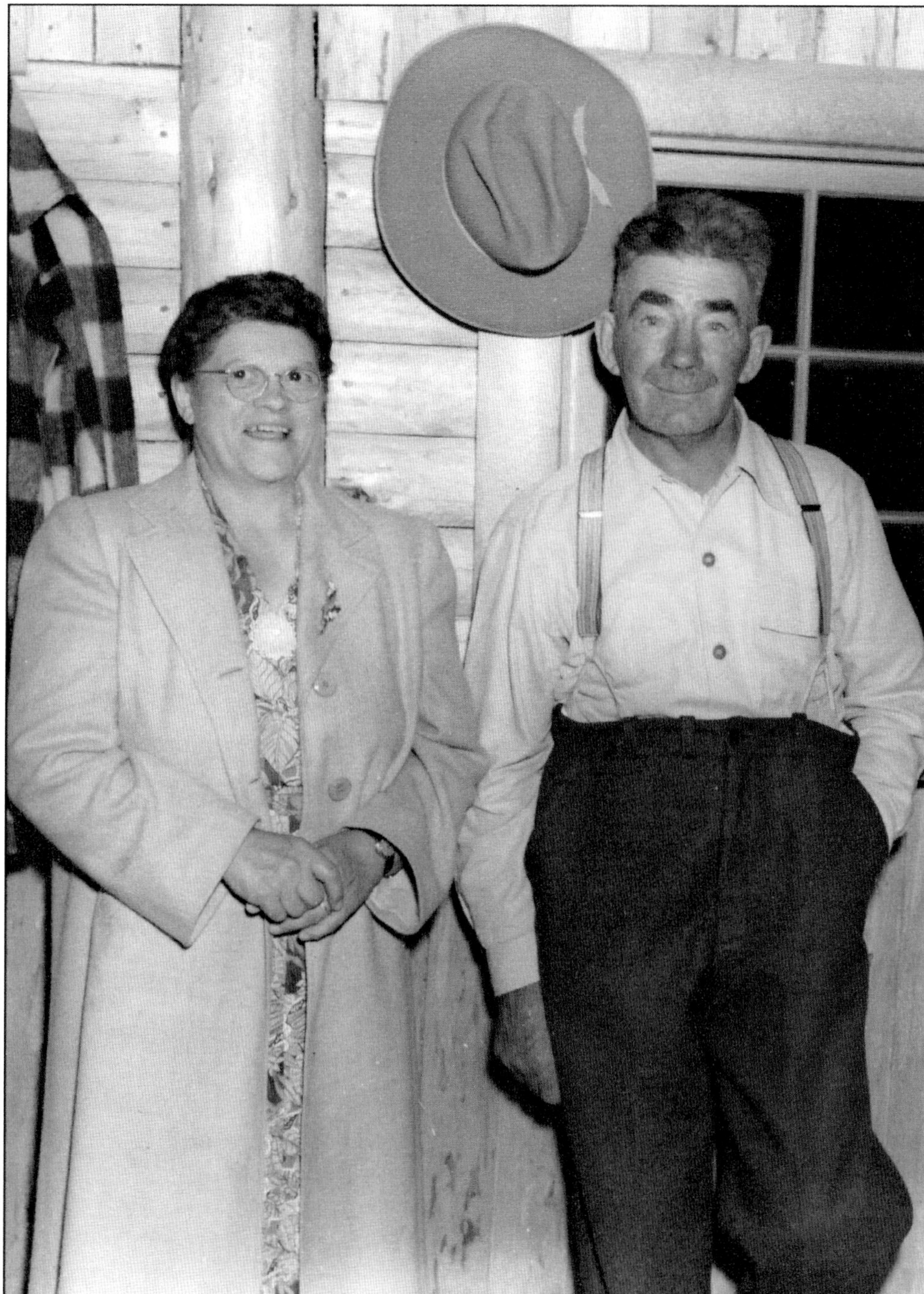

EMMETT AND ANNIE'S WEDDING 1949. After a decades-long relationship, Emmett and Annie Breneman finally married. The February 17, 1970, special edition of the *Gallatin County Tribune* published a story straight out of local lore. Reportedly, Emmett, the laconic and droll cowboy, entered a barbershop on his wedding day and told the barber to fix him up nice as he was going to a wedding. "Oh," said the barber, "Who's getting married?" "Annie Breneman," was Emmett's answer. "The nice schoolteacher from Butte? Who's she marrying?" "Me." (HCRC.)

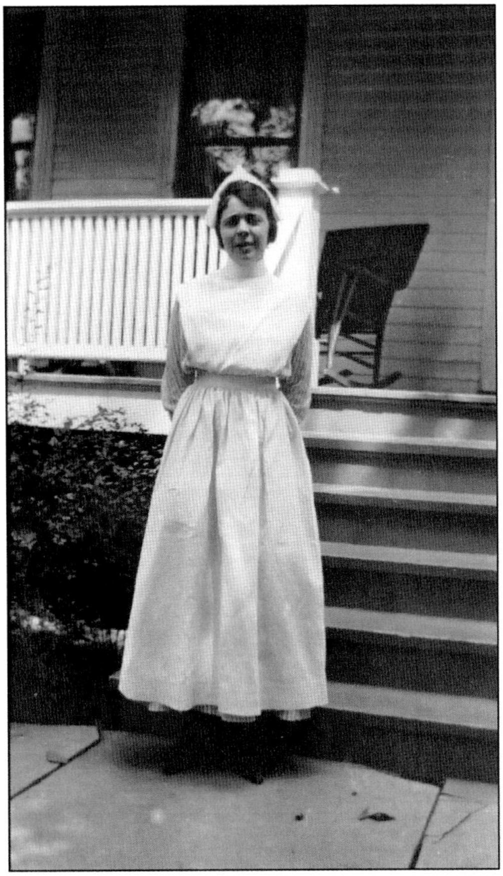

Lilian Crail (Left); Lilian and Kitten (Below). Lilian Crail was born in 1896, just a few years before her parents moved the family to the West Fork Basin. Lilian grew up on the ranch. Like her mother, she loved animals, particularly horses and dogs. She was comfortable in the kitchen and the barn. She was a great shot and an equestrian. Lilian did not inherit any part of the land as she had received money from her father to study nursing at the Illinois Training School for nurses, from which she graduated in 1921. After serving an appointment as floor director at Cooke County General Hospital in Chicago, Lilian moved to Long Beach, California. There, she met Hal DeWaide, and in 1957, at age 61, they married. During their retirement, Lilian and Hal moved to Salem, Oregon, where Lilian died in 1981. (Both, HCRC.)

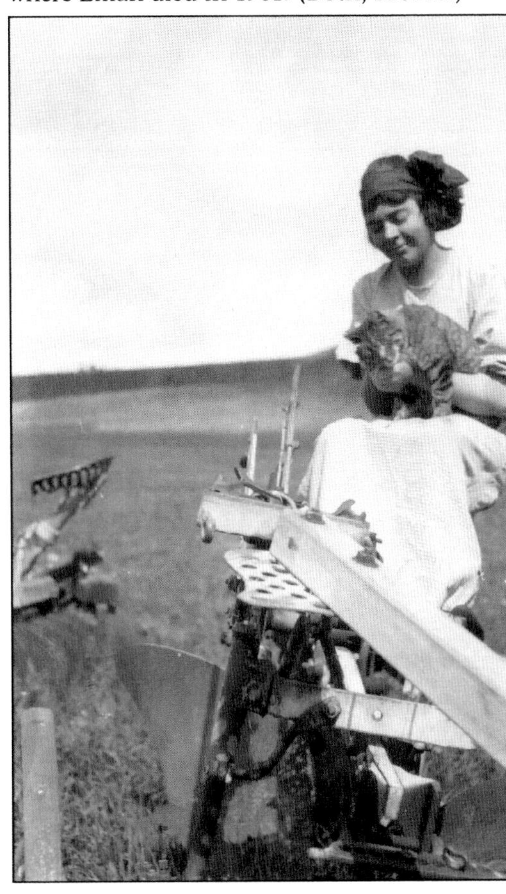

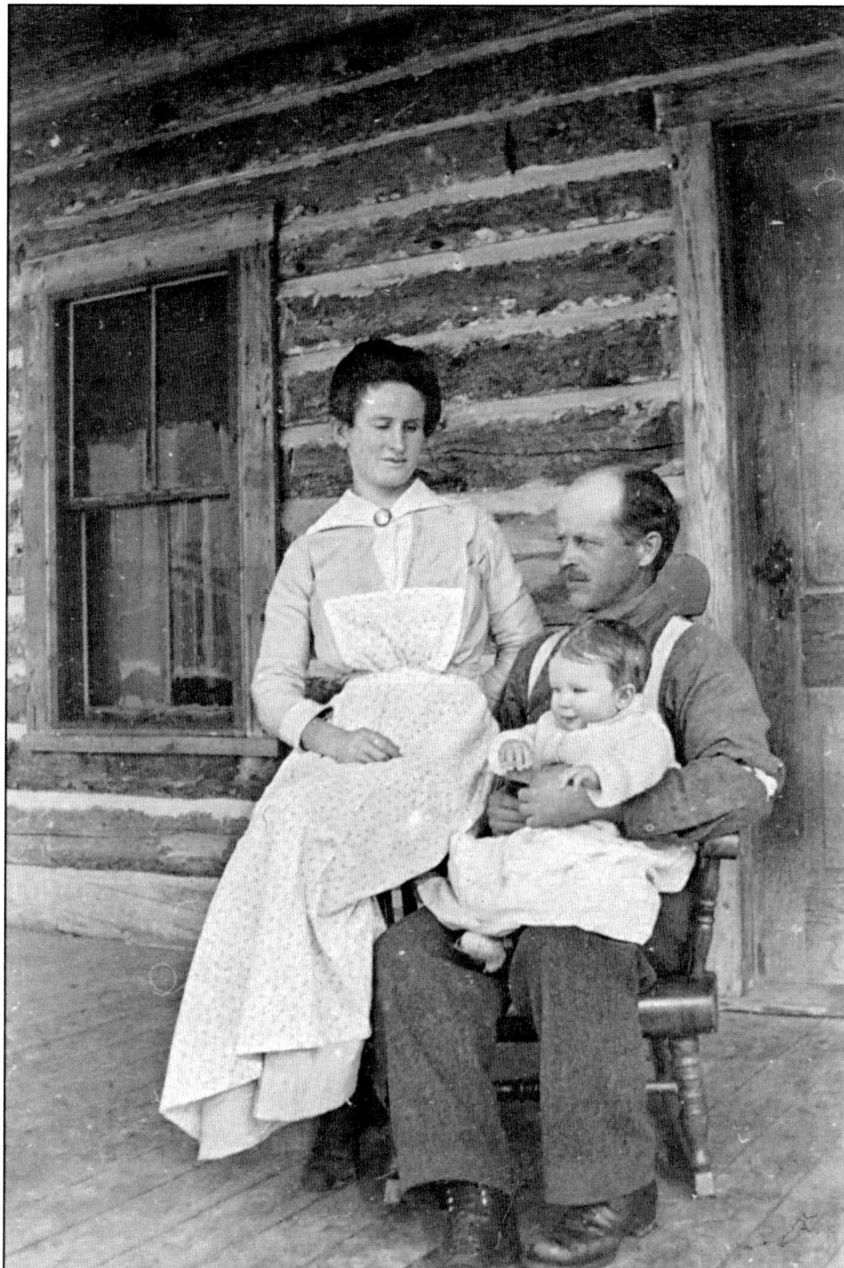

William, Pearl, and Willabelle Lytle. Billy Lytle arrived in the canyon as a prospector and farmer in 1897. He and Pearl Lockhart, sister of Mary Lockhart Michener, married and proved up their homestead south of Porcupine Creek in 1905. Their daughter Willabelle was born in 1915. Billy was reportedly a great skier. The Lytle family was strong on education, and after they married, Pearl donated her cabin to serve as a school. William was the Ophir School Board's clerk for 13 years and later a trustee. Pearl was board chair in 1920. Sadly, Pearl died in her 40s in 1926. Billy was remarried in 1935 to Winifred Kirk. Daughter Willabelle eventually relocated in the Gallatin Gateway and Bozeman area. She married Ken Tonn and had several children. She died in 1998 in Coos Bay, Oregon. (PM.)

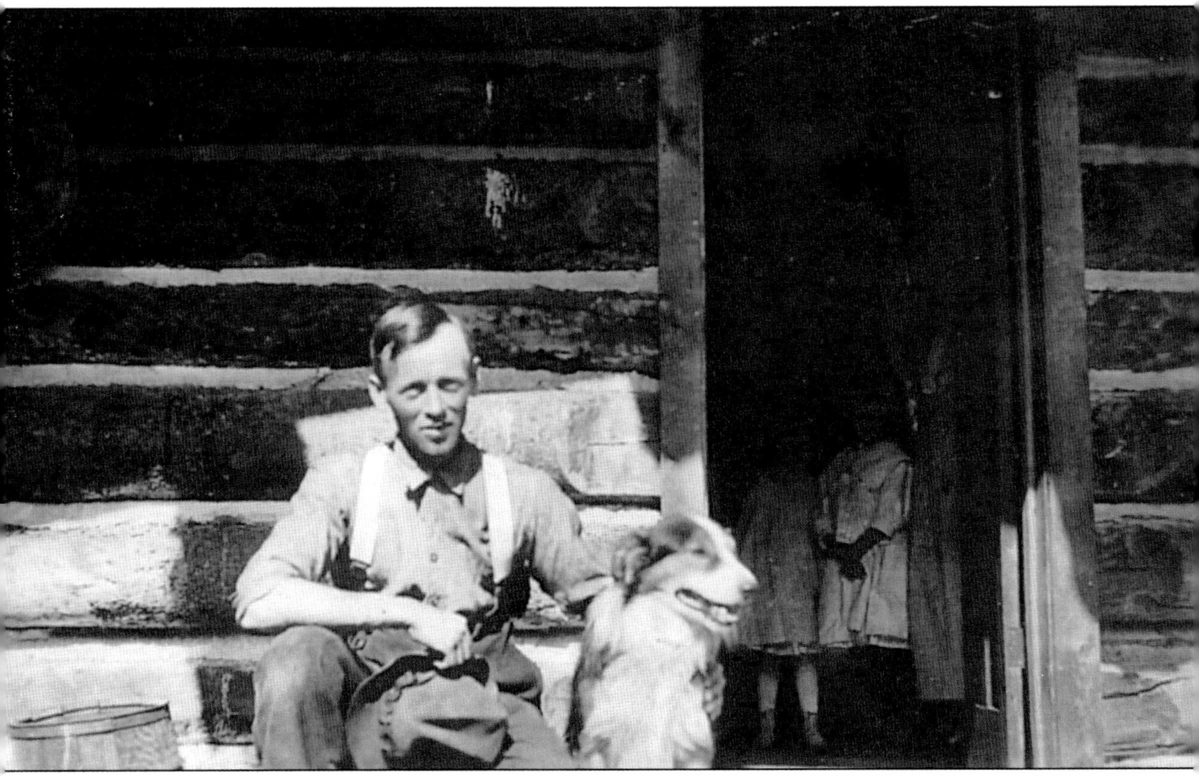

Clarence Lytle. Clarence Lytle, William's brother, first came to the Gallatin driving cattle with Tom Michener. In 1915, he homesteaded the quarter section near the Crails that was to become Lone Mountain Ranch and raised cattle, horses, and hay. Although unmarried, Clarence served the community on the school board and, during World War I, on the draft board. He sold the property in 1926 to the Chicago paper mill tycoon J. Fred Butler, who created the B-K. (Lone Mountain Ranch.)

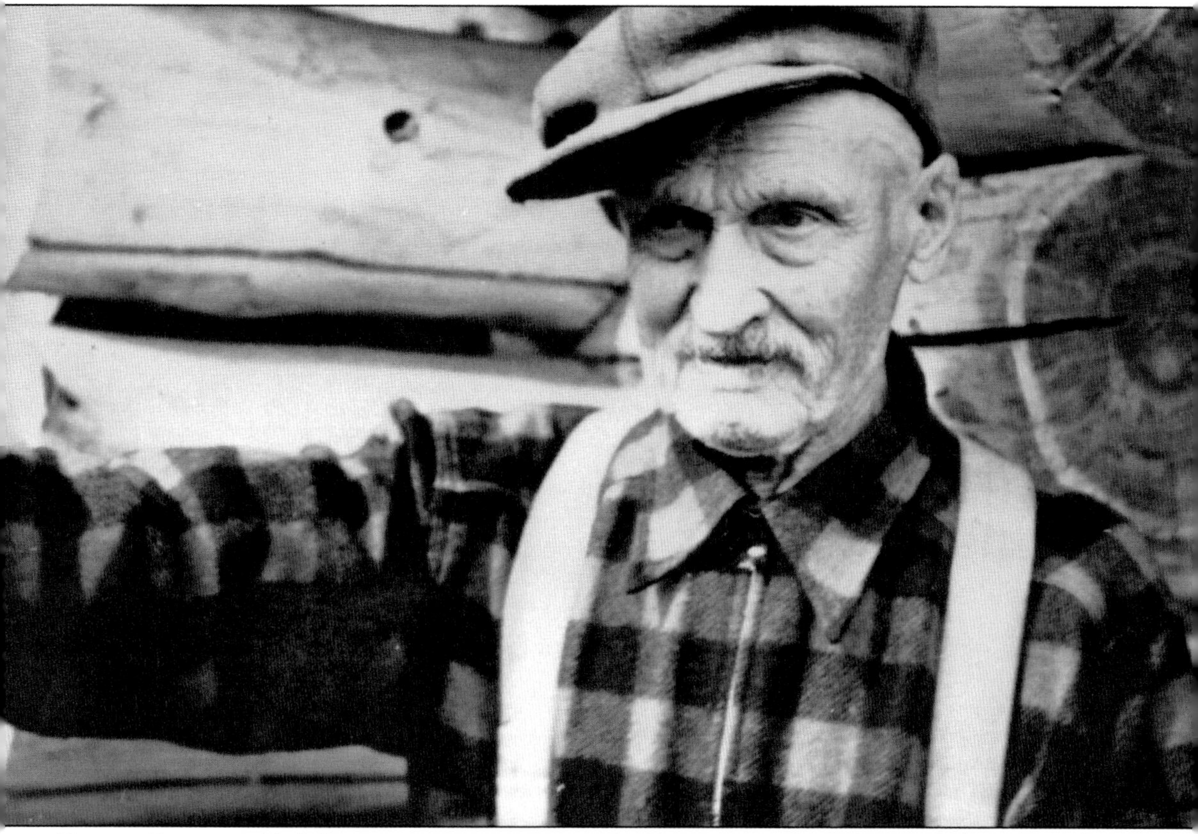

Thomas Lincoln. Fledgling economic ventures in the Basin required employees' dedication and hard work. Both Thomas Lincoln and Lew Bart were childless and landless but are remembered as trustworthy and persistent men. Born in England, Lincoln supported himself as a trapper in his early days here. The 1930 census indicates that at age 77 he managed the 9 Quarter Circle under M.S. Cunningham's ownership. Bart, short for Lewis Cass Bartholomew, was born in Ohio to an itinerant family that moved frequently to eke out a living. "Big Lew" settled here in 1886 when he was 30. During the next half century, Big Lew built and lived in many structures. A squatter on the Karst property and at Twin Cabins, before the Lemons arrived, he failed to prove up. In the early 1930s, he lived at the Michener place before the Vicks. Whether mining at the Apex Developing Mine, sawmilling at Robbers' Roost, or caretaking a summer resort like his father, Big Lew tried his hand at many livelihoods to sustain himself. Through it all, he stayed here. (HCRC.)

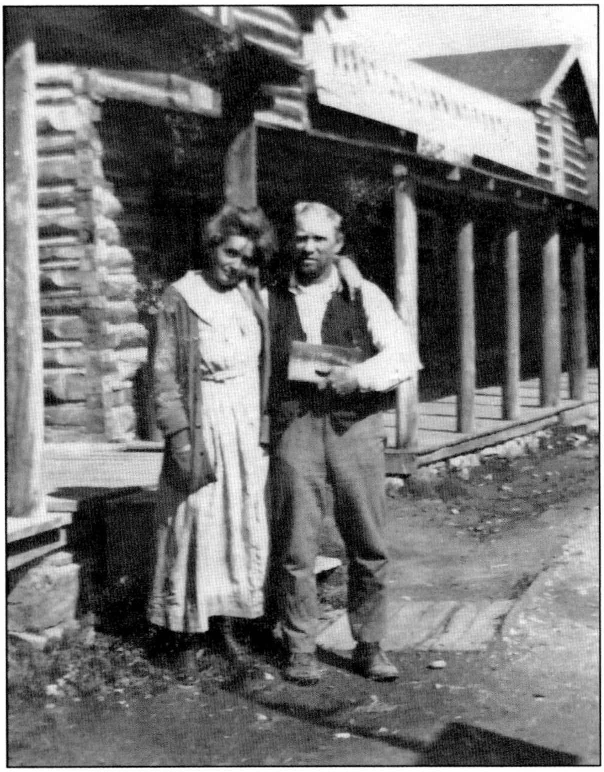

Pete and Jennie Karst (Left); Pete and Nellie Karst (Below). Pete Karst was born in Manitowoc, Wisconsin, in 1875 and died at age 90 in 1966. He came to the Gallatin Valley in 1898 and began freighting to the Cooper Tie Camp. He soon opened his dude ranch, Karst Kamp, one of the first in Montana, which he ran for 50 years. He married Jennie Dickinson in Wisconsin in 1913, and together they ran the ranch and raised Isabelle. Jennie died in 1931. Nell Severance worked for the Northern Pacific Railroad, promoting tourism in the West for its patrons. She met Pete through work and in 1938 gave up her job to marry him and run a Western vacation spot. Nellie died in 1960. (Both, S. Anderson.)

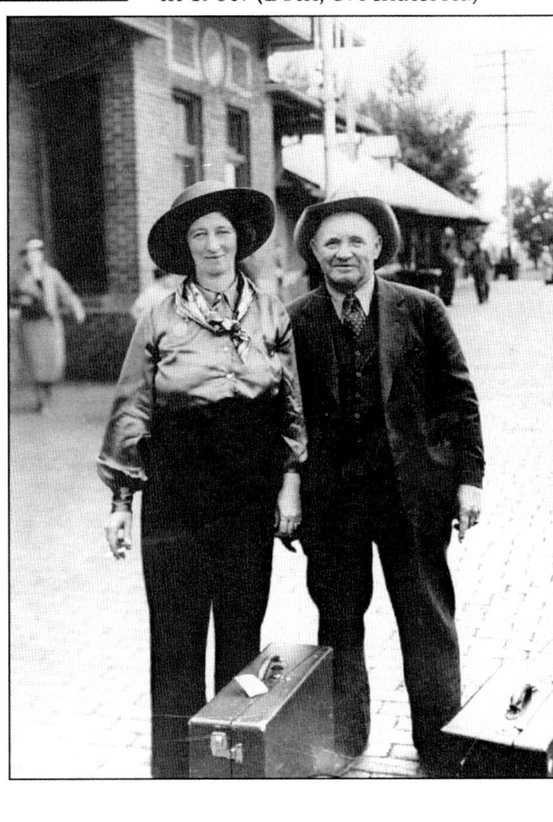

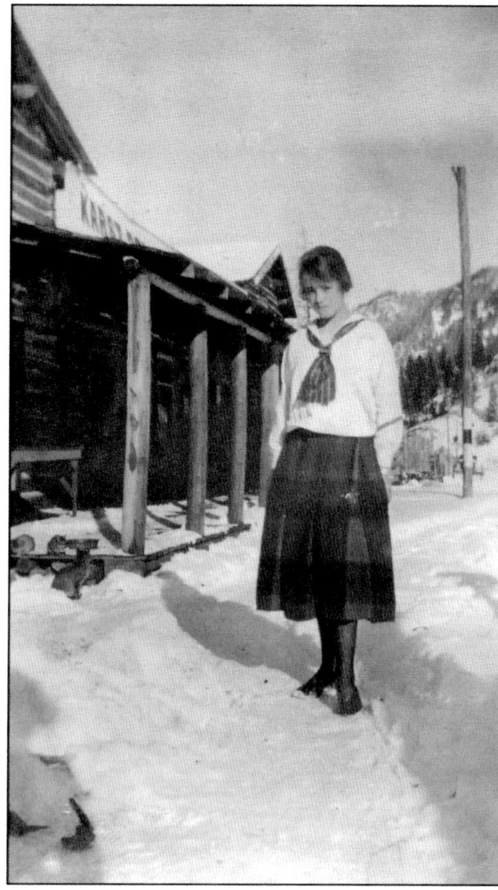

Isabelle Karst Durnam (Right); Ed Durnam (Below). In 1914, Ed Durnam, a golf professional from Minneapolis, came to the canyon to work for Pete Karst. Isabelle was born in 1906 and came into the Karst family at age seven when Jennie married Pete. Ed and Isabelle married in 1923 and worked for Pete until 1936. The homestead on nearby Moose Creek is still in the family. The lettuce farm in Durnam Meadows just south of Karst ran from 1936 to 1955, when they switched to Hereford cattle. These meadows have been returned to the Gallatin National Forest as a conservation easement. In her later years, Isabelle was asked in an oral history interview what it was like growing up on a famous dude ranch. In her own simple and direct manner, she said, "We worked." (Both, S. Anderson.)

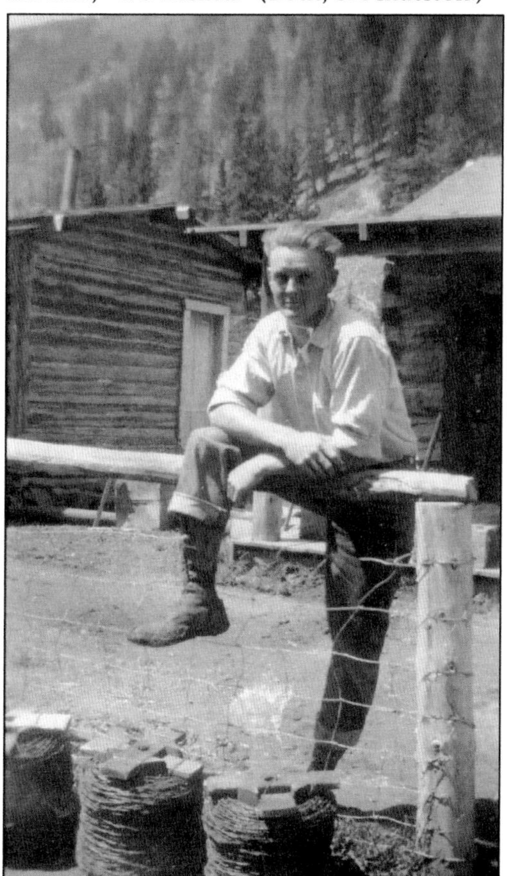

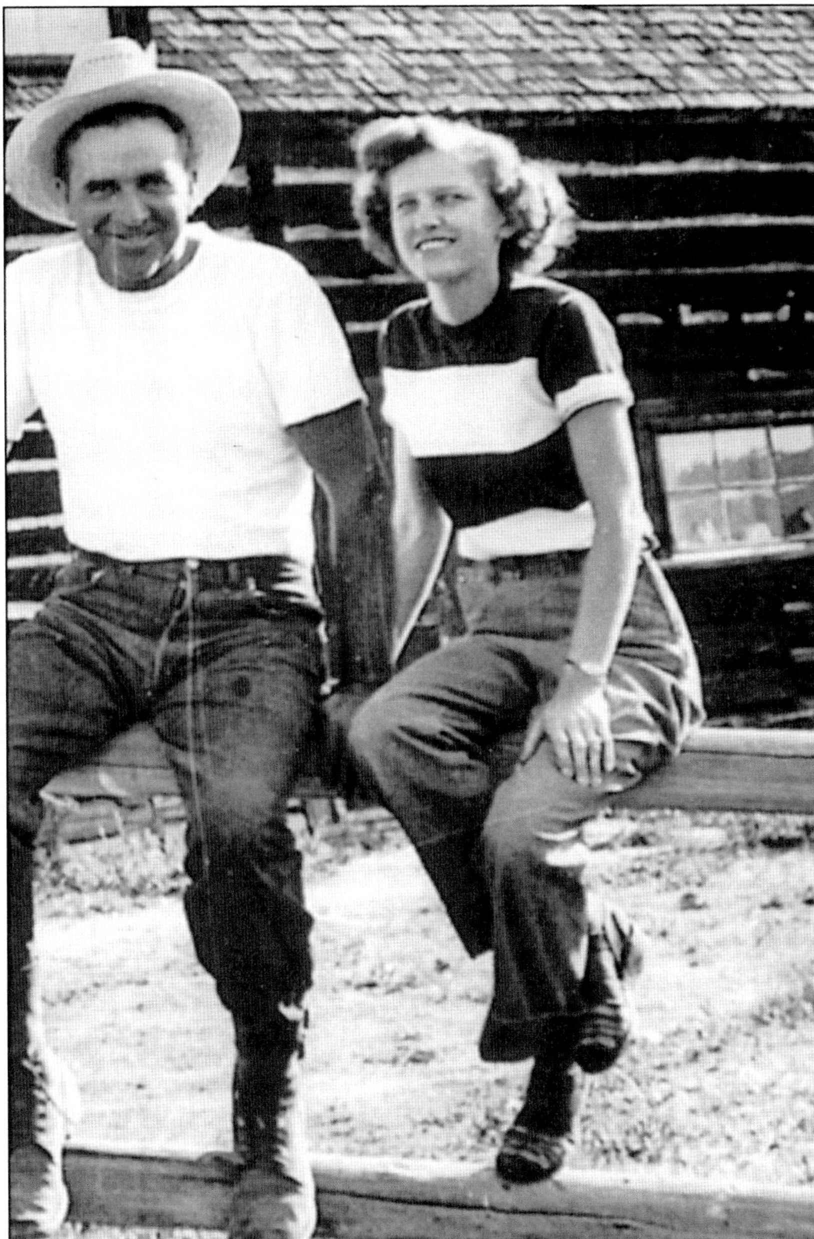

Jack and Elaine Hume, 1950s. Jack Hume lived in Oakland, California, but he often came to this area to hunt. In 1947, a year after Bucks T-4 opened for business, Jack brought his bride, Elaine, to honeymoon here. Hume asked Buck Knight to alert him to any ranches coming onto the market. Three years later, the Humes, along with Thomas and Florence Boa, purchased the Crail Ranch from Emmett Crail. After annexing the Lone Mountain Ranch properties, the entire expanse became a 2,000-acre dude ranch where Jack and Phyllis Bowles managed the operation. The Humes relocated the original Crail cabin to the north of the main house to gain a better view of Lone Mountain. They also razed many of the ranch buildings and plumbed the main house. The next owner, Sam Smeding, ranched the spread for a few years. He sold to Big Sky Corporation in 1970, and the modern era was born. (Lone Mountain Ranch.)

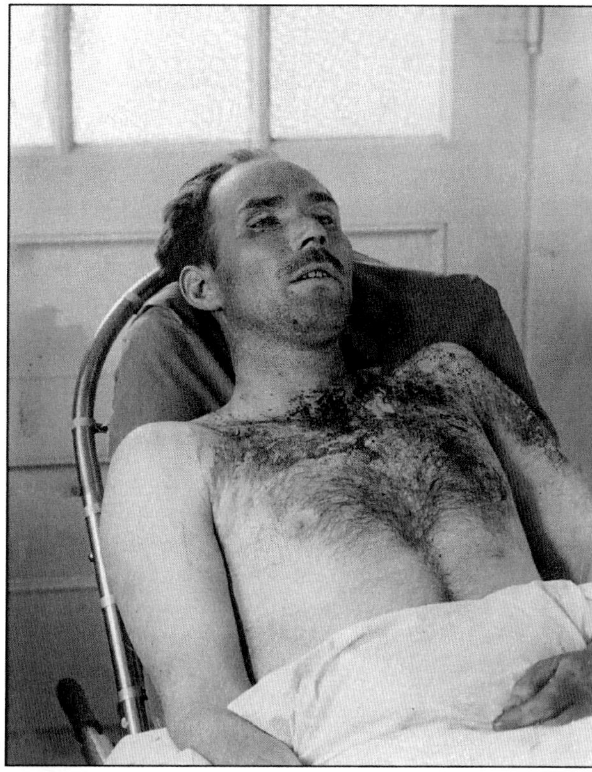

ANDREW HUNTER (RIGHT); PAUL RUSHTON (BELOW). The Gallatin and West Fork had its share of the "Wild West." In 1918, Andrew Levinski shot and killed two men that he thought were claim jumping. In July 1932, the two men in these police morgue shots robbed the Security and Trust of Bozeman and headed off up the Gallatin Canyon. They were chased by Paul Bohart on a motorcycle and, after an inconclusive shootout, headed up into the hills by Cinnamon Creek to hide. Not planning well, hunger drove them to mistakes. Food was hung in a tree, and when one of the robbers came for it, the posse shot him. They then flushed and killed the other robber, who had wounded the sheriff. Although sounding a bit like Butch Cassidy's Wild Bunch, these two were really more inept Depression-era gangsters. (Both, PM.)

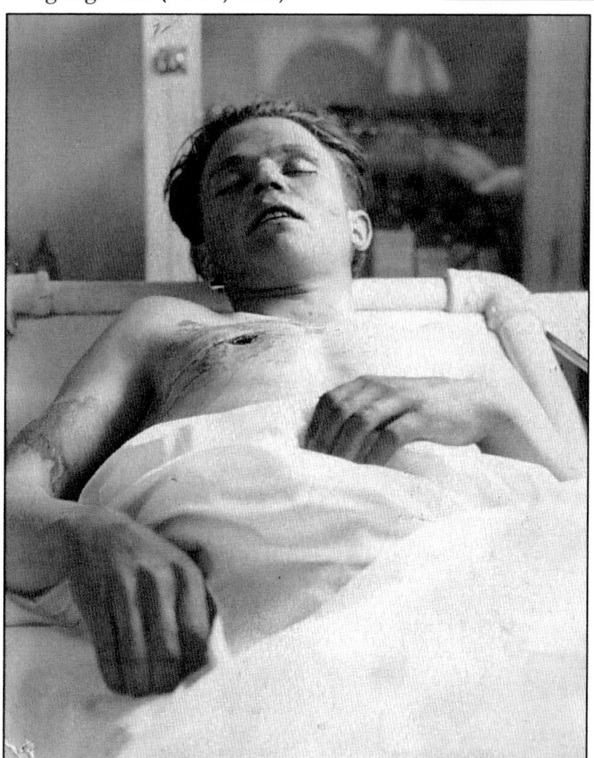

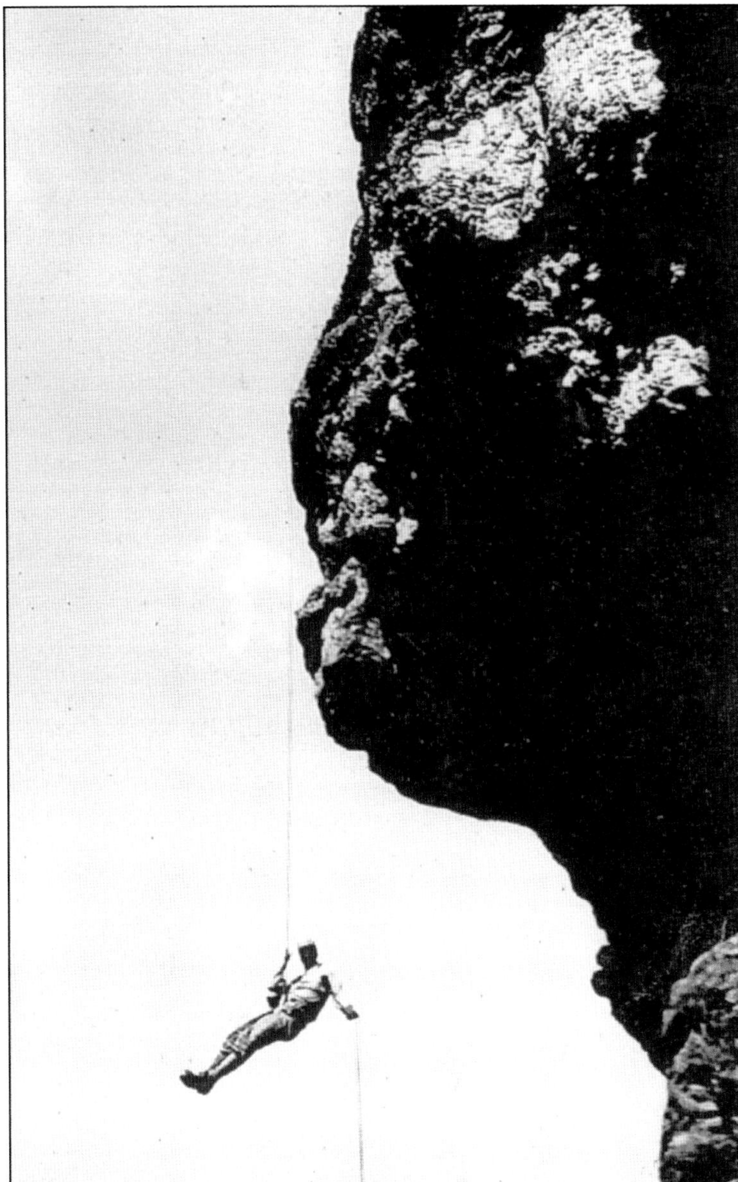

George Lemon, Alpinist, Rappelling. George Lemon (1919–2010) grew up at the Half Way Inn (now the Rainbow Ranch.). He served with the 10th Mountain Division, the county's first rugged-terrain soldiers, and as a "Ski Trooper," George saw fierce fighting in Italy. Although he sustained shrapnel in his eye, he returned to combat. George's bravery and service were recognized with the following awards: the American Campaign Medal, the European-African-Middle Eastern Campaign Medal, Good Conduct Medal, and the World War II Victory Medal. After his discharge, George worked at the Idaho Pole Yard in Bozeman for several winters and then the Montana State Highway Department, plowing Highway 191 for 22 years. Although his family sold the Half Way Inn in 1946, George stayed on in the canyon. He and Clara Lou married in 1950 and raised two daughters, Verna and Donna. Their home, across 191 from the Half Way Inn, was constructed from logs that George cut. He served on the Ophir School Board throughout the 1950s and 1960s. (Beth Naert and Verna Sene.)

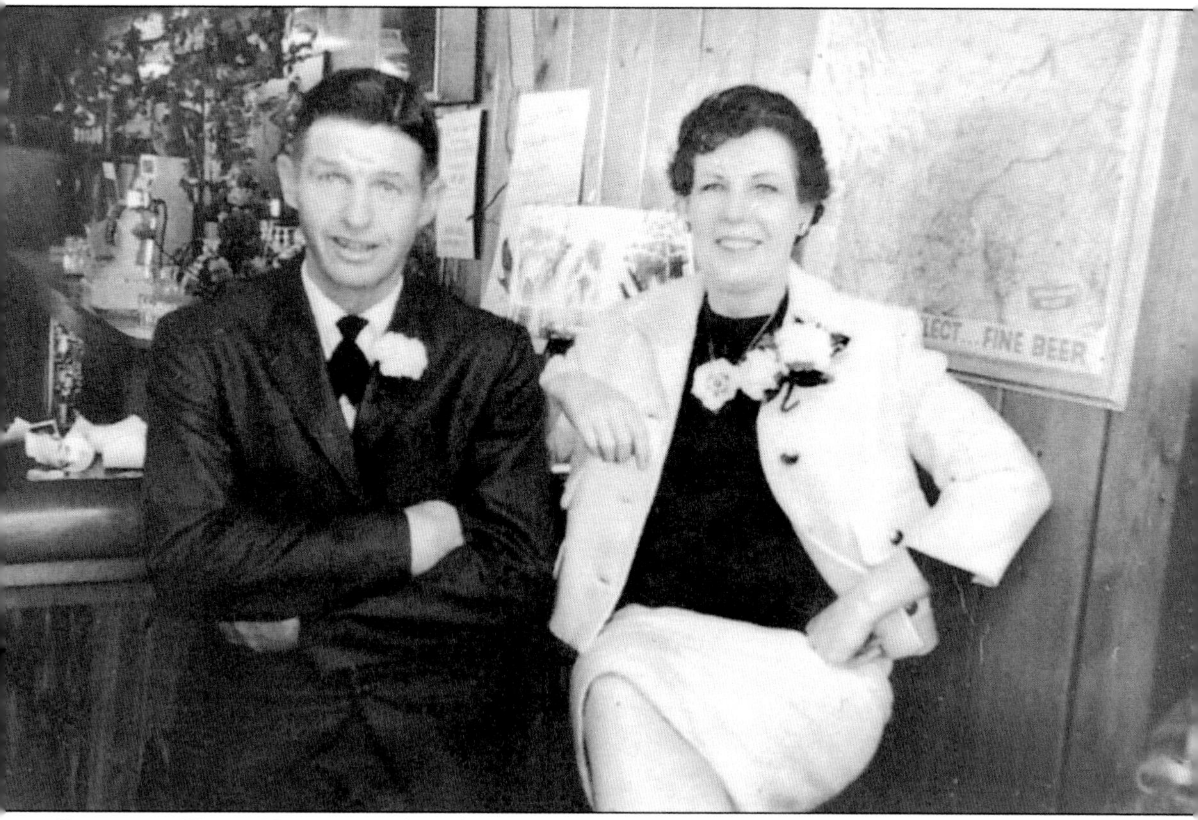

Buck and Helen Knight. Buck and Helen Knight were both born in the Paradise Valley and came to the Gallatin to work on the Elkhorn Ranch. They bought 10 acres of what had been the Stillman homestead and opened Buck's T-4 in 1946. Starting with a few cabin rooms, a restaurant, and a bar, they added more rooms, a dance hall in 1950, and an additional 160 acres. A summer and hunting season resort, it gained a reputation for Western hospitality. They were a team, and Buck often said, "Without Helen there would be no business." Helen would respond, "Without Buck, there would be no customers." They ran it until their retirement in 1970, when it was sold to the Scholz family whose son Mike turned it into the premier motel and dining place on US 191. (Beth Naert.)

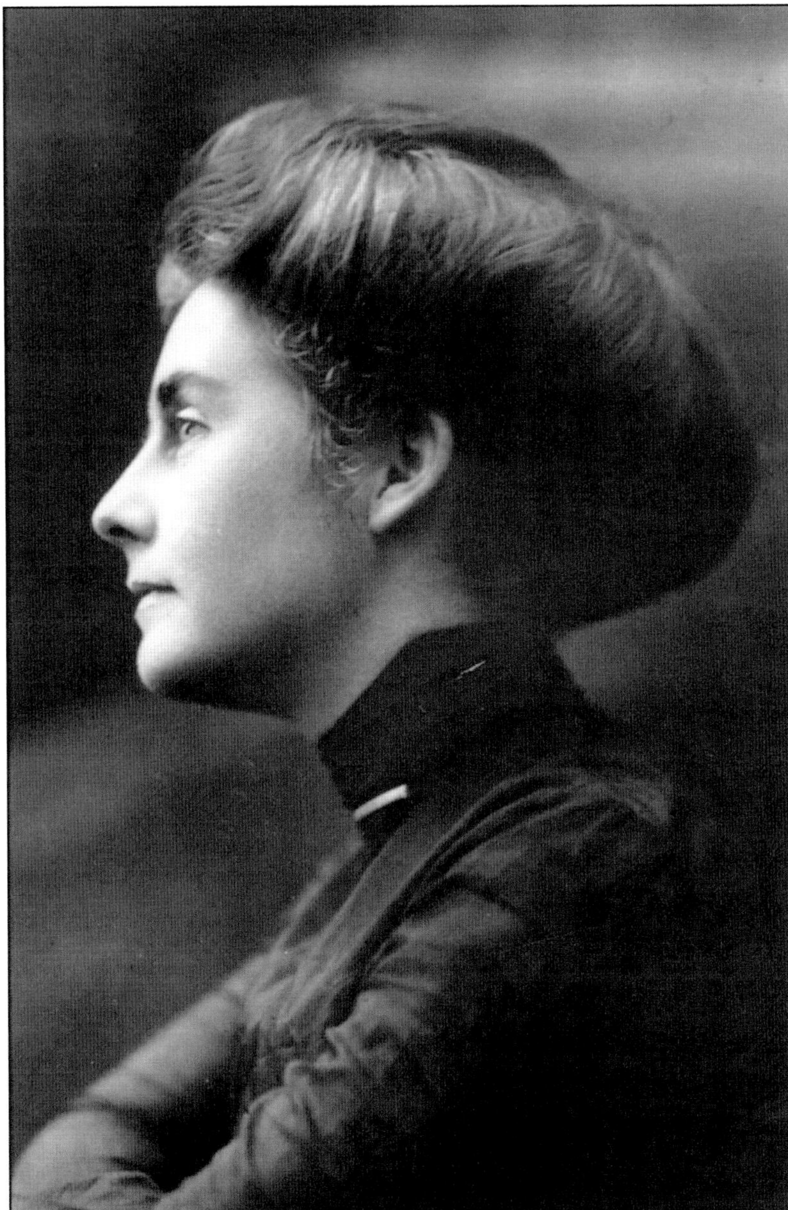

Dr. Caroline McGill. First employed as a schoolteacher, Dr. McGill continued her own education and became the first pathologist in Montana. She loved to hunt, fish, and hike, and she believed in the restorative properties of the outdoors. In 1936, Dr. McGill purchased the Buffalo Horn Resort from Josephine Wilson and used it as a retreat for her patients and friends. Renamed the 320, the ranch was crammed with items reflecting McGill's fascination with antiques and artifacts. Many remain, but most became the basis of a collection that would ultimately evolve into the Museum of the Rockies at Montana State University. When she died in 1959, McGill generously bequeathed money to the women's club for a public project, which was used to build a new school. She also gave the Goodrich family, who had managed the 320, the option to purchase the ranch, which they did. McGill's generosity to many local families during her time in the area and through her estate is fondly remembered. (PM.)

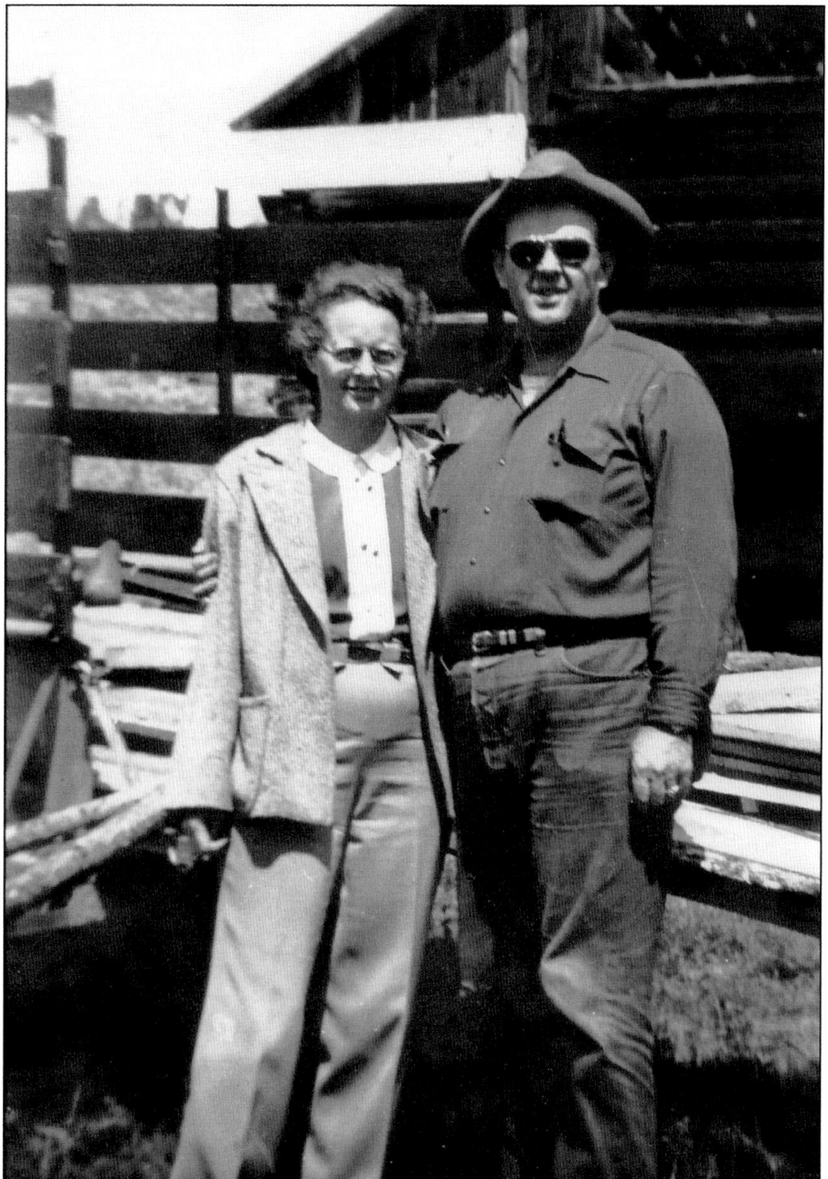

KEN AND LADORA MCBRIDE. Ken and Ladora McBride graduated from Montana State College in 1935 and worked several occupations, from teaching to working the chrome mill in Nye, Montana, to the 5 Spot Bar in Absarokee. In 1952, they purchased the 171 acres that cornered the B-K and Crail Ranches and had been homesteaded by Henry and Ella Johnson. The two-story structure on the property, previously a barn, was converted into a house. A half-century later, it still stands at 111 McBride Lane. The McBrides raised sheep and seasonally guided clients on hunting and fishing trips. Their 5-K Ranch provided cabins, meals, and licensed guides. In the winters, when deep snow made the roads impassable and snowshoes mandatory, the McBride family returned to Bozeman. As the Big Sky Resort became a reality, Ken developed the Westfork Meadows subdivision. Always "independent minded," Ken successfully sued the US Forest Service to move a road to avoid sheep collisions. At the McBride memorial service in 2008, the family celebrated Ken's passion for "feeding the mountain sheep at Big Sky." (McBride family.)

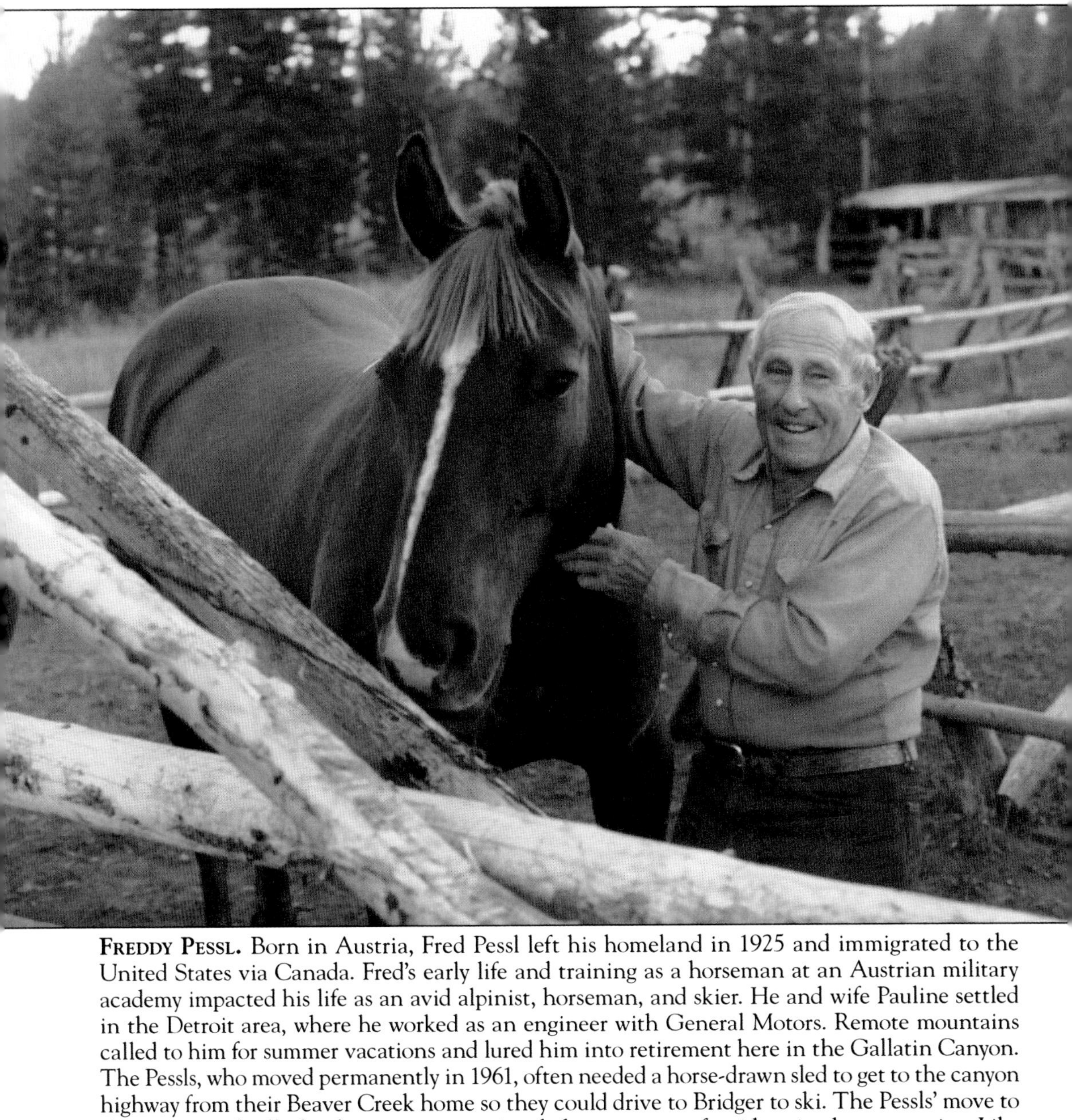

Freddy Pessl. Born in Austria, Fred Pessl left his homeland in 1925 and immigrated to the United States via Canada. Fred's early life and training as a horseman at an Austrian military academy impacted his life as an avid alpinist, horseman, and skier. He and wife Pauline settled in the Detroit area, where he worked as an engineer with General Motors. Remote mountains called to him for summer vacations and lured him into retirement here in the Gallatin Canyon. The Pessls, who moved permanently in 1961, often needed a horse-drawn sled to get to the canyon highway from their Beaver Creek home so they could drive to Bridger to ski. The Pessls' move to the area specifically for their retirement signaled a new type of resident in the mountains. Like many retirees today, the Pessls were active in the community. Within a year of moving here, Freddy joined the school board and Pauline joined the women's club. Since a new school needed to be built, his engineering expertise proved valuable during the planning stages. (Pessl family.)

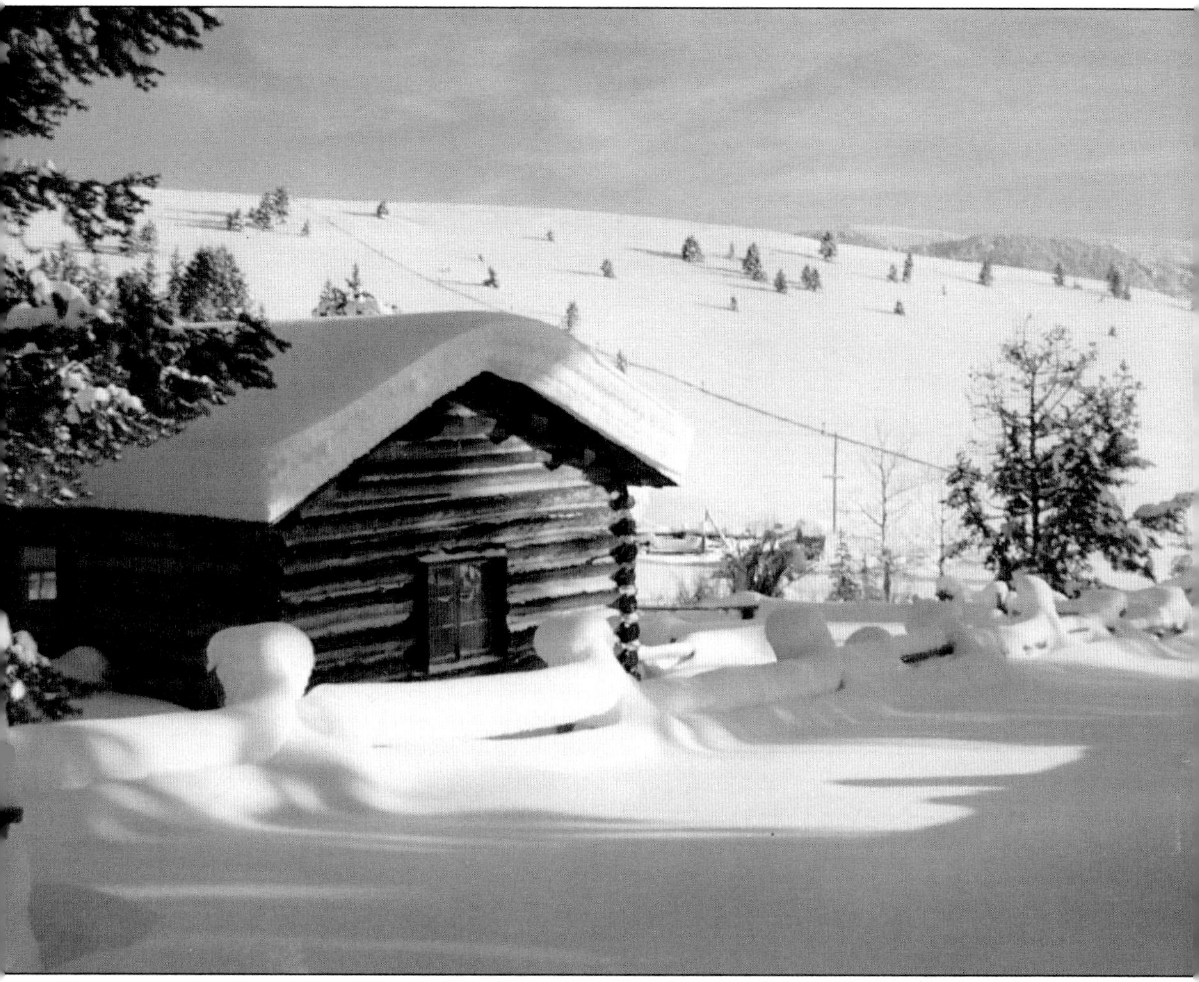

Cabin and Ski Rope Tow. This 1904 cabin, which had been built by a Norwegian woodcutter, was later converted to a Pessl guest cabin. It is clear that Freddy loved kids, as he taught local youngsters to ski using the rope tow seen on the hillside. Pessl explored the mountain ranges and hiked Andesite and Lone Mountain to ski, presaging the area as a resort. Freddy maintained a close personal relationship with Hans Gmoser, the Canadian mountaineer and father of heli-skiing, and in 1970, Pessl experienced his own exciting heli-skiing. After meetings with Chet Huntley and Chrysler Corporation investors at the Lone Mountain Ranch and the 320 in 1970, he heli-toured the mountain with 1968 Olympic gold medalist Jean-Claude Killy. Together, they skied what would come to be called Andesite Mountain's Ambush trail. "It will be quite some development," Fred wrote in his diary on February 12, 1970. Instead of flying in Killy to consult and survey the terrain, the resort development team could have just asked local expert Fred Pessl! (Pessl family.)

Bibliography

Clark, Kenneth William. *A History of the Economic Ventures Employed by the Karst and Durnam Families in the West Gallatin Canyon 1898–1955*. Unpublished paper. February 6, 1981.

Crail, Augustus Franklin. Ten Personal Letters 1868–1897. The Historic Crail Ranch Archives.

Cronin, J. and Vick, D. *Montana's Gallatin Canyon, A Gem in the Treasure State*. Missoula, MT: Mountain Press Publisher, 1992.

Hayden, F. V., "Sixth Annual Report of the United States Geological Survey of the Territories, Embracing Portions of Montana, Idaho, Wyoming, and Utah; Being a Report of Progress of the Explorations for the Year 1872 (1873)." All US Government Documents (Utah Regional Depository), Paper 575. www.digitalcommons.usu.edu/govdocs/575

Hume, Elaine. *Life at the Crail Ranch*. Unpublished memoir. 1992.

Kerson, Michael. *Horse-Drawn Loose Haying at Grant-Kohrs Ranch National Historic Site Using the "Beaver Slide."* Video Mike Productions, 2007.

Malone, Michael P. "The Gallatin Canyon and the Tides of History." *Montana the Magazine of Western History*. Montana Historical Society, Vol. 23, No. 3 (Summer 1973).

Marble, Charles. *Fifty Years In And Around Yellowstone Park*. 1932-02-06. Theodore Roosevelt National Park. www.theodorerooseveltcenter.org

Ophir School Board minutes 1912–1964. Ophir School District No. 72, Gallatin Gateway, Montana.

Russell, Osborne. *Journal of a Trapper*. Library of Western Fur Trade Historical Source Documents. www.mtmen.org

About the Organization

Preservation of the Crail Ranch began in the late 1970s as a grassroots effort of a group of women and men from the rapidly growing Big Sky resort area. Through their efforts, the buildings and grounds of this exemplary Montana homestead were added to the National Register of Historic Places.

Established in 2006 as a committee of the Big Sky Community Corporation, the Historic Crail Ranch Conservators has expanded the original mission of preserving the property. The group raises awareness and appreciation of local ranching heritage. Through the work of the HCRC volunteers, the ranch has become an educational resource that captures the history and essence of the American West.

The Crail Ranch is open for tours on weekends throughout July and August from noon to 3:00 p.m. There is a featured heritage event on most weekends.